Teaching Native America Across the Curriculum

Studies in the Postmodern Theory of Education

Joe L. Kincheloe and Shirley R. Steinberg
General Editors

Vol. 349

PETER LANG
New York • Washington, D.C./Baltimore • Bern
Frankfurt am Main • Berlin • Brussels • Vienna • Oxford

Curry Stephenson Malott, Lisa Waukau,
Lauren Waukau-Villagomez

Teaching Native America Across the Curriculum

A Critical Inquiry

PETER LANG
New York • Washington, D.C./Baltimore • Bern
Frankfurt am Main • Berlin • Brussels • Vienna • Oxford

Library of Congress Cataloging-in-Publication Data

Malott, Curry Stephenson.
Teaching Native America across the curriculum: a critical inquiry /
Curry Stephenson Malott, Lisa Waukau, Lauren Waukau-Villagomez.
p. cm. — (Counterpoints : Studies in postmodern theory of education; v. 349.)
Includes bibliographical references.
1. Indians of North America—Education.
2. Indian philosophy—United States.
3. Education and state—United States. 4. Indians—African influences.
I. Waukau, Lisa. II. Waukau-Villagomez, Lauren. III. Title.
E97.M343 371.82997'2—dc22 2009018350
ISBN 978-1-4331-0405-3 (hardcover)
ISBN 978-1-4331-0404-6 (paperback)
ISSN 1058-1634

Bibliographic information published by **Die Deutsche Bibliothek**.
Die Deutsche Bibliothek lists this publication in the "Deutsche
Nationalbibliografie"; detailed bibliographic data is available
on the Internet at http://dnb.ddb.de/.

Cover art by Alexander Joseph "Gokey" Menore, Jr.

The paper in this book meets the guidelines for permanence and durability
of the Committee on Production Guidelines for Book Longevity
of the Council of Library Resources.

© 2009 Peter Lang Publishing, Inc., New York
29 Broadway, 18th floor, New York, NY 10006
www.peterlang.com

All rights reserved.
Reprint or reproduction, even partially, in all forms such as microfilm,
xerography, microfiche, microcard, and offset strictly prohibited.

Printed in the United States of America

Table of Contents

Introduction: The Significance of Who We Are and This Book 1

Native America and World History

1. Why Is Philosophy Important in Teaching the Americas? 9

2. African Influences in Ancient Central America 39

3. The Menominee: Sovereignty and Education in a Changing World 57

4. A Closer Look at Menominee Sovereignty:
   A Discussion between Sisters 83

Teaching Native America across the Curriculum

5. The Social Studies and Epistemological Diversity 93

6. Indigenous Children and the Social Studies:
   A Menominee Case Study 113

7. Native American Philosophy and Western Science
   with Andrew Gilbert 131

8. Native American Democracy and Western Mathematics Curricula ... 155

9. Native American Literacies and the Language Arts Curriculum 173

Conclusion

10. Knowledge Production in an Age of Economic Meltdown 203

Appendix A 231

References 237

Introduction: The Significance of Who We Are and This Book

Curry Stephenson Malott: When white folks, such as myself, write about people of color, Native peoples in particular, there are always multiple dangers associated with the legacy of colonization. For example, when producing scholarship from the positionality of white privilege about the experiences of oppression, even when it is done with the intention of challenging abuse, one runs the risk of reproducing the essentialized constructions of hierarchy where the Indigenous are reduced to a single experience or perspective, such as the *Noble Savage*, and whites are afforded the unstated status of *expert*. A related danger is when whites take books like this and use them to position themselves as more knowledgeable about indigeneity than the Indigenous themselves.

There is also a tendency for white people to not explore these and other problematic issues associated with whiteness because in the current hegemony it is incorrectly assumed that most *white people are self-actualized*. Instead, liberal whites, oblivious to their own internal contradictions, tend to sympathetically and paternalistically explore all the reasons why they believe *Indians and people of color are so damaged*. A closely related product of this deficit thinking is when whites attempt to speak *for* rather than *with* the oppressed. In most instances, however, whites are hardly equipped to speak *with* and would therefore be wise to find the humility to *listen* to the experiences and perspectives of those marginalized by the long tradition of racialized imperialism.

Perhaps even more damaging and possibly one of the most exploitative tendencies is when progressive whites falsely position themselves as the *other*. Typically, this is done as an attempt to dodge responsibility. The most common story told by those with white skin privilege is that they have a distant Native American relative and therefore have a right to their *white privilege*. These historical accounts are more often than not true. However, having a distant relative who was of Native American ancestry does not make white people indigenous or absolve them from the process of colonization and capitalist exploitation that much of our European background is connected to.

In other words, the significance of the *Indian relative story* is missed. The reason why so many white people in the US have Native American descendents is because significant numbers of Native Americans were absorbed into white society as the result of a series of grossly unjust removal and relocation programs, especially during the 1800s, from the Cherokee's *Trail of Tears* to the Miami's of the Miami Valley of Ohio relocation to Okalahoma. The *white Native American relative story* is therefore part of the tragedy and cultural genocide that defines whiteness in the Americas and beyond.

Sometimes this racial posing occurs when whites marry into families of color. For example, just because my wife is a Jamaican national of African descent and I am a father of a biracial daughter, it does not relieve me of my white skin privilege and the responsibility to act as an agent of social change it demands. What it has done, however, is exposing me to more views from below, in both hegemonic and counter-hegemonic manifestations, and, as a result, making me *even* more aware of my whiteness. For example, oppressed people, such as African Jamaicans in the US, in order to survive and resist their oppression, must develop an understanding of their oppressors, that is, the white managers and bosses that serve as America's economic and social gatekeepers. Being exposed to a Black immigrant analysis of white people and whiteness allows whites, such as myself, an opportunity to critically self-reflect and grow.

The first line of defense against these hegemonic traps, outside of *listening*, is for whites attempting to work counter-hegemonically to self-identify as *white*. In so doing the white person begins the process of taking responsibility for the legacy of abuse, deception, genocide, and naked plunder that has given way to the existence of white-skin privilege in North America, and much of the world. Another practice that white progressive scholars might be wise to follow, when possible, is to work with critical colleagues of color in counter-hegemonic collaboration. However, this must be more than an act of tokenism. In other words, they must be genuine engagements where every contributor has the opportunity to both contribute to the project and grow. This book represents one of those mixed authorship engagements.

* * *

As a white man born in Oxford, Ohio in 1972 into a working/middle class family and raised by his single-mother, it is my intention to show other whites that it is in their best interest to resist the negative structure of white supremacy. Speaking directly to whites, I also want to note that self-identifying as white does not lock us into reproducing whiteness. I would argue that proclaiming we are white paves the way to become self-conscious of our privilege, thereby creating the opportunity to choose to resist such injustices as anti-racist educators/world citizens. That is, to fight white-skin privilege, as whites, we have to start by identifying ourselves as white and therefore unjustly privileged. We can then begin making connections to how whiteness divides the working class as part of maintaining the basic structures and relationships of class power. That is, whiteness is a hegemonic construction of the ruling capitalist class.

While those deemed "white," on average, receive more material privileges than non-whites, most people who fit within current definitions of whiteness would also be better off without the institutionalization of white supremacy. Simply stated, a united working class/human species would be far better equipped to create a socially just world than a divided one. In *A Call to Action* (2008) I made the point that white people, while at times made to feel special or superior because we are white, have been left to rot and die of cancer at alarming rates in de-industrialized areas like Niagara Falls, New York. My intentions here are similar. That is, this book, in part, is designed to offer white people (and others) a worldview not based on the false supremacy of Europeans, but one that acknowledges the contributions of Africans, Native Americans, and others to modern democracy and scientific knowledge production. Solidarity, in this context, is not a polite gesture made by the assumed *superior* to the assumed *inferior*, but rather, it is an acknowledgement of the awe-inspiring achievements of the non-European world that paved the way for Europe (and those of European descent) to begin emerging from the Dark Ages—a process still underway.

* * *

Lisa S. Waukau: I was born and raised on the Menominee Indian Reservation. I have spent the majority of my life on the reservation. I am a member of the Bear Clan, the protectors and teachers in the Tribe. I have been a teacher at the Menominee Indian School District for almost 27 years. I wanted to work on this book because I have been a teacher of native children for most of my teaching career. I also had the opportunity to teach non-native children in the distance-learning program at Menominee High School. I found that there are more similarities than differences between the groups. Native children, of course, have a different worldview of themselves in relation to the dominant society than the non-native child. Both groups, however, have innate curiosity and a joy of learning that makes it a pleasure to teach. At the same time, I found a deficit in the knowledge of the non-native about Native American history, which I think is a detriment to the non-native child. These children will grow up to be the policy makers in the American government and for them to engage their practice democratically and with social justice, they need to understand the world of natives and other non-dominant group peoples and perspectives.

In addition, I hope this book will assist those strong people who have taken on the most important of all job—teaching. These important people are the ones who give voice to the children of America. I have found in my time as a teacher that you never know that *thing* that is going to ignite the minds of young people. The pedagogical and curricular choices teachers make today will impact policy two generations from now. An example of this is Richard Nixon's wonderful experience with his football coach, who happened to be a Native American. Nixon went on to become President of the United States and he just so happened to be responsible for landmark legislation that reversed the policy of termination for Indian Tribes. He established a new way of doing things for tribal governments called Indian Self Determination. Who knew that would happen?

Many times, as a teacher, I have influenced my students. It is never that lesson plan that I spent hours on, but it is rather that story or that activity that students will remember years later. I still run into my children in the grocery store, and, after asking me if I have retired, they will say, "remember when we talked about…?" That is the unknown in the teaching profession and I am hopeful that this book, as teachers and pre-service teachers engage it, will create many of those "remember when we talked about…" moments.

* * *

Currently, I am the chairwoman of the Menominee Indian Tribe of Wisconsin. I am charged with defending the Tribe's sovereignty and interpreting government policy. I take this responsibility seriously. Dealing with the government is a constant battle, and one can never weary or bad things can happen to the Tribe. As we try to open an off-reservation gaming operation, I am amazed at the red tape and bureaucracy Indians face. The government hopes we will just give up or we will run out of money for lawyers. I am a fighter and this will not happen on my watch. I hope my stories can be an inspiration to others dealing with difficult situations.

* * *

Lauren "Candy" Waukau-Villagomez: My spirit name is Keskesakaeh, which means "the time just before dawn." My mother was from the Crane Clan and my father from the Bear Clan of the Menominee Nation. I was born and raised on the Menominee Indian Reservation for most of my early life. My stepfather, Mani Boyd, gave me my Indian name when I was a young girl, who had a major influence on my life. Mani was a traditional Menominee man, who spoke the Menominee language and was a member of the Big Drum religion. Mani shared with my sisters and me Menominee culture and traditions. More importantly, he lived as he believed and he was a role model for us to follow.

One of the many values and teachings he passed on to us was the importance of passing on traditional teachings and knowledge to others. This has become a focus of my life and why I became an educator. This belief has made me appreciate the importance of passing on my knowledge to the students with whom I work. I have worked in a number of different places and in a number of different positions during my career as an educator. I worked on the Menominee Indian Reservation, the Pine Ridge Indian Reservation in South Dakota, and the Lac du Flambeau Indian Reservations in northern Wisconsin. These experiences have all had an impact on my world view.

Life for Native American people has always been difficult to say the least. I have tried to use my education and knowledge to change the educational institutions that have had such a traumatic and devastating effect on Native American people through the years. This has been a frustrating and challenging endeavor. I have moved through the years from the hands-on and in the trenches approach to trying to change the mind-set of the teacher in the classroom. Only time will tell which approach is better.

* * *

At this point the reader may be wondering how this book came about. That is, how did this young white man with radical ideas develop a relationship with two older, reservation women from Wisconsin? Curry and I had been colleagues at the same college (D'Youville College) for a number of years with similar friends and research interests. We both attended a conference in Pomona, New Jersey and Curry needed a ride back to Buffalo after our presentations were completed. We spent the long trip back exchanging life stories about his work in New Mexico and my work on reservation schools. As a result, Curry asked me to write a chapter on Native American education for his book, *A Call to Action*. After that endeavor was completed, I shared with him my sister's dream of writing her own textbook on Native American history for high school students. While we continue to strategize about the most effective way to present that book to the world, we wrote this one for our (and other) teacher education students.

* * *

On behalf of my sister and myself, I would like to say "Waewaenon" (which means thank you in the Menominee language) to Curry Malott and the wonderful people at Peter Lang, Shirley Steinberg, the late Joe L. Kincheloe, Bernadette Shade, and Chris Myers, for the opportunity to share our knowledge and our stories. It is always difficult for marginalized people to have their voices heard. We hope others will read our words and use them to make a difference in the education of all children.

Native America and World History

CHAPTER ONE

Why Is Philosophy Important in Teaching the Americas?

Underscored in this introductory chapter is the notion that history is not neutral. That is, it is not an objective retelling of past events. Rather, histories are written from particular perspectives informed by very specific assumptions that are philosophical in nature. The history of Western philosophy, for example, within dominant North American society tends to be written not only from a Euro-centric perspective, but also from a capitalist class vantage point. Challenging these constructions—constructions we argue are invalid—we point to the Black Egyptian and Native North American influences on Western philosophy as a way to begin conceptualizing knowledge production from a non-Euro-centric perspective as part of the process of developing democratic identities for a democratic society.

* * *

Before we proceed with the task of contemplating the relevance of philosophy in *Teaching the Americas*, we must first begin to define what we mean by "philosophy" because there are as many conceptualizations of what philosophy *is* as there are diverse traditions. For the purposes of the discussion at hand, we can begin to understand what philosophies are, at their most basic level, by viewing them as evolving interpretive frameworks for making sense of, and guiding our practice in, the concrete, physical world. Philosophies are said to differ from one another in how they answer fundamental questions, such as: What is knowledge (epistemology)? How are the world's entities related (ontology)? And, what is the nature of good and evil (axiology)? From this place of departure we might then come to the conclusion that philosophy is a universal human phenomenon that necessarily exists—socially constructed and therefore not predetermined—within every *population*, however conceived. If this universalism thesis is to be accepted, then we can begin to analyze the similarities, differences, and relationships between philosophies created by distinct human groups that are situated in specific geographical contexts at particular moments in time.

However, in Western societies (and others) the dominant perspective/philosophy/worldview/paradigm is hegemonized—that is, it is presented as a non-perspective, as normal and natural, in short, as just "how it is." Hidden within the resulting claims of operational objectivity in the construction of knowledge and ways of knowing are the immense political implications of the practice of the dominant paradigm. It has been argued (Malott, 2008) that the dominant paradigm in the Americas, the U.S. in particular, can be accurately defined as the Columbian pedagogy of conquest and plunder. It is worth repeating that the ideological apparatus that justifies this violent, genocidal process of wealth extraction, depopulation, and repopulation—a highly political endeavor—is hegemonized: it is presented as the only rational (i.e. scientific) way to understand and operate in the world.

The lesson to be learned then, *if* we are good students, is that *resisting* enslavement and being externally commanded or controlled is irrational, and, at the same time, coddling the aggressor *is* rational—from this analysis we can conclude that the vast majority of humanity, at various levels of severity, depending on racism and other variables, are taught (successfully *and* unsuccessfully) to hate themselves and forfeit their political power through inactivity, with the exception of lending their weight to one of two members of the business class every four years. It is incorrectly assumed that advanced intelligence is exceptionally rare rendering those uniquely endowed with this special gift of the natural leaders—the bosses—which renders them morally obligated to civilize the savage, of whatever cultural, ethnic, or regional background—*the* white man's burden.

This is the epistemological backbone of the dominant philosophy (a form of idealism discussed below); as its hierarchies tacitly waft through the political smog of civil society, its self-destructive symptoms become most visible among those who unconsciously hold themselves in contempt for not being that which is associated with the ruling elite, either real or imagined—smart, white, male, just, and thus rich—while simultaneously animated by a bitter hatred toward those or that identified as being responsible for nurturing and encouraging this tragic and deeply saddening hatred of self. Comprehending the too often deadly inner-battles such conflicted senses of self-engender is so challenging for those who have not experienced it, that it rarely happens. Not only is it difficult for privileged people to imagine the lived experience of an internalized oppression that is so deep and seemingly fixed that it becomes internally visible, but also the problem of comprehension is compounded by the normalization of the dominant epistemology that occludes an engagement with the subjugated knowledge that lends itself to a critical reading and understanding of, and practice in, the world.

Thus, while we are all informed by philosophy, we are not all equally aware of the paradigms we possess, and, therefore, how we are influenced by them. For example, a white middle-class male uncritically raised in the dominant U.S. society in the twenty-first century is probably not going to be as aware of himself as uniquely situated on stolen Native American land as is a contemporary traditional Hopi grandmother, whose philosophical orientation, and its practice in sacred geography, is being physically attacked and threatened by U.S. capitalist imperialism. We study philosophy, therefore, in part, to become more aware of ourselves (and each other), and in the process, the possibility arises for us to dehegemonize our minds and become true owners of self and, as a result, democratic participants.

Philosophy therefore not only shapes how we see the world, but philosophies are always human constructs born in history as they, through people, shape history. When we strive to bring any philosophical perspective as it currently exists into focus, and if we are successful, what we witness are a set of ideas at a particular moment in their development. Our interest here is to chart the historical development of human thought as a way of better understanding the present moment because such insights are indispensable for making informed decisions. Marx described this imperative as one that is not merely interested in understanding the world, as philosophers tend to be, but with transforming it against oppression and suffering and for the social arrangements most conducive to universal self-actualization—the process of becoming self-actualized is conceived here as being self-directed rather than externally imposed, therefore critiquing the behaviorist position of Maslow (1968).

As a result of this hegemony, through the various socializing institutions, such as schools, especially working class schools, young people tend not to be actively engaged in the construction of their own philosophies, but are rather far too often indoctrinated by teachers who themselves have been indoctrinated with the same dominant approach as the sole producer of valid knowledge and creator of the *one* "right" answer, such as *Columbus discovered America*, and *the U.S. is the world's most democratic nation because it was founded by wise believers of free market enterprise*. These "facts," which are refuted in later chapters, are part of the knowledge base of the dominant paradigm, that, again, is not taught as informed and motivated by a specific set of interests, values, beliefs, and ideas (philosophy), but rather, as *objective* reality.

Consequently, every curriculum presupposes a philosophical perspective. That is, the process of creating a curriculum is always informed by a particular reading of the world and idea about what knowledge is and how it is obtained. In the chapters that follow we provide substantial evidence that clearly suggests the dominant Western scientific approach to education is not only epistemologically and ontologically inadequate, and therefore only minimally useful, but also its exclusionary impulse has proven catastrophically damaging to the ideological diversity indicative of human existence. This volume therefore sets out to contribute to the monumental task of not only restructuring settler-state educational curricula as we know them, but also challenging taken-for-granted assumptions about what curriculum *is* and what it *can* be—as is most forcefully demonstrated in chapters twelve through fifteen.

But of course we invite you, students of the philosophies and interconnected histories of humanity, which are the stories of our ideas and how we have put them into practice, to participate in the re-construction of our curricula, and thus our philosophies, and how we use them. Ultimately, the invitation is to become educators that are critically conscious creators of history and activists for a more just world. This is something that can be done *now* because there are currently many educators in public schools and colleges and universities doing critical pedagogy—and doing it successfully building vast communities of subversive producers and engagers of subjugated knowledges. Winthrop Holder (2007) stands as a steadfast example of a veteran New York City (the Bronx and Brooklyn) high school social studies critical pedagogue who has been "giving voice to the voiceless" for over twenty years publishing, and in the process empowering, the critical insights of the hundreds upon hundreds of students he has worked with over the years. Holder began reproducing student work decades ago in a series of self-produced and student-run journals, which quickly gained the support of parents, university professors, school districts, school janitors, and schoolteachers.

These critical approaches to education deserve much celebration and reflection because they successfully embrace diverse ways of knowing allowing educators and students to "hang out in the epistemological bazaar listening to and picking up on articulations of subjugated knowledges" (Kincheloe, 2005, p. 127). It is therefore not saying too much that restructuring the curriculum (at least within our own classrooms) for social justice (however defined) is within our *immediate grasp*. It is precisely because the act of challenging the formal process of knowledge production requires the use of our creative capacities, that is, our labor power, which is embodied within our bodies, and thus in our control, that renders direct action in the here-and-now a matter not of ability, but rather, one of *will*—always acutely aware of possible personal costs. However, *will* alone is not enough. One must be sufficiently prepared to engage in the work of critical pedagogy. The issue of competence is overcome through the process of *genuine* practice and the life-long study it demands. From here, we might say that this volume is designed to facilitate the development of professional competence within those who have chosen a critical pedagogical approach to teaching and learning.

* * *

In the following discussion we begin our analysis with the dominant/hegemonic "Western" perspective because it is this approach that currently presents the most significant barrier to the development of critical consciousness (discussed below) and agency within much of the world, including the Americas (the focus of our present inquiry), which is a central goal and objective of our critical pedagogical approach to *Teaching the Americas*, that is, the facilitation of critical consciousness against human suffering and all other forms of irresponsibility, such as environmental destruction. It is worth briefly noting that the degree of irresponsibility embedded within the foundation of U.S. society, the epitome of Western civilization and the self-proclaimed world's number one proponent of democracy and freedom, is highlighted by recent findings that demonstrate that the simple act of living in America, and, as a result, becoming Americanized, has proven to be a significant health risk. It has been found that the degree to which immigrant families can maintain their cultural traditions and family ties and not internalize the values and habits of Americans, the less likely they will develop serious health issues. For Black women, it is the perpetual stress of living in a racist context that contributes to their substantially higher rates of premature births, and, as a result, higher rates of infant mortality (Byrd, 2002)—a nation that causes such high levels of stress within sub-groups of its own population effecting their health in serious ways can only be identified as irresponsible. Because it is our intention to demonstrate the interconnectedness of all ideas, peoples, and places throughout time, the narrative below includes many perspectives. In other words, the philosophies at work in the Americas are not only those that are Native to the Americas, but they are also ones that can be traced directly to Europe, and from there, to Africa, the Middle East, and Asia.

Again, before we explore the implications and indispensability of *consciously* drawing on philosophical insights in *Teaching the Americas*, we must first outline the archeology and genealogy of the dominant paradigm, that is, what is commonly understood to be "Western" philosophy. This is no small task, and we risk missing key insights in this introductory format, but we must nevertheless proceed conscious of the risks we are taking. In the following section we trace the history of Western philosophy from antiquity to 1492 when Columbus began the process of American colonization. The section that proceeds this initial investigation explores some of the fundamental ways in which Native American philosophy forever transformed what we know to be "Western" philosophy. In the final section of this chapter we consider, in some detail, what the implications are for *Teaching the Americas* informed by this history of philosophy. In the process, we provide *an* answer (not the only answer) for the question of why philosophy is important for the interconnected tasks of teaching and learning the Americas.

However, before we proceed with our historical discussion of philosophy, it is worth briefly considering two anthropological approaches to such endeavors—diffusion and convergence—and a third one we call *indoctrination*. The notion of diffusion suggests that the products of human creativity, that is, technology or inventions, were "made in but one place" and if "worthwhile" their underlying knowledges "spread" to other regions (Sarton, 1952, p. 17). Many critics of Euro-centric history, such as Martin Bernal and Cheikh Anta Diop (discussed below), take this position in regard with Egypt as being the cradle of Western civilization. Convergence, on the other hand, is a theory that is based on the premise that because all distinct human groups essentially have the same needs and the same biological endowments to meet those needs, the history of humanity is marked by "simultaneous discoveries...made at about the same time by different people in separate places" (Sarton, 1952, p. 17). As the concept of convergence is a direct response to the notion of diffusion, it should not be surprising that "the theory...of convergence...does not deny the frequent occurrence of borrowings and imitation between one people and another" as it acknowledges the existence of "simultaneous discoveries" (Sarton, 1952, p. 17).

While the combined use of convergence and diffusion lends itself to a more complex understanding of the history of philosophy than drawing on either one by itself, as we will see below, a third classification is necessary to depict the transference of ideas that has occurred through the process of colonization. In other words, due to the passivity implied within the concept of *diffusion*, the result of trade or other types of relatively peaceful interactions, we need a term that names the *active* imposition of ideas. For the purposes of this discussion we will call this third category *indoctrination* or compulsory diffusion. Highlighted in the following discussion are therefore the convergence, diffusion, and indoctrination of ideas (philosophies) throughout history—always situated in a particular social context. Again, we begin with "Western" philosophy.

THE ROOTS OF MODERN EMPIRE: FROM EGYPT TO ROME

The philosophical traditions associated with European-based civilizations (including Spain, Britain, and France, and Mexico, the U.S., and Canada, for example) tend to be traced back to a most European-looking ancient Greece through the lens of what has been described as a perverted form of racist diffusion perpetuated by a tradition of modern Euro-centric historians of science and philosophy. Martin Bernal (1987), in his critically acclaimed and highly responded to *Black Athena: The Afroasiatic Roots of Classical Civilization*, identifies this "model of Greek history" as the "Aryan Model," which views "Greece as essentially European or Aryan" (p. 1). Contextualizing this approach to Greek history, Bernal (1987) notes that it "developed only during the first half of the nineteenth century" and "flourished during the twin peaks of anti-Semitism in the 1890s and again in the 1920s and 1930s" (pp. 1–2). According to this Aryan perspective, the Indigenous inhabitants of Greece were civilized by "invading" or "infiltrating" northern "Indo-European speakers sometime during the fourth or third millennium BC" (Bernal, 1987, p. 2).

Those who advocate for this model of white cultural diffusion also tend to support what we can call the *multiple-emergence* thesis of evolution, which is based on the assumption that *man* evolved into *man* at different times and in different regions of the world, which account for what is hegemonically claimed to be the natural hierarchy of intelligence found between the so-called different races, with Europeans consistently coming out on top. Advocates of such an approach spend a considerable amount of time attempting to make the case for the existence of vast differences between Greek and Egyptian civilizations. Underscoring this point mainstream scientists have gone so far as to argue that tracing the roots of Greek society to Egypt is a Euro-centric construct because it suggests that Egyptians, Africans, and people of color in general need to be connected to that which is identified as European, such as ancient Greece, to be viewed as legitimate, when, in reality, they do not need such false connections due to their own unique richness.

Challenging the scientific validity and cultural bias of the multiple emergence approach to human evolution, Diop (1987) reminds his audience that it is a mathematical impossibility for the same species to have multiple emergences. In other words, it is not feasible for a single species to *descend* more than once and produce many genetically compatible *lineages*. What is more, all known evolutionary evidence points to Africa (Kenya) as the sole birth place of humans, who, through twenty to forty thousands years of migration and *adaptation*, developed into what we know the world's people to consist of. The implications of Diop's (1987) scholarship—the conclusion that if humans had not migrated out of Africa, then today all humans' would be Black—remains highly controversial among elite academics. But he does not stop there, Diop (1987) stresses that the hierarchy of intelligence thesis is nothing more than a myth as no scientist or researcher has ever found any scientifically significant differences in the brains of people from the unsubstantiated social construction of different races (the issue of evolution will be more fully explored in Chapter Twelve). That is, human intelligence is consistent and indistinguishable across the species.

In the end, the white supremacists deny what seems undeniable: that the Egyptians, Phoenician, Africans, and all of humanity are related, and that central and fundamental aspects of early Greek, and thus "Western," civilization, were externally adopted through both diffusion *and* indoctrination—including philosophy, science, mathematics, religion, language, and governance. While Diop (1987) maintains that the assertion that the totality of humanity stems from a single African origin is a conclusion of science and thus incontestable, human history becomes more complicated when considering the social development of culture because it has always been the result of diffusion, convergence, and, at times, indoctrination. In other words, only in very rare instances, if any, have human cultures manifested themselves in isolated, homogenous contexts.

For example, the tendency toward hierarchy might have already been established in what would become Greece as a result of the process of subjugation initiated by the northern invaders that predates Egyptian colonization. Egyptian imperialists therefore might have just contributed to a tendency that was already underway. If there is any truth to this speculative hypothesis, then we might say that social relationships based upon hierarchy emerged within separate human communities simultaneously—communities already separated by thousands of years of migration—through the process of convergence, and later by indoctrination and diffusion. However, these ideas and the rigorous science informing them have been antithetical to establishment scholarship and research.

One of the most prominent of such Euro-centric scholars, Bertrand Russell, who, despite his shortcomings, remains one of the great Western philosophical thinkers of the twentieth century offering many valuable insights to the field such as, "science tells us what we can know, but what we can know is little, and if we forget how much we cannot know we become insensitive to many things of very great importance" (Russell, 1945/1972, p. xiv), a point we return to in Chapter Twelve. For now, we will focus on the Euro-centrism in Russell's (1945/1972) widely influential *The History of Western Philosophy* where he situates his work, through implication, within the theoretical context of what we might call *racist-diffusionism* highlighted in his reproduction of the white supremacist assertion that "philosophy, as distinct from theology, began in Greece in the sixth century B.C." (p. xiv). Implied within Russell's discourse— the discourse of the conquerors, or, more subtly, the dominant society—is the modern manifestation of Plato's myth of the metals metaphor (Malott, 2008) where the belief in the natural hierarchy of people within a given society is replaced by the fabrication of a universal scale that can rank civilizations from advanced to primitive, and, of course, the European inventors have always positioned themselves (at least the rulers) as specially endowed with logic and science, and therefore responsible for having led the rest of the *savage* world out of the darkness of mysticism, superstition, and emotional impulse, and thus, the inventors of philosophy, reason, and the good society.

Commenting on this tendency within Euro-centric history to dichotomously portray Greece as essentially "rational" and Egypt as "irrational," which misses the complexity of the existence of both rational *and* irrational ideas and practices in *both* Greece and Egypt, Bernal (2001) comments that "the centrality of madness and shamanism" in "Greek life and thought" is distorted by emphasizing the "'rational' Greek texts" and ignoring "the many more 'irrational' ones" (p. 392). Emphasizing such instances of historical complexity Bernal (2001) continues, "in Egypt too, there were areas of 'rationality'—sophisticated and rigorous mathematics...wonderfully observed medical symptoms...and more—amidst what we now consider to be magic and superstition" (p. 392). We might observe a similar context in today's U.S. society that simultaneously legitimizes right-wing Christian fundamentalism and a rigorous tradition of scientific investigation.

Russell does acknowledge the indisputable fact that before the rise of Greek society, "civilization had already existed for thousands of years in Egypt and Mesopotamia" (p. 3). However, Russell disregards the significance of this fact arguing that ancient Egypt, burdened by the "terrifying gloom" of its own internal aristocratic mysticism, lacked the ability to acquire the necessary freedom to become competent in the "purely intellectual realm"—needed to conceive of more advanced levels of civilization unhindered by the primitive nature of reflex and impulse—which, he argues, represents the contribution of the Europeanized Greeks—the "Indo-European" invaders of present-day Greece. In other words, Russell suggests that those responsible for bringing philosophy and science to the barbarism of Egyptian civilization were the "fair-haired invaders from the North" (p. 7).

Russell even manages to turn one of humanity's greatest inventions, the symbolic representation of words—writing—into evidence of Egypt's assumed inferior status next to their European superiors noting that Egypt's form of writing, comprised of pictures, was "cumbrous" or clumsy, which was developed, thousands of years later, by the intellectually advanced Greeks, into a more useful and efficient form of civilized "alphabetic writing." Many historians raise serious caution against judging too harshly the "imperfections" in the Egyptian and then Phoenician systems because "...our own alphabets and especially...the English one...is a real monstrosity," and therefore, aware of these insights, rather than assuming a position of arrogance, "be a little humbler" (Sarton, 1952, p. 110).

While the Aryan Model of Greek history, as perpetuated by Russell, for example, seems to be hindered by the hegemony of a politically motivated form of propaganda negatively impacting its status as a legitimate scholarly undertaking, the "Ancient Model" (Bernal, 1987) of Greek history, on the other hand, while also based on the premises of diffusion, does offer the rigorously inclined an analysis with a great deal more substance and, as a result, an enhanced attempt at historical accuracy. The Ancient Model, as articulated by Bernal (1987), while accepting the Aryan hypothesis that Greece was invaded by northern Indo-Europeans around the fourth or third millennium B.C., it is based on evidence that the core influences on ancient Greece stem not from those with "fair hair," but from the residual effects of having been colonized by the Egyptians and Phoenicians around 2000 B.C. The idea that Black, or "Negro," Africans could have dominated and indoctrinated "white" Europeans is so fundamentally contrary to the dominant paradigm of racial hierarchy that it remains a rejected idea within the discipline. For example, prominent Egyptologists and classicists, such as Mary Lefkowitz (1997), argue passionately against Bernal (1987) asserting that in the second millennium Egyptians were not a *colonizing people* and to claim they were is to rely on Greek myth and *strange* interpretations of archeological evidence.

Because Bernal's approach challenges Euro-centric history, it has been harshly attacked by mainstream Egyptologists—a field Diop (1987) argues was created to prove that ancient Egyptians were White because of the mountains of evidence that clearly suggests they were in fact Black. It is safe to assume that if *Black Athena* were not so rigorously grounded on an examination of the evidence, it would not have received the attention it has. While this exclusionary tendency within the academy is significant in and of itself, we are presently more interested in our exploration of the historical context of philosophy.

We use the terms diffusion and indoctrination as tools to assist us in our comprehension of this complex history. For example, it is clear that, on one hand, you have ancient Greek aristocratic philosophers admirably referencing the African sources of much of their own culture and internal structure, and, in the process, contributing to the development and refinement of that which they understood to be Afro-Asiatic, such as the written manifestation of human thought. On the other hand, there is evidence of Greek resistance against external influences, such as the art of writing, highlighted in Socrates' seething diatribe *Phaidros*. Summarizing this complexity Sarton (1952) concludes that, "the intense rivalry that obtained between the Greeks and the Phoenicians did not separate them so much that they could not influence one another" (p. 111). Despite the Greeks' apparently conflicted relationship with writing, at least initially, and seen from the Ancient Model perspective, it becomes abundantly clear how influential the Egyptians and Phoenicians were, and remain, on Western civilization.

Casting the invention of writing in the light offered by this Ancient Model approach to diffusion, and informed by a significantly more rigorous engagement with the anthropological and archeological evidence, George Sarton (1952) plainly states that, "the greatest achievement of the Early Egyptians was the invention of writing" (p. 20). Rather than portraying the unfinished-ness of ancient Egyptian text as evidence of inferiority, Sarton celebrates the Egyptian genius embedded in the essential epistemological idea of standardizing a system of symbols capable of translating and recording the infinite creative spontaneity of human thought. Underscoring this perspective Sarton notes that, "the great inventions were seldom completed by the great inventors" (p. 21), and writing, which developed within multiple locations and over the course of as much as 4000 yeas or more, renders the *single-inventor* conception utterly and completely short sighted, or perhaps just Euro-centric and anti-Black. From a diffusionist perspective, it was the combined efforts, over time, of first the Egyptians, then the Phoenicians adding consonants and a more efficient format for commerce, and finally, the Greeks with the addition of vowels, that paved the way for modern "Western" writing. Outside of this development, simultaneously in other regions, we find many examples of the convergence of writing—within the Mesopotamian Sumerians, the Chinese, the Maya, and others, who, therefore, had maintained, at times, independent existences, although this is difficult to verify (see Chapter Two). Regardless, the history of humanity is the history of its "monogenius." The diversity is found within the values informing how this genius has been manipulated.

Sarton (1952) observes that such complex cultures, like that of ancient Egypt, require the unification of large populations of people, which, he argues, is only possible "in relative peace and comfort," and, therefore, "share their many tasks and the fruits thereof, and stimulate one another" (p. 19). However, we know that large complex societies can be built not only through democracy, as suggested by Sarton, but through physical coercion and/or ideological indoctrination. As already noted, ancient Egypt, at the pinnacle of the Old Kingdom, was a society built on the divine-right logic of aristocratic hierarchy. It is not too far of an historical stretch to argue that the wealthy aristocracy of ancient Greece modeled their own system after the Egyptian approach, especially when one refers to the historical documentation of the ancient Greeks themselves. Consequently, it should not be surprising, that proponents of the Aryan model tend to discount these sources as fictional myth. However, examining a little closer the ideological motivation behind foundational inventions, like writing, might provide more clarity concerning these issues.

Sarton (1952) underscores the importance embedded within the creation of symbolic representations of language in his observation that "the invention of writing" had a "deeper purpose," which he identifies as "the preservation, correction, and standardization of the language itself" (p. 67). These observations concerning not only the mechanical act of writing, but also the political ends for which the technology was designed to meet, are crucial here in our attempts to come closer to comprehending what early Egyptian society was like. The legitimacy of the

Egyptian Dynasties seems to have been based, in part, on the national story and the divine connection between the leaders and the cosmos. These stories, documented, fixed, and advertised through hieroglyphic writing, unified the people around their ruling class. The Egyptian state was religious-based and dedicated to the enrichment of itself through colonization. In this context writing became a necessary tool of bureaucratic bookkeeping. These tendencies, it can be argued, set the stage for the mechanistic standardization and categorization of knowledge and knowledge production indicative of "Western" science.

This insight is fundamental in our understanding of the history of Western approaches to what we might call the science of philosophy—conceived as theoretically informed interventions in the world—because, from a Western perspective, "no scientific work of any kind could ever be published without a linguistic tool of sufficient exactitude" (Sarton, 1952, p. 67). In ancient Egypt and Mesopotamia philology (the science of record keeping and categorizing associated with libraries), therefore, was not "one of the latest sciences," but rather, "one of the earliest" due to the need "from the beginning" to "standardize," "refine," and "increase" the "precision" of their interacting languages (p. 67)—and all languages are always pregnant with political implications as they are intimate aspects of the social contexts in which they are found. Placing his analysis in practice, Sarton (1952) concludes, "philologic consciousness was a part, an essential part, of scientific curiosity" (p. 67). However, we must note that this analysis, while important, does not posses universal applicability as evidenced by the high degree of "exactitude" achieved through oral traditions demonstrated in Chapter Fourteen.

Again, none of this would have happened at all, or at least when it did, if it were not for the very early intellectual brilliance of Egyptian epistemological and ontological orientations. Even Galileo (1564–1642), who Russell (1945/1972) himself credits with being "the greatest of the founders of modern science" (p. 531), identified the creation of writing as the most significant human invention for its ability to accommodate humanity's infinitely creative use of language within the parameters of a relatively finite system—"24 little characters" (Galileo Galilei, 1632, quoted in Chomsky, 2000a, p. 4) originally developed by the Egyptians of the Old Kingdom between 3400 and 2475 B.C. (Sarton, 1952). However, at the same time Galileo justly reflects on the genius of antiquity, he digresses by reproducing the false hierarchy that situates all that is presumed to be Western as representative of the pinnacle of advanced civilization, and everything else as inferior, barbaric, and not as advanced.

This grand-narrative perspective is based on the assumption that there is but one true linear standard for human social development that can be used to measure where any given society falls on what we might call the civil-savage scale. While we remain highly skeptical of all hierarchies—because of their socially constructed nature—especially this one that is based on an invented conception of literacy that has been put to work in the service of empire building by privileging the "Western" written word and forms of knowing over the vast richness of the philosophies informing Native American's oral traditions while simultaneously denying the existence of pre-Columbian Alphabetic texts Indigenous to the Americas (discussed in Chapter Two and Fourteen), we cannot deny the brilliance of ancient Egypt's invention—a brilliance stripped from Black Egypt and handed over to the Indo-European Greeks by modern Euro-racist historians.

From the Egyptian invention of writing alone, no doubt, the Western world has benefited tremendously. Imagine the world without writing, without books—but what of the content of these books? To what does the Western world owe ancient Egypt for the West's ideas, that is, European philosophy? What insights might our anthropological concepts—convergence, diffusion, and indoctrination—offer our efforts at answering this question? World-renowned Afro-centric Egyptologist, Marxist scholar and historian, and Senegalese Professor, the late Cheikh Anta Diop (1955/1974), after reviewing, and collecting himself, mountains of evidence, supports the Ancient model of diffusion concluding that:

> The ancient Egyptians were Negroes. The moral fruit of their civilization is to be counted among the assets of the Black world. Instead of presenting itself to history as an insolvent debtor, that Black world is the very initiator of the "western" civilization flaunted before our eyes today. Pythagorean mathematics... Epicurean materialism, Platonic idealism, Judaism, Islam, and modern science are rooted in Egyptian cosmology and science. (p. xiv)

Diop is not ambiguous in his critique of the European racism that has clouded the West's historical lens in the modern era. It is worth noting that the subject areas Diop identifies as Egyptian-based—math, science, and philosophy—were not originally conceived as distinct. That tendency is a relatively recent form of reductionism. In the ancient worlds of Egypt and Greece these areas of inquiry were not viewed as separate from one another, but rather, part of the same paradigm or view of the world. In other words, the philosophies about the world, how it operates, and what aspects of it can be known for certain, for example, were scientific and mathematical—unified. The completeness of the unification of all areas of inquiry will emerge toward the end of this volume as each study or chapter will conflate into the next. We have begun, in this chapter, taking up the issue of philosophy, Platonic Idealism in particular. We will take up the issue of the African roots of Pythagorean mathematics in the context of Native American mathematics in Chapter fifteen. Epicurean materialism will be taken up in Chapter Twelve in the context of the science curriculum. For now we will explore the Egyptian roots of Platonic Idealism.

However, before we proceed, it is especially important that we pause at this juncture and make sure we do not over-extend our analysis in our attempts to counter the racism of Euro-centric conceptions of history, and falsely romanticize ancient Egypt, as ancient Greece often is, as a perfectly worked out democratic utopia. Our task when engaging ancient *Black* Egypt is therefore to highlight the genius of their accomplishments while simultaneously not ignoring aspects of their civilization that influenced ancient Greece that were based on hierarchy and thus oppressive to large segments of their populations. As we will see, from the Egyptian bosses the Greek rulers adopted an ideological model that the Romans would later put to work for empire building—idealism. In our discussion we pay particular attention to the ways in which the Greeks (and later others) reformulated it and put the philosophy to use fulfilling the class-based dreams of what developed over a few thousand years into European imperialist superpowers and European-based colonialist settler-states in the Americas and elsewhere (however, our analysis here is limited to the context of the Americas).

The evidence is fairly conclusive that Egypt did emerge as the first world (at least the world as it was known by those people at that time) superpower. It should therefore not be surprising that Egyptian society embodied the same contradictions and antagonisms as found in modern capitalist empires, such as the U.S. Portraying the ancient kingdoms of Egypt as consisting of single national interests is as incorrect as presenting the U.S. as consisting of a single national interest because it ignores that in class-based societies what is good for the bosses, such as more profits, tends to be bad for those relegated to the status of worker/slave because more profits/capital/wealth usually requires lower wages or standards of living.

Diop (1955/1974) goes so far as to argue that in rural and urban centers during the Middle Kingdom (2160–1788 B.C.) there existed "marginal capitalism" as evidenced by the labor force being "free" and "contractual" and the existence of "a business class who rented land in the countryside and hired hands to cultivate it" motivated by the sole purpose of generating "huge profits" (p. 210). In the cities, Egyptian capitalists engaged in what seems to be very modern business practices such as "interest-bearing loans, [and] renting or subletting personal property or real estate for the purpose of financial speculation" (Diop, 1955/1974, p. 210). While Diop (1955/1974) argues that it was the "inalienable liberty of the Egyptian citizen" (p. 210) that prevented the development of "strong capitalism" with more power over the populous than the state or nobility, the contradictions within Egypt's hierarchical arrangements did lead to a series of unsuccessful internal revolutions.

Diop's analysis, examined next to Marx and Engels' (1848/1978) history of human social development, underscores the latter's European-centered perspective.

That is, naming what they understand to be the stages of conflicting interests, beginning with ancient Rome, which transitioned into the Middle Ages, and finally giving way to the modern bourgeois era, Marx and Engels (1848/1978) comment: "freeman and slave, patrician and plebeian, lord and serf, guild-master and journeyman, in a word, oppressor and oppressed, stood in constant opposition to one another, carried on an uninterrupted, now hidden, now open fight, a fight that each time ended, either in a revolutionary reconstitution of society at large, or in the common ruin of the contending classes" (pp. 473–474). Again, Diop's study, which uncovers early African forms of capitalist economic arrangements that gave way to very early social revolutions, challenges the Euro-centrism of Marxism. This is not a casual point. The historical development of human social arrangements are far too complex to attempt to fit them into a single linear scale.

Before we continue let us briefly return to Diop's observation that ancient Egypt experienced revolutions. Revolutions are enormously costly and very rarely do they materialize into outright physical and forceful challenges to the basic structures of power, and even more rarely are they successful. For full-blown revolution to occur large segments of whatever population must have come to a series of philosophically-informed conclusions resulting from their practice in the world: the system does not, or ever will, serve their interests; reforms, under these conditions, are forever futile; and the only way to relieve themselves from perpetual suffering and degradation is, therefore, to risk ones life through the social organization and implementation of rebellion (Chomsky, 2007). There is no reason to believe that this would have been any different in antiquity than as it is now. In other words, this may prove to be one of the few universal tendencies present within the human condition.

As revolutions or counter-hegemonies always suggest a particular critique or reading of the world, it should not be surprising that it has been found that at the same time Egyptians were developing the art of writing during the Old Kingdom, some of their imaginations were also animated by axiological conceptions of right and wrong situated in the ontological context of the movement and interaction of ideas or minds. We might call this philosophical idea the dialectic, born out of the tension between competing interests. According to Martin Bernal (2001), "Plato's theory of ideas and moral dialectic were anticipated in Egypt by over a thousand years" (p. 390). For example, Diop noted that "there is no doubt that the theory of the dialectical movement due to the action of opposite couples (thesis, antithesis, synthesis) originates from the Hermopolitan cosmology, which explains all the phenomena of the universe by the action of the law of opposites" (quoted in Crawford, 1995, p. 137).

David James (1995) provides a detailed description of what this dialectical movement looked like in practice through his analysis of a discussion between an

Egyptian father, Any, and son, Khonshotep, on the nature of moral instruction written before or during the fourth century B.C. on papyrus. The banter begins with Any equating moral instruction with the taming of a wild animal (thesis) similar to Freire's (1999) critical description of the banking model of education. Khonshotep returns fire holding that only with reason and inward acceptance can one truly learn the virtues of morality (antithesis) alluding to an active rather than passive engagement with ideas. The debate continues, and the tension from which gives way to new understandings (synthesis).

Sarton (1952) argues that ancient Egypt's two thousand eight hundred and seventy five year long history provided the stability needed to maintain the cross-generational continuity for the development of such rich philosophical traditions. We might also reason that it was the exploitation suffered by the masses (over time) that fueled the development of philosophical perspectives based on morals and ethics. Again, even as far back as the Old Kingdom some Egyptians were developing a kind of early *moral philosophy* and *conscious*, which certainly must have been a result of the contradictions of their own hegemonic hierarchies because it is only the presence of suffering that creates the need for a philosophy and practice of liberation, that is, a moral philosophy and critical consciousness. In other words, without the lived reality of oppression and subjugation there is no need for counter-hegemonies (Malott, 2008).

Ironically, it is the oppressive idealist philosophy of divine superiority that European leaders have claimed as their own creation and evidence of their own supremacy (along with Egyptian math and science). Before the fading memory of history allowed the European architects of empire to claim aristocratic philosophy as the fruits of their own labor, advocates of Greek culture and independence—advocated for in the face of Egyptian colonialism—looked admirably toward Egypt as they organized their own societies. Summarizing this position Bernal (1987) points to Isokrates, "the outstanding spokesman for Panhellenism and Greek cultural pride" (p. 103) during the early fourth century:

> Isokrates admired the caste system, the rulership of the philosophers, and the rigor of the Egyptian philosopher/priests' *paideia* (education) that produced the contemplative man, who used his superior wisdom for the good of the state. The division of labor allowed a "leisure," which allowed for "learning." Above all, he insisted that philosophy was, and could only have been, a product of Egypt. This word seems to have been used by the Egyptianizing Pythagoreans for some time—possible since the sixth century. (p. 104)

Within this brief sketch—written from the perspective of diffusion—we can begin to make out the root structures of the Platonic Idealism that would go on to influence Christianity and then animate the minds of those European colonizers responsible for the most grievous of all human atrocities—the American Indian Holocaust that was part and parcel of "taming" the "wild frontier" and the African Holocaust that was a by-product of the trans-Atlantic slave trade. As part of fully engaging the philosophical implications of ancient Greece, we briefly revisit the connections between Greek, Phoenician, and Egyptian civilization through the combined use of our three concepts—diffusion, convergence, and indoctrination. Because of the unavoidable implications of the practice of empire-building, the following discussion takes the form of a sort of history of empire from Egypt to 1492, and then in the next section, from 1492 to the present. Because every practice in the world, including, and especially, empire-building, presupposes a theory, the following investigation pays particular attention to the dynamic and tension-filled relationship between the concrete and theoretical/philosophical contexts of *empire*.

* * *

It has already been established that Egyptians and Phoenicians colonized Greece. Bernal (1987, 2001), Diop (1987), G.M. James (1954/2005), and many others argue that Egyptians "civilized" the Greeks, not the other way around, and, it seems, once literate in the functional knowledge of civil society and a sufficient degree of political and economic independence was established, while still informed by the ethics of dominance, not democracy, the "light haired" northerners super-exaggerated the Egyptian hierarchy, and, after spreading it west and north and the elapse a few thousand years of successive failed and successful attempts at empire building, discursively reversed the order of who originally developed the modern roots of Western empire. From our brief examination of this *fact* of history, we have begun to provide an answer to the question of how our three anthropological concepts (convergence, diffusion, and indoctrination) can inform our understanding of this ancient colonial process. However, our investigation has just begun, this is but our place of departure.

Let us examine a little closer the specific structural features of the Egyptian, Roman, and then, after Europe's "dark ages," the Western European model of this universal, colonialist system of *empire*. Before continuing, however, it might serve our conceptual interests to clarify what we mean, operationally, by *empire*. First and foremost, the concept of empire conjures images of vast mobile armies—the ranks of which perpetually expand and contract with the strength, influence, and tactical decisions of its architects—deployed in the service of the expanding impulse of the system. At their heart, empires are military-based, profit-seeking societies with the goal of political, ideological, and economical world-domination. Ultimately, the tendency toward empire is a way for a ruling class (or an emerging ruling class) to emerge as *the* universal one-government master of the world. Some incorrectly describe empire as a relatively recent phenomenon and thus the last stage of capitalism. However, as we have seen thus far, empire is an ancient and recurring tendency, and, therefore, conceived as either the first stage of capitalism or simply pre-capitalist (Perlman, 1985). Perhaps it is sufficient to say that empire in general is inherently capitalistic, that is, a form of governance that consistently places the quest for profit far above the needs and interests of people. Idealism might be one of the earliest philosophies conducive to empire building.

Within idealism we find a philosophical universalism based on natural hierarchy, and, as a result, embodies a tendency conducive to empire. Through Plato this was expressed as the myth of the metals metaphor (Brosio, 2000; Malott, 2008). For Plato knowledge was not created but unequally distributed among humanity by God into three groups: a small number of the population was assumed to be of Gold metal quality (the most intelligent and thus the natural leaders—hence, the white man's burden, that is, the arduous responsibility of the master race to civilize the savage); a slightly larger group of Silver quality individuals (highly intelligent but still in need of guidance); and finally the vast majority of humanity were said to be of Bronze value, and thus unfit to be citizens (slaves and brutes with little or no intelligence and therefore capable of only being directed).

However, the mysticism embedded within Plato's system of ranking did not go un-critiqued, even by his contemporaries such as Aristotle. A guiding assumption behind Aristotle's realist science is the belief that all objects are endowed with an internal, unchanging order, or *essence*, that can be uncovered through objective, systematic, observation. In other words, for Aristotle, to *know* is not merely the act of remembering the knowledge that God equipped you with upon your creation. Rather, to know is to engage the senses in uncovering hidden truths embedded within the natural, material world. Thus, unlike Plato who argued the senses are a hindrance to pure thought, Aristotle argued that the senses are an indispensable tool in bringing to consciousness that which is hidden by the mysteries of nature.

After the rise and fall of ancient Greece, the Roman Empire emerged not necessarily as a contributor to what had been established by the Egyptians, Phoenicians, and Greeks, but, through political maneuvering, offering foreign regimes a mode for social control, the Romans were responsible for bringing the knowledge of antiquity to Western Europeans "accustoming" them "to the idea of a single civilization associated with a single government" (Russell, 1945/1974, p. 271). Diop (1987) notes that these universalisms were slow to come in ancient Greece as conceptualizations of government were limited to the concept of the city and the Gods associated with its particular rulers, and enforced with repressive impunity. It was not until Plato's *Republic* and the Stoicism of Zeno who controversially proposed the notion of a universal God and single government that would unify all free *men* (only about one to six percent of ancient Greece's population were free *men*, nearly the opposite as ancient Egypt) informed by justice and morals freed from religion (these ideas, in an earlier time, caused Socrates his life). Situating this analysis of the ancient Greek world and its relationship with universals in a larger context Diop (1987) notes that, "these universalist ideas derived from the southern world and in particular from Egypt. A thousand years before the Greek thinkers…the Egyptians…had clearly conceived the idea of a universal God…of all humankind" (pp. 31–32).

According to Diop (1987), Christianity was originally an offshoot of Judaism based on its *chosen people* conception of religion, but failed in its conversion attempts, and therefore turned to unconverted "barbarians" and adopted the one-God universalism thesis of the Egyptians. These notions transcended the class distinctions of ancient Greece allowing the poor to worship on a far more equal footing. These tendencies, already underway with the Stoics, allowed the Romans to organize the population against the "municipal regime" and "establish the empire" (Diop, 1987, p. 33). What made the empire possible was what we might call *the monopolization of governance*. The tradition of Athenian and Spartan statesmen competing for city dominance gave way to the universal government of Rome. What Rome offered was a model for hegemonic stability. As a result, many of the Mediterranean cities wrought with internal class conflict "offered only a semblance of resistance" to Roman conquest, which "led to the establishment of the Roman Empire" (Diop, 1987, p. 33).

After the fall of the Roman Empire, unable to sustain the "achievements of antiquity," the West was overcome by a prolonged period of "intellectual regression," the Dark Ages, while the "barbarian" or tribal kings of what would become Europe, inspired by the memory of Rome, repeatedly attempted to "rebuild a universal Christian empire" (Diop, 1987, p. 35). The knowledge produced in antiquity "vegetated in the monasteries" rendering the Church one of Europe's only foci of intellectualism during their Dark Ages (Diop, 1987, p. 35). Diop (1987) concludes that it was the "Arabs" during the seventh century who reinserted the knowledge of antiquity back into the societies of Western Europe through a series of colonizations. For example, Islamic scholars and philosophers, such as Avicenna and Averroes, introduced the West to the life, work, and social and political contexts of Aristotle. Islamic colonizers also brought to the West "advanced metallurgy," "the navigator's compass," "gunpowder," "naval maps," "the axial helm," and chemistry and mathematical knowledge from the East (Diop, 1987, p. 36). Placing the role Islamic colonizers played in helping the West out of its darkness, Diop (1987) comments that "the fact that Spain was the first European country to acquire technical supremacy at the dawn of modern times…can be explained only by the Arab contribution during the time of its colonization" (p. 36).

Wherever this universal empire has gone, its fruits have been the same: great wealth, greater poverty, and the simultaneous and contradictory existence of internalized oppression and widespread rebellion and resistance. Encouraging resistance at the expense of internalized oppression has been the historic work of critical pedagogy—that is, empowerment and agency over enslavement and subjugation. But to where can we trace the roots of this democratic impulse and propensity for independence and liberty?

THE NATIVE AMERICAN ROOTS OF MODERN DEMOCRACY

The history books of the West are filled with romantic stories about the brilliance of Christopher Columbus and his great achievements. That is, discovering the "New World" and, in the process, bringing civilization (i.e. Christianity) to the untamed wilderness—a wilderness either described as "empty" of people or empty of civilized people. Columbus is said to have been inspired by God and motivated by an insatiable appetite for adventure. However, a closer look at the scholarly literature and available primary sources provides an historical account about as far removed from the official story as one could imagine. It appears that Columbus was not so much motivated by *good will* and the *Christian spirit of brotherly love*, but by the cruel and utterly barbaric practice of plunder for wealth (and fame) supported by a desperate Europe nearly bankrupt from a long series of unsuccessful holy crusades. Columbus was therefore not so much seeking what we might call the X-treme-game adventurism of the wealthy and bored, but a get-rich-quick scheme and, therefore, a way out of the depravity of a decaying Europe (Malott, 2008). From the historical documents it is more than clear that Columbus' quest for wealth in the Americas manifested itself in a form of genocidal barbaric cruelty never before witnessed by humankind—not in Egypt, not in Phoenicia, not in Rome, no where. We review this history in Chapters Five through Eight, and will therefore not rehash it again now. What we will focus briefly on here are some of the ways in which Native American social philosophy had a civilizing effect on Europe, Europeans, and much of the world (this discussion will be more fully explored in Chapter Ten) because that history is important to the final section of this chapter that considers the theoretical implications of curriculum development and reformulations.

* * *

> Nineteenth-century historians created the Greeks as the fountainhead of that culture by consciously omitting references to the Semitic or Egyptian origins of mathematics, philosophy, and literature...A parallel history of conscious omission of...American Indians has been practiced in mainstream American history. (Mohawk, 1992, p. 61)

While Columbus seems to have noticed a fundamental philosophical difference between Europe and the Taino Indios he encountered in present-day Haiti and the Dominican Republic as evidenced by his own journals (Malott, 2008), his thirst for wealth occluded any desires he may have had to learn from their example. As a result, a mere twenty years after Columbus and his men arrived in the Caribbean Basin, the once fertile and populous islands were desolate and forever stained with Indigenous blood and heartache. It was not until the sixteenth century that Europeans began actively learning from Native American philosophical perspectives. According to Oren Lyons (1992), the Spanish and English, in the Americas, were decidedly more genocidal than the French. Arguing this point, Lyons (1992) notes that during the sixteenth century the French, more than anyone else, "joined the Indians on the Indians' terms" (p. 27). Jesuit missionaries in particular wrote extensively on their adventures with Native Peoples, such as the Huron in contemporary northeastern Canada, focusing on their egalitarianism and respect for the dignity of the individual, which sparked an intellectual movement in Europe, the Enlightenment. In other words, generations of French and English writers working in close proximity with Native peoples in North America influenced Europe's intellectual community, which, eventually, would influence a global re-conceptualization and revitalization of democracy. We can understand this history as a form of diffusion—the diffusion of democracy.

When Columbus washed up on the shores of present-day Haiti and the Dominican Republic, Native Americans, in general, had developed perhaps the world's most democratic philosophy, and therefore democratic political context. It is therefore not surprising that Native societies were especially attractive to Europeans and Africans brought to the Americas as labor. It should therefore also not be surprising that the colonizers, in many ways, were themselves philosophically transformed in profoundly democratic ways as a result of their interactions with Native Americans. For example, in *Exiled in the Land of the Free*, John Mohawk and Oren Lyons (1992) note that there was an "ironic twist" to Europe's conquest of the Americas:

> The conquerors were themselves conquered. For along with the exportation of gold and slaves from the New World, something else was exported: democracy. This export item, perhaps Native America's greatest contribution to the world, toppled European monarchies and ultimately resulted in the formation of the USA. (p. 2)

In *Exiled in the Land of the Free* Peter Matthiessen (1992) casts this diffusion in a slightly different light alluding to the universalism of the democratic impulse, which he characterizes as the state of being "at one with…Mother Earth," commenting that it "had been lost to all but a few 'traditional' Europeans in the very farthest corners of that continent" (p. xii), such as the Saami Nation of Finland,

Norway, Sweden, and Russia who are known for their ancient, Indigenous management practices of the vast Reindeer herds who migrate near the Arctic Circle (Seurujarvi-Kari, 1994). The traditional Hopi of the four-corners region (New Mexico, Colorado, Arizona, and Utah) of present-day U.S. offer an even more concrete democratic context in which they trace the convergent origins of all of humanity to. According to Hopi profits (whose spirituality is so thoroughly grounded in the concrete physicalness of the Earth that it is authoritative in the realm of the world's ancient Indigenous traditions) at the beginning of this world, the fourth world, like at the beginning of the previous three worlds, all of humanity was given the same simple democratic directions by the mysterious force that makes possible the existence of life, which people call many things such as God and The Great Spirit: to take care of the world and everything in it (including each other). Again, this worldview had tremendous transformative implications on Western philosophy sparking the Enlightenment.

For example, Enlightenment scholar Jonathon Israel (2006) argues that what was unique about the Enlightenment, contrary to accepted scholarship, was not the methods of science and reason, but rather, the democratic interpretive framework for understanding such data that would prove to have revolutionary implications. Israel (2006) argues that the modern conception of revolution, the product of this new interpretive framework, emerged in France, and is therefore compatible with the Indigenous analysis of Lyons (1992). Situating this struggle over the hearts and minds of men and women and therefore the relationships that define our existence in the context of philosophy, Jonathan Israel (2006) notes:

> Only philosophy can cause a true "revolution"... A revolutionary shift is a shift in understanding, something which, though intimately driven by the long-term processes of social change, economic development, and institutional adaptation, is in itself a product of "philosophy" since only philosophy can transform our mental picture of the world and its basic categories...Most modern readers [however] resist attempts to envisage 'philosophy' as what defines the human condition. (p. 13)

Philosophy, from this perspective, is the lens through which we view the world, and ultimately, informs our daily interventions and interactions in the world. Every conscious, functioning person has a particular way they think about and make sense of the world, which we can call our philosophy—everyone therefore has one. Israel (2006) argues that before *The Enlightenment* Europeans were "too steeped in tradition, theological doctrine, and the mystique of kingship" (p. 3) to embrace the paradigm shift and radical break from the past implied within the modern conception of revolution. However, what Israel fails to explain is how this radicalism managed to flourish in the context of such Euro-conservative rigidity. The modern manifestation of the revolutionary impulse did not just appear out of nowhere. Again, it was the example of the lived practice of democracy in the Americas that offered those foreigners willing to listen a concrete, practical example that could be advocated for and emulated in other contexts.

For example, Donald Grinde (1992) in "Iroquois Political Theory and the Roots of American Democracy" notes that early Enlightenment thinkers such as the French scholar Jean Jacques Rousseau and the British writer John Locke "derived much of their ideas about democracy in a workable form from travelers' accounts of American Indian governmental structures" (p. 231). The modern conception of revolution, as described by Israel (2006), can therefore be attributed to the internalization of American Indian conceptions of "unity, federalism, and natural rights" (Grinde, 1992, p. 231). This analysis is clearly informed by diffusion.

Modern Euro-centric historians, however, argue that American democracy can be traced back to the democratic example of ancient Greece or to the more recent Magna Carta (the Great Paper) of 1215, which was an English charter designed to establish basic rights for the King's subjects. Countering such arguments Grinde (1992) notes that because the Magna Carta failed to achieve freedom and equality within the narrow limits of an authoritarian parliamentary framework, when Europeans came to the Americas, there had not been a working democracy in Europe for over two thousand years, that is, since the fall of the "Greek city-states of Athens" (p. 230), rendering American democracy, for example, a direct result of American Indian influence.

As suggested in the quote at the beginning of the present subsection, this Native American influence that has forever transformed Western philosophy tends to be as unreferenced as the Egyptian and Phoenician influences on European culture. Another similarity is that the omission of these influences is a relatively recent practice. For the greater part of the nineteenth century "…the American Indian, as a symbol of liberty and things distinctly American, was commonplace" (Grinde, 1992, p. 249) among Euro-American politicians and propagandists. However, the rigor of this historical accuracy within mainstream, settler-state anthropology, historiography, and politics gradually gave way to a Euro-centric, white supremacist national story conducive to the manufactured civil-savage scale. Grinde (1992) concludes that the American political system is the result of an amalgam of European and American Indian influences. As we will see in Chapter Four the founding of the United States was centered around two competing imperatives: capitalism and private property against freedom and democracy. As a result, and as we will see later in this volume, there always existed two Enlightenments, one radical and more or less true to the democratic gifts of Indigeneity, although not always properly referenced, the other, a form of cooptation and therefore a continuation of European social hierarchy and dominating practices.

Philosophy and the Contextualization of Curriculum

What do these insights offer the construction and manifestation of our educational practices, and why is philosophy important to the task of *Teaching the Americas*? The combined use of philosophy and history demonstrates that to rely too heavily on the epistemological concept that there is but one correct answer and way to construct knowledge is to risk missing many invaluable opportunities to learn from diverse perspectives. A typical example illustrating this point: The settler-state education system presents Columbus as the great discoverer who brought civilization to the "New World." A Taino Indian in 1493 of present-day Haiti, on the other hand, might have complained that, "when the Europeans realized that we were here, they murdered us and took everything they could from our homeland and our people." The idea is that in oppressor/oppressed situations there are two primary perspectives (that of the aggressors and that of those under attack) that result in the creation of very different knowledges and theories concerning particular events and views of the world, such as colonization and the legitimacy of operating a capitalist enterprise.

Upon closer examination, however, we uncover a tendency that indicates that as the colonization process develops and expands in the use of indoctrination as a tactic for social control and subjugation, its complexity and contradictions in alliances and relationships within and between oppressed and oppressor groups too expand. We find, for example, the oppressed both resisting the process of plunder and dehumanization and simultaneously internalizing the legitimacy of predation and thus their own oppression. One also witnesses oppressors deepening and intensifying their commitments to violent exploitation, and simultaneously former bosses attempting to renounce dehumanization working to end the process of value-production associated with colonialist plunder. There are therefore not just two perspectives, that of the bosses and that of workers, for example, but many overlapping and competing perspectives. The critical theoretical tradition informing this very analysis and the reformulation of curriculum, in part, can be traced directly to North American indigeneity, as demonstrated in the preceding subsection.

* * *

The democratic example of indigeneity is informed by the belief that people posses the cognitive ability to tend to their own interests. According to Donald A. Grinde (1992) in "Iroquois Political Theory and the Roots of American Democracy" many of the "founding fathers" of the U.S., Benjamin Franklin most notably, rejected the anti-democratic European model drawing instead on the brilliance of the Iroquois system of shared governance designed to ensure democracy and peace by putting power and decision making in the intelligent hands of the people united in a confederation of nations and not in the divine right or assumed superiority of a ruler. Grinde and others in *Exiled in the Land of the Free* (Lyons & Mohawk, 1992) document, in great detail, the generosity of the Iroquois leaders in assisting Euro-Americans, before, during and after the American Revolution, in creating a unified Nation composed of the original thirteen colonies as the foundation for long-term peace, freedom, liberty and democracy in North America. Putting the American Revolutionary war in a context foreign to traditional social studies instruction, Grinde (1992) notes that "the first democratic revolution sprang from American unrest because the colonists had partially assimilated the concepts of unity, federalism, and natural rights that existed in American Indian governments" (p. 231). It is abundantly clear that the gift of democracy received by the United States government by the Haudenosaunee has all been but subverted. For examples of the democratic tradition in contemporary times, outside of Native communities themselves, we have to turn our attention to the highly marginalized critical tradition.

However, we might say that this democratic tradition, commonly associated with European critical theory (i.e. Marxism), is an appropriation because the Native American source of these generous gifts, in the contemporary context, tends not to be cited, as argued above. For those already engaged in the lifelong pursuit of knowledge, this is an easily amendable flaw—requiring of such Western-trained critical theorists/educators an active epistemological and material engagement with Native Studies and Indigenous communities the world over (Ewen, 1994; Kincheloe, 2008). We might say that the critical theoretical tradition, rooted in Indigenous conceptions of freedom and liberty, represents a rich history of opposition to anti-democratic, authoritarian forms of institutionalized power—private (corporate), federal (state), and religious (Clergy/Church)—for it is this unjust power that poses the greatest barrier to peace. The example of the Haudenosaunee is relatively indicative of this tradition, which stands in stark contrast to the anti-democratic Aryan model. What follows is therefore a summary of the origins and fundamentals of Haudenosaunee political thought.

* * *

According to "Haudenosaunee oral history," millennia before the arrival of Europeans, "Native peoples of the northeast woodlands [including present-day western New York] had reached a crisis" indicative of the existence of rampant violence and "blood feuds" between "clans and villages" (Sotsisowah, 1978/2005, p. 31). Amongst this atmosphere of terror there emerged a young man with a vision of peace. Because his name is only used during ceremonies, he is commonly referred to as the Peace Maker. This Peace Maker has been credited with being "one of the great political philosophers and organizers in human history" (Sotsisowah, 1978/2005, p. 31). His story begins in the now predominantly Canadian-controlled regions north of Haudenosaunee territory. After failing to persuade his own countrymen to adopt his message of peace, the Huron, he traveled to the land of "the people of the flint," the Kanien'Kehá:ka, or Mohawk, where he sought out the most feared "destroyers of human beings" and "brought to each one his message" (Sotsisowah, 1978/2005, p. 31). The warriors took his message and became his disciples, assisting in its dissemination and perpetuation.

Eventually, these efforts resulted in the peaceful union of five of the Nations in the region, the Oneida, the Onondaga, the Mohawk, the Seneca, and the Cayuga, which stands as one of the first, and therefore one of the oldest, democratic confederacies in human history, which, eons later, after the arrival of Europeans, became Six Nations, a history, however, beyond the scope of this essay. While these histories are very interesting themselves, what is of particular importance here is the fundamental principles of the Peace Maker's Great Law of Peace.

The "first principle" that was presented by the Peace Maker was that the world in which we live was created by the "Giver of Life" who did not intend for humans to "abuse one another" as had been the case amongst the Native Americans of the northeast (Sotsisowah, 1978/2005, p. 32). Essentially, the Peace Maker reasoned that "human beings whose minds are healthy always desire peace, and humans have minds that enable them to achieve peaceful resolutions" (Sotsisowah, 1978/2005, p. 32). Towards these ends "government would be established for purpose of abolishing war and robbery among brothers and to establish peace and quietness...by cultivating a spiritually healthy society" (Sotsisowah, 1978/2005, pp. 32–33). Particularly significant was the Peace Maker's conception of peace because it went further than advocating for the absence of war, but for "universal justice." The practice of peace, it was said, could only be established within societies that had established power, reason, and righteousness, which constitutes the heart of the Peace Makers' democratic challenge. Haudenosaunee leader, Sotsisowah (1978/2005), defines these *dispositions*, which, because of the value of hearing his voice and considering his perspective, are quoted at length

> "Righteousness" refers to something akin to the shared ideology of the people using their purest and most unselfish minds. It occurs when the people put their minds and emotions in harmony with the flow of the universe and the intentions of the "Good Mind" or the Great Creator. The principles of righteousness demand that all thoughts of prejudice, privilege, or superiority be swept away, and that recognition be given to the reality that the creation is intended for the benefit of all equally—even the birds, animals, trees, and insects, as well as the humans. The world does not

belong to humans...Nothing belongs to human beings, not even their labor or their skills, for ambition and ability are also gifts of the creator. (p. 33)

"Reason" is perceived to be the power of the human mind to make righteous decisions about complicated issues. The Peacemaker began his teachings based on the principle that human beings were given the gift of the power of reason in order that they may settle their differences without the use of force...and that force should be resorted to only as defense against the certain use of force...and there is an ability within all human beings...to grasp and hold strongly to the principles of righteousness. (p. 33)

The "power" that the Peacemaker spoke of was intended to enable the followers of the law to call upon warring or quarreling parties to lay down their arms and to begin a peaceful settlement of their disputes...It was power in all the sense of the word—the power of persuasion and reason, the power of the inherent goodwill of humans, the power of a dedicated and united people, and, when all else failed, the power of force. (p. 34)

Sotsisowah (1978/2005) continues, explaining that the Peacemaker's law, in a sense, "anticipated" the emergence of social classes, and was therefore designed to "eliminate" any arrangements that might resemble the competing interests of class society, especially in the area of property, and, as a result, banned the existence of separate territories that had previously caused much jealousy and conflict. Toward these classless ends, and therefore through the establishment of a highly complex system of *direct* democracy, the leaders were positioned to be *direct* conduits through which flowed the power and authority of the society held in the hands of the people.

Even though the content that has just been presented is a somewhat incomplete description of Sotsisowah's (1978/2005) summary of the Peacemaker's law, it fulfills the task of highlighting the rich democratic tradition within the Iroquois Confederacy. Again, while this framework was conceived by the Peacemaker as a gift to all people, it is especially relevant to those who live within the United States because the creation of the U.S. government was highly influenced by Six Nations leaders informed by the Peace Maker's Great law of Peace. Sotsisowah (1978/2005) argues, and I would concur, that the law of the Peacemaker, which survives despite tremendous odds, has yet to be fulfilled, rendering its central themes currently relevant because "...the possibility remains that the Peacemaker's vision of a world in peace and harmony may yet be realized" (p. 40). Not only is the world at war, but the entrenchment of class antagonisms only seems to be growing. The Haudenosaunee form of direct democracy against class interests is therefore perhaps more needed now than ever. The observation that Indigenous worldviews influenced the Enlightenment sheds light on the Indigenous roots of modern democracy and revolution and thus progressive and radical forms of education. Indigenous philosophy has therefore been indispensable to the task of teaching and learning because it represents the interpretive framework that transformed

Western philosophy providing very different ways to think about questions fundamental to education, such as: What is the mind and how does it work?

* * *

It is the struggle between competing ideas about how the mind works and how we learn that guide the creation of most educational experiences. From Plato the West adopted the idea that the minds of people, as represented by intelligence, are predetermined by God, and God has an unwavering record of only creating a few supremely advanced ones in each generation, rendering a very small minority natural leaders and controllers of the vast majority. This authoritarianism and the divine right to rule informing it is an ancient European tradition whose current structures can be traced back to the hierarchal and "temporal organization" of the Roman empire—the western most provinces of which extended into the heart of northern Europe (Diop, 1987). Again, Europeans brought to the Americas the basic idea that the King is the King and the world is his domain because God said so (Malott, 2008). It is worth repeating that this European model was largely rejected by many Euro-Americans drawing instead on the brilliance of Iroquois Democracy, and, in the process, becoming counter-hegemonic, critical-scholar revolutionaries. Aristotle's Egyptian-influenced materialist science—realism—has taken on new meanings in this democratic context. A guiding assumption behind realism is the belief that all objects are endowed with an internal, unchanging order, or *essence*, that can be uncovered through objective, systematic, observation challenging the argument for divine epistemological hierarchy. Since the Enlightenment, in the Western tradition, it has been argued that the essence of what it means to be human, that is, human nature, is not divine determinism, but the ability to independently think and to become aware of much of what animates our minds. This notion of relative autonomy and free will, and the resulting revolutionary agency, stands in stark contrast to the Western conception of the universal holy empire, and thus, God's will.

French philosopher Rene Descartes is often credited with laying the conceptual foundation for the modern Western interpretive framework, which, at the time, was highly subversive. Descartes' work is seldom connected to its Indigenous North American influences, which we attempt to rectify while simultaneously exploring critiques of Cartesian reductionism. Descartes' "mechanistic worldview" was profoundly influential changing "western civilization profoundly" as it was conceived as "something that changes everything" (Israel, 2006, p. 5) because it takes as its place of departure the possibility that everything that is believed to be true is actually false, therefore demanding sufficient evidence to prove the certainty of assumed truths. Signifying his attempt to break with European hegemony represented in Plato's myth of the metals hierarchical idealism, Descartes describes his democratic conception of human intellectual endowments on page one of his *A Discourse on Method* (1637/1994) noting that, "good sense is, of all things among men, the most equally distributed," which is determined "by nature" (p. 3). Because "reason and sense" are equally distributed, reasons Descartes (1637/1994), they are "found complete in each individual" and therefore "the difference of greater and less holds only among the *accidents*, and not among the *forms* or *natures* of individuals of the same *species*" (p. 3). Considering this universal characteristic among the species, clearly influenced by North American indigeneity, Descartes (1637/1994) observes that, "I rightly conclude that my essence consists only in my being a thinking thing [or a substance whose whole essence or nature is merely thinking]" (p. 122). From here it has been routinely argued within the Western modern scientific community that, unlike other species, humans do not operate solely at the level of instinct due to the unique ability to think before acting, and, as a result, possess the ability to change our minds or alter the schema that mediates how we understand the world.

While the Native American democratic conceptualization of human nature (i.e. the Iroquois), which Descartes (1937/1994) clearly embraces, remains popular within the West's critical theoretical tradition (although almost always incorrectly attributed to European sources), he was also informed by dichotomous logic leading him to believe that "the mind or soul of man is entirely different from the body" (p. 128) even though "the whole mind seems to be united to the whole body" (p. 127). Upon closer investigation, however, Descartes (1637/1994) observes that when, "a foot, an arm, or any other part is cut off…nothing has been taken from [the] mind" leading him to believe that the mind and the body are separate and distinct—representing an inability to completely break from Western hegemony. In other words, while Descartes counter-hegemonically challenges the false hierarchy of intelligence, he embraces a reductionistic ontology and therefore an analysis of mind that distorts the interconnectedness of all that is. Chomsky (2000a) disregards the question entirely noting that there is no clear distinction between where the body ends and the mind begins—the mind is simply matter designed to produce thought. Descartes advocated for an ontology that conceived the mind as separate and distinct from the body, which suggests the existence of a world not whole and unified, a common view of indigeneity, but one consisting of separate parts that can be reduced to their *essence* through scientific investigation. From this perspective it is assumed that truth and certainty are to be found within *essence*. Lost, however, is an understanding of the deep, rich, ever-developing relationships between all *essences*—essences conceived here not as static, but also in a perpetual state of change and thus tension. In short, it is a form of Platonic idealism that is reproduced in Descartes' dichotomy between the mind, the realm of God and reason, and the body, the Godless, untamed wilderness of the flesh.

The danger of Cartesian reductionism in education is the tendency to disconnect the production of knowledge from the social political context in which it is situated. Conceiving the world as chopped up into areas of study or disciplines is another fundamental feature of Western reductionistic and thus decontextualized education. Ignoring the political implications of the scientific method of knowledge production informing industrialism, for example, has been catastrophic. Reducing humans, geography, and all forms of life to their wealth generating potential through the disinterested science of capital is the result of the mechanistic and thus utilitarian view of the body after it has been disconnected from the soul or the mind. Summarizing this "machine cosmology" (Kincheloe, 2005) Descartes (1637/1994) theorizes, "if the body of man be considered as a kind of machine, so made up and composed of bones, nerves, muscles, veins, blood, and skin, that although there were in it no mind, it would still exhibit the same motions which it at present manifests involuntarily, and therefore without the aid of the mind [and simply by the dispositions of its organs]" (p. 126). Descartes attempts to further mechanistically depoliticize and thus neutralize the body by arguing that is was formed by God as a machine "for the sake of motions" (p. 127). Choosing to reject this false dichotomy, it is our intention throughout this volume, to provide a unified, interdisciplinary approach to the production of knowledge and conceptualization of the world and all that it encompasses.

CHAPTER TWO

African Influences in Ancient Central America

The role of Africans in ancient South America is discussed throughout this chapter providing additional evidence countering the Eurocentricism of the dominant paradigm. These discussions are particularly significant because they challenge the paternalistic assumption that Europeans developed the most advanced technological and scientific traditions bringing them to the Americas, integrating what was fast becoming a global economy, in an inevitable advancement of civilization. Through our investigation we discover that the Europeans came to the Americas quite late compared to their African counterparts. Like Chapter One, the chapter that follows offers a significant perspective for non-Euro-centric knowledge production for a democratic society.

* * *

It is widely accepted in the settler-states of North America that Columbus discovered the Caribbean basin and the Americas, and in the process, "enlarged the world" (Russell, 1945/1972, p. 486), rendering recent Europeans the first (or at least the first substantial) foreigners in America and therefore the rightful *owners* of these so-called *unclaimed* lands (see Chapter Six). However, there exists a much different hegemony among the many Maya communities of Central and South America due to their pre-Columbian experiences with North and West African visitors and settlers. A few semesters ago in a teacher education course at D'Youville College in Buffalo, New York Curry Malott had the opportunity to make use of these insights. It happened in a philosophy of education class, which he had constructed in a way that challenged the students to consider what it meant for them as future teachers to be a part of socializing the next generation of the settler-community with Western philosophy on stolen land Indigenous to particular human groups with their own rich philosophical traditions. The texts included *Rethinking Columbus* (Bigelow, 1994) and *A Call to Action* (Malott, 2008). One of the students in the course, *Luis*, would often come to class excited to share how happy it made his Mayan grandmother that white people were finally discussing the implications of the "truth about Columbus" and his legacy in the contemporary era. On one such occasion Curry suggested that Luis ask his *Abuela*, "Who came before Columbus?" Luis looked puzzled responding that he didn't think she would know because she had never been to college or formally educated, that is, Westernized. Curry responded noting that "it didn't matter" and that he "ought to go ahead and ask her." Luis returned the following week anxious to tell the class that he had asked her, and without hesitation, she matter-of-factly responded "los Negros," as if to say "what a silly question, everyone knows the Blacks came here long before Columbus and the Gringos."

* * *

Highlighted within this story is the richness of the subjugated knowledge excluded by Western reductionism (see Chapter One). These Indigenous insights are particularly important from a critical constructivist (Kincheloe, 2005) perspective because the act of learning or acquiring knowledge here is understood *not* to be the passive and objective transmission of predetermined *facts* that occurs when we "detach" the "mind from the senses," as Descartes (1637/1994) argued was possible, leading him to believe that he was able to "abstract my mind from the contemplation of [sensible or] imaginable objects, and apply it to those which, as disengaged from all matter, are purely intelligible" (p. 103). Challenging this Cartesian idea that the mind and the production of knowledge can be disconnected from the social context of "corporeal objects," criticalists have observed that because humans are inherently social beings, everything we do, including learning, occurs in the highly political terrain of society—*the mind and society* can no more be disconnected from one another than can *the mind and the body*. Learning is therefore never objective and can thus be described as an active process of creation that is unavoidably and always situated in a social-political context.

Because the mind is designed to socially develop *schema* for the production of thought—schema that are not predetermined, and therefore always subject to change—the process of becoming conscious of the content of our schema is of extreme importance. That is, for critical constructivism (and critical pedagogy) self-awareness is indispensable. For example, if we are not aware that we have been indoctrinated with self-destructive schema and thus are not aware that we are acting self-destructively, we cannot be expected to independently alter our behavior. The normalized and naturalized, that is, hegemonized, belief that everything assumed to be non-white, Western, and European is inferior or savage, has a direct consequence of producing self-destructive knowledge and perpetuating the practice of oppression.

Unfortunately, because Euro-centrism is the norm, the historical discussions that follow are important for a number of interrelated reasons. That is, the history of African visitors in the Americas is the story of the movement of ideas across both time and space determined by various Native American and African peoples and the relationships they negotiated throughout their pre-Columbian contact periods (outlined below). Pedagogically, these narratives are presented here to challenge readers to critically examine their own schema/interpretive frameworks/worldviews. We find this more academically rigorous historiography joyous and epistemologically invigorating, and therefore, conducive to *sparking a passion to know* (Freire, 2005) within our audience, such as students, and, in turn, has the potential of dialectically informing our schema advancing the production of socially just knowledge and educational (and society-wide) practices as future or current educators.

That is, when we de-hegemonize our schema through the never-ending process of critical self-reflection and action (Freire, 2005), we pave the way for dehegemonizing the knowledge we produce. For example, when the Euro-centric history curriculum is reformed and the central roots of Western science are accurately understood as essentially African, the production of anti-Black knowledge and practices face severe challenges. We can describe this as social justice scholarship, which is the choice of critical pedagogy because it serves the best interests of humanity—and we conclude that it is in the best interest of humanity to be united around democratic principles, such as an appreciation of diverse epistemologies, paving the way for universal self-actualization. This conclusion stems from our rejection of the myth of natural hierarchy, which is based on the assumption that the establishment of social equality can only ever be an attack on freedom because it prevents the naturally superior individuals or groups, however conceived, to rise to their predetermined state of domination. Consequently, teachers' loyalties, critically conceived, should be to the communities they serve, based not on hierarchy, but on the Cartesian conclusion that (Descartes, 1637/1994), "good sense is, of all things among men, the most equally distributed" (p. 3).

Transgressing the narrow epistemological borders of the dominant, Euro-centric paradigm we will now turn to a detailed review of the evidence *of* and consider the implications *for* the African presence in the Americas that *began* as much as perhaps 3000 years or more before Columbus (von Wuthenau, 1992/2002).

Again, the view of the world the following histories provide are counter-hegemonic because of the constructions and practices they have the potential to foster in the white supremacist context of global capitalism.

Before we proceed, however, we must offer a brief caution. The idea here is not to simply replace the old and immutable subject matter with another curriculum to be passively absorbed. Rather, the goal is to demonstrate that *absolute certainty* is a very slippery fugitive that no isolated person, acting alone, has ever been able to grasp in its entirety. As a result, anyone claiming absolute ownership of the one true reality ought to be received with great suspicion. A more healthy and democratic approach, however, is to view the production of knowledge and the practice of politics only as strong as its active participants—that is, societies where political power and venues for the production of knowledge are equally distributed and therefore marked by large numbers of actively engaged members are democratically stronger than those where power is concentrated in the hands of a few and organizing ideas about the world come from a very limited array of sources. We therefore invite you to engage the following chapter not passively and mechanically, but actively. That is, as you read on you may ask yourself:

- How might the ideas and analyses presented here inform my schema, and, as a result, my future practice?
- What arguments or ideas do I not agree with and why?
- What counter evidence do I have to support my criticisms?
- What ideas brought me joy, and why?
- What evidence was the most compelling or convincing?
- What evidence presented here was the most surprising?
- What other questions did this chapter lead me to ask?

* * *

Because the dominant Euro-centric story of Columbus traces the knowledge that enabled Europeans to come to the Americas to the Copernican theory that one could reach India by sailing west from Spain (Cadiz in particular) and to the earlier work of prominent *Franciscan Schoolmen* such as Roger Bacon's geography conducted in the mid-to-late thirteenth century, for example, and from these sources to Plato and other early Euro-Greek thinkers (Russell, 1945/1972), the science and practice of African and Islamic maritime inventors and sailors that diffusively came before them is downplayed or ignored outright (Covey, 1992/2002; Van Sertima, 1976/2003). What is Euro-centrically glossed-over here is that while the Greeks knew much about the planet, such as its round shape and size (Covey, 1992/2002), their navigational and map-making skills were limited, which Europeans, centuries later during their age of exploration (marked by Columbus) were unable to overcome. For example, the limitations of European naval technology and science, even in the fifteenth century, are most strikingly represented by the fact that "they could not find longitude at sea" (Covey, 1992/2002, p. 123). This, in part, was due to their lack of "trigonometry," which, consequently, is needed to "transfer points on the spherical surface of the earth to a flat plane in such a way as to preserve correct distances" (Covey, 1992/2002, p. 118) for the purposes of map making.

Neither the European Renaissance explorers nor the Greeks of Alexandria possessed this knowledge. However, in the sixteenth century maps were made of South and North America that "seem to be based on ancient maps" (Covey, 1992/2002, p. 118). Europe, as a possible source of this knowledge, has been ruled out by the rigors of scientific diffusionism. That is, not only had they not developed the mathematics needed to produce accurate maps, but the only "Europeans" of antiquity capable of such achievements, the Greeks, do not suggest "even a hint of America" (Covey, 1992/2002, p. 119) in their ancient world maps. As we will see below, it was those Black Africans and Phoenicians that this sophisticated mathematical knowledge of geography can be traced to.

Departing from *the facts*, the dominant Euro-colonialist paradigm portrays Columbus as having taken the technical knowledge of navigation and geography, said to be invented by "white" Europeans, and put it to work for God imbuing it with a holy purpose, which was to spread Christian civilization to the untamed wilderness—the white man's burden as highlighted in Chapter One. Again, upon closer examination, however, it becomes obvious that the technical knowledge Columbus and Europe's elite *did* possess was of African and Phoenician origin and the Euro-Elite motivation was not one of good will and brotherly Christian love, but one of hierarchy and domination, and were thus determined to achieve their desires by whatever *genocidal* means necessary (Malott, 2008). As we saw in Chapter One, the practice of genocide represents a model of empire that has unabashedly hyper-inscribed the idea of universal-hierarchy with a savagery and barbarism never before witnessed by human civilization.

Placing Europeans at the pinnacle of civil achievement represents a form of cultural genocide, paving the way for physical genocide and domination. Put another way, this propagandist approach to history serves to credit West and North African achievements, for example, to Southern Europeans as part of the myth of white supremacy needed as an ideological justification for Euro-Christians to accept the genocide and enslavement of all non-European and non-Christian peoples, Africans and Native Americans in particular (Diop, 1987). Challenging this white supremacist diffusionism with a more academically grounded diffusionism, von Wuthenau (1992/2002) argues that it is not enough to document the genocidal cruelties of Europeans engaged in the West African, trans-Atlantic slave trade, but scholars should also work to re-write the official curriculum to include detailed accounts of "the nobility of Black rulers who had their portraits carved in colossal stone monuments on American soil" which underscores "the glorious past of African lords in Ancient America" (pp. 82–83). While it has become increasingly acceptable in academic circles to discuss "the enslavement of Black people in the New world" it remains bitterly unacceptable to examine "the role of Blacks in the Americas prior to the slave-trade" (Clegg, 1992/2002, p. 231). From a critical constructivist perspective, we might therefore observe that under the current hegemony it is acceptable to produce knowledge that critiques Europe's atrocities, if their victims, in this case Africans, are presented as inferior. At the same time, it is not acceptable to produce knowledge informed by schema grounded in the evidence that highlights the African role as a world leader in science and technology. Within this counter-hegemonic history we find the African navigational and map making skills that, thousands of years later, would find their way into the hands of Europeans. Again, this ancient model of diffusionism is a direct challenge to the Euro-centric diffusionism of the process of colonialist plundering and predation (Malott, 2008), which, at times, has manifested itself as *the white man's burden*, as noted in Chapter One.

As a result, when we hold our studies to such higher standards of rigor, and therefore, reference the technical and scientific knowledge present within fifteenth century Europe back to Black African antiquity, we discover that the original architects too put it to work to travel abroad spreading it not only west to Europe (Scobie, 1985/2007) and east to China, but to South and central America as well. From this perspective, as demonstrated below, we gain new insights that identify a common Black African diffusive influence in the empires of both Rome (see Chapter One) and that of the Aztecs from the twelfth to the sixteenth century. Coming to a similar conclusion Wayne Chandler (1992/2002) argues that ancient Egypt was not only essentially Black, but it influenced subsequent African empires, as well as being "the mother of mankind" and, as it turns out, the "midwife of many a civilization" (p. 248) such as the sudden emergence of a Mesoamerican empire marked by hierarchical social organization and the construction of large-scale centers of ceremonial worship and hegemonic power. West African and Maya perspectives on ancient interactions between these two regions of the world (West and North Africa and Central America), therefore, offer considerable insight in better understanding and *Teaching the Americas*, and, "as a result of these revelations, a new drama of man begins to unfold on the Meso-American stage" (Chandler, 1992/2002, p. 248). Continuing with the ontological perspective advocated for in Chapter One that embraces the interconnectedness of all that is, and therefore the unification of all subject matter, the focus of the present inquiry on Africa and America contributes significantly to this approach.

This history represents an important, but far too often ignored or distorted, part of the experience, and thus curriculum, of humanity. In other words, it is part of our collective story, so we must strive for the discipline to be accurate in our historical investigations ensuring we *get it right* and thus operate under accurate schema. In *getting it right*, we must caution against confusing the mere *inversion* of the civil-savage scale, where Black Africans, as the primary architects of the major advances in "Old World" antiquity, replace Europeans' privileged position as the genetically superior "race," with transgressing it completely. In challenging the argument that Europeans are responsible for creating the most advanced and superior civilizations and technologies, it is easy to get romantically caught up in tracing the trail of Western philosophy, science, and technology away from Europe and into Africa and Native America, and, as a result, leaving the hierarchical framework in tact.

When we challenge the hierarchy of civilizations paradigm, we are not only concerned with the roots of modern Western democracy, for example, but we are also highly interested in exploring multiple philosophies of practice and ways of being that are not based on hierarchy and the romanticization of "lords" and nobility, regardless of descent, European, African, or American. We are therefore not only interested in acknowledging the fact that much of modern Western society can be traced to ancient Africa, but we are particularly concerned with challenging the very idea that industrial-techno global neo-liberal capitalism represents the most advanced manifestation of human civilization. In other words, we must continuously ask ourselves what we can learn from yesterday about today and what we might do as we inevitably move forward into the future. As argued in Chapter One, this is the critical pedagogical project/movement that this book is designed to contribute to, and is therefore addressed, in great detail, in later chapters. Because of the great complexity characteristic of the pre-Columbian exchanges between Africa and South America, this chapter has been focused on better understanding this history. In so doing, we contribute to our understanding of Empire outlined in Chapter One. In the final section of this chapter we briefly review the critical pedagogical implications of the analyses presented herein. First, however, we continue our study of the interconnected histories of Central America and North and West Africa.

* * *

In the centuries before the European *conquest* of the "New World," rumors of civilizations to the west across the vast oceans, previously unknown to Europeans, emerged from Africa, Guinea in particular, which Spain, reeling from a series of very costly and unsuccessful crusades, eventually chose to take seriously, and consequently, led to the financing of Columbus' expeditions to the Caribbean Basin (Van Sertima, 1976/2003). As we will see below, these *rumors*, emanating from Africa, were informed by first hand accounts and long-standing relationships with South Americans. An appropriate place of departure here might be a brief summary of the accounts of the conquistadors in the Americas at the start of the sixteenth century.

When Spanish *religio-military* speculators began exploring South America in the early sixteenth century, Black Africans, in some areas, turned out to be an already established presence in social life. The early Spanish colonists—early from a strictly Euro-perspective—on the mainland of continental South America made special notes in their journals of "sightings of Africans in the New World" (Van Sertima, 1976/2003, p. 25). For example, in 1513 Spanish imperial representative Vasco Nunez de Balboa and his regiment, starting out north east (Atlantic side) of the isthmus between North and South America, made their way south in search of gold, each new Indigenous community they encountered pointed the wealth-crazed men further south informing them of another ocean (the Pacific) on the other side of the narrow strip of land where there sailed "boats as big as theirs" and endowed with "more gold than they could ever weigh" (Van Sertima, 1976/2003, p. 23). Balboa and his men, driven by their insatiable appetite for gold and wealth, made it across the mountainous and highly treacherous land bridge to the other side of the isthmus—to the Pacific Ocean—where they stumbled upon a Mayan village, and, "to their astonishment," noticed a group of "war captives who were plainly and unmistakably African" (Van Sertima, 1976/2003, p. 23).

Additional physical evidence of this significant African presence throughout South America includes areas where the population is significantly darker than surrounding tribes suggesting that Blacks "mixed with the local races" and "formed" what has been identified as "small isolated groups" (Van Sertima, 1976/2003, p. 25). These two examples suggest that there was not one single type of pre-Columbian relationship established between Africans and Native Americans. That is, what is suggested is that the African cultural influence in the Americas, discussed below, that, in some respects, persists, can be understood as the result of diffusion through inter-marriage, for example, *and*, later, in some instances, simply did not occur due to a change in the political context resulting in the existence of African "war captives."

Let us examine a bit closer the African cultural influence in South America. It should be expected that accompanying the African presence in the Americas are cultural artifacts, such as, "realistic portraitures of Negro-Africans in clay, gold, and stone" found in "pre-Columbian strata" unearthed by relatively contemporary archeologists (Van Sertima, 1976/2003, pp. 25–26). Perhaps the most striking artifacts found in southern Mexico of a pre-Columbian African presence are "colossal" granite heads with distinctly "Negroid features" (discussed below), the earliest of which have been dated between 1200 and 700 B.C. (Van Sertima, 1976/2003, p. 26). As we explore this evidence, we are particularly concerned with what we can learn about the relationships between African travelers and settlers and Native South Americans, that is, Maya. From the interactions between these ancient worlds we gain insight into how Ancient African culture spread to the Americas, that is, we look for evidence of both diffusion and compulsory diffusion/indoctrination. What we know about human culture and the fact that Africans were present in South America over a long period of time, we expect to find a great deal of complexity, as previously alluded to.

From Ivan Van Sertima (1976/2003), Alexander von Wuthenau (1992/2002) and other's accounts, we get the impression that a great deal of diffusion occurred—diffusion that grew from the love and admiration that the visited Mayan communities had for their African guests. Van Sertima (1976/2003) notes that because many of these African explorers came from Noble/elite classes, they carried themselves in a particular way that led the Maya to view them as gods. Looking at the artifacts from each major time period, this image begins to appear: African influence in the Americas can be observed from the Olmec culture around 800 B.C., "when they arise in massive stone sculptures," to what is identified as Mexico's medieval Maya period, "when they appear not only in terra-cotta portraits but on golden pectorals and on pipes," and finally to "the late post-Classic period" (Van Sertima, 1976/2003, p. 27), which coincided with European conquest and colonization. From this account it should not be surprising that Van Sertima (1976/2003) concluded that the Aztecs regarded the African portrait as a "scared face" and that they had a number of Black Gods, such as the God of jewelers, Nauslpilli and the God of the traveling merchants, Ek-chu-ah. The existence of not only ancient African artifacts, but the incorporation of Africans into their religion clearly suggests that a great deal of diffusion occurred as Native Americans seemed to hold their African friends in high regard.

The ancient Olmec's placing of the six to nine foot granite heads that weigh as much as forty tons is highly significant as an example of cultural/religious diffusion. Summarizing this point Van Sertima (1976/2003) notes that these heads "stood in large squares or plazas in front of the most colorful temple platforms" and at the center there were "great altars" and "one of these was made out of one of the Negroid heads, flattened on top for that purpose" thereby providing more evidence that suggests that their African visitors "were like gods among the Olmecs" (p. 32). When we consider the enormous amount of human labor power that was needed for "the construction of these Negroid figures," it becomes possible to comprehend that it "is a fact of staggering proportions" (Van Sertima, 1976/2003, p. 32). That is, the massive forty-ton basalt rocks were quarried and transported eighty miles to the holy Olmec cites.

Summarizing this diffusionist analysis Van Sertima (1976/2003) notes that the Olmec culture of antiquity bears the "stamp" of a "signature both unique and foreign" (p. 33). For example, Van Sertima does not think it a mere coincidence that the first appearance of the "Negro-African" in Mexico coincides with both the emergence of "pyramids, mummies, trepanned skulls, stelae and hieroglyphs" because there is no "evolutionary precedents" (p. 34) in America, and achievements of such extraordinary complexity represent a long development rather than the initial stages of a society. It should be noted that the presence of Egyptian hieroglyphs, that is script or writing, found in the late 1950s on a number of seals excavated in Chiapas, Mexico and carbon-14 dated to be as old as 1000 B.C., for some anthropological scientists, is perhaps the strongest piece of evidence that has been unearthed. For Chandler (1992/2002), "writing can be used to identify a culture" (p. 251) as accurately as DNA evidence can identify an individual.

While this discovery of hieroglyphic writing in Mexico, said to be of Egyptian influence, for some scholars, should be interpreted as providing strong evidence of ancient African cultural diffusion in Mesoamerica, it is far more common in mainstream liberal academia to not even deny the possibility of an African presence, but rather, to ignore the question entirely treating the Mesoamerican civilizations of antiquity as untouched by outside influences. For example, leading anthropologist Michael Smith (1996/2003), who himself directed many excavations at numerous Aztec locations, never mentions the possibility of any Egyptian *or* African influences of any kind in his widely read *The Aztecs*, not even in his discussions of Aztec writing.

Prominent figures in other related disciplines such as Manuel Aguilar-Moreno (2007) working in Art History leaves the question similarly unanswered. For example, Aguilar-Moreno (2007), in his *Handbook to Life in the Aztec World*, attributes Aztec hieroglyphic writing to the much earlier Olmec civilization never mentioning or alluding to the possibility of ancient African travelers who were fully equipped with what turned out to be widely-influential epistemological and ontological cargo. Attempting to contextualize the unfathomably brutal and deceptive Spanish conquest of the Aztec Empire and the enslavement of the Indigenous peoples of South and Central America, Aguilar-Moreno (2007) argues that "the Aztec civilization…grew out of its predecessors—the Olmec…" and was not able to defend itself from the conquistadors due to their ignorance of the formers' foreign military philosophy, which stemmed from "still being isolated from the rest of the world" (p. xx). As a result, Aguilar-Moreno (2007) suggests that South Americans experienced no transcontinental cultural exchanges before the arrival of the Spanish. However, despite this ontological shortcoming, the literature contains many valuable insights regarding the philosophical underpinnings of Aztec writing and the socio-political context in which it flourished.

For example, Smith's (1996/2003) anthropological work led him to the conclusion that "the Aztec's, like most ancient peoples, did not distinguish categories of 'science' and 'art' as we do today" and that "Aztec art, too, was integrated into religion, politics and society" (p. 238). From this analysis we can begin to understand the unified approach to the production of knowledge that dominated Aztec society. However, while the Aztec's held a unified approach to epistemology, their empire, like all empires, was based on hierarchical social arrangements where "the nobles and lords composed only 5 percent of the...population" but were "firmly in control" (Smith, 1996/2003, p. 131) as their power and privileges were stipulated by law and transferred only through a rigidly enforced system of heredity. Below the nobility was a class of lords who ran large estates by birth-right granted to them by the nobility. The vast majority, however, were commoners whose sole function was to serve the owners and bosses of the Aztec world.

Trades, such as scribe which was a well respected profession, were also passed on from father to son. Summarizing this point Smith (1996/2003) notes that "the occupation of scribe was hereditary" (p. 241). It is worth repeating that some of the Aztec's hieroglyphic symbols mastered by the scribes have been identified as indistinguishably Egyptian. It appears that not only were the symbols similar, but the ways in which the Aztecs used writing bears striking similarities to the ways in which the Egyptians put it into practice. Smith's (1996/2003) account provides a concise summary of the role of writing in Aztec society at the time of Spanish colonial intervention

> The Aztecs produced codices and other manuscripts or books for a variety of purposes. Religious books...contained depictions of gods and rituals, along with much information on the 260-day ritual calendar. These books were used by priests for divination and to keep track of rituals. Historical books typically consisted of a list of years in the year-count calendar accompanied by representations of key events in the history of a dynasty...There were several types of administrative books, including tribute [taxes] lists, maps of city-state territories, and records of landholdings. (p. 240)

Smith's depiction here is of a society informed by a bureaucratic, divine-right hierarchical logic very similar to the ancient Egyptian model. The argument is therefore that the Egyptians brought the epistemological idea of standardizing a system of symbols capable of recording human thought to Mesoamerica, which, through a process of cultural diffusion, the Olmec embraced and began applying to their own language, and because the science was intimately connected to social-political-religious knowledge, their society too was transformed.

* * *

What is more, the "ascendancy" of the "Negro-African dynasty" in Upper and Lower Egypt was "passing through a very unstable period" (p. 34) as their fleets (as well as those of the Phoenicians) were perpetually on the move searching for tin, which was becoming scarce, "to pay the black Nubian rulers of Egypt" (p. 34). Connecting this context of ancient Egypt to America Van Sertima comments that "ships on this metal run, moving in the vicinity of the North African coast, could have been caught in a storm and swept off-course by the North Atlantic currents" (p. 35), some branches of which would have taken them right into the Gulf of Mexico. Because of the many documented accounts of such storm-induced accidents occurring, even in modern times, this is a likely scenario of the "startling appearance in the Olmec heartland of Negroes with elements of Egyptian culture" (p. 35).

Another indication of the role Africans played in a later period of America—middle South America (the few hundred years before Columbus)—can be found within certain dialects of the Mayan language. The historical accounts take us out of antiquity and into the eleventh and twelfth centuries when Mandingo traders from Mali began to trickle into southern Mexico from the south and southeast. This point should be the most obvious and expected because language is the primary vehicle through which people communicate. These Mandingo West Africans were traders who had learned Nahuatl, "the lingua franca of the Aztecs" (Van Sertima, 1976/2003, p. 94). It is said that these merchants could be found in Mexico's growing urban markets, the largest of which would see as many as 60,000 consumers in a single day. The Mandingo, in Mexican markets, sold many unique items such as the skins of exotic animals not found in the Americas like lions, colorful fabrics, and gold jewelry. These luxuries that the Mandingo made available in the common marketplace, in earlier times, were items typically only available to the "noblemen and kings of Mexico, who seemed to have had some earlier contact with them" (Van Sertima, 1976/2003, p. 93). These merchants settled and built towns spreading their language and in the process, their religion and philosophy, largely due to their mixing with the local population. For example, "the verbal root *na*" and what we might call the philosophy of Nagualism, which is concerned with the hidden and mystical knowledge embedded within things of nature and the natural world, can be found only in those isolated Mayan communities that mixed with the Mandingo (Van Sertima, 1976/2003, p. 98).

While this mountain of evidence (only touched on here) has led many scholars to the conclusion that the cultural traditions of South America rest on the Olmec base from antiquity, suggesting that the Central America the Mandingo came to had already been touched by Africa because the earlier Egyptian cultural influences were of great significance. However, within mainstream academia there remain many scholars who seem unable to see the world outside the Eurocentric paradigm that places Africans on the lower end of a civil-savage scale—a scale that is erroneous to begin with, no matter who is placed where- -which is as incorrect of a conclusion that one could draw as perhaps possible. What follows is a brief summary (sometimes a restatement) of some of their arguments, which are important to keep in mind because this hegemonic white supremacy continues to provide the conceptual fuel for the dominant paradigm.

* * *

The evidence that suggests that there was a significant diffusionary African presence in the Americas, like the evidence that suggests that ancient Egyptians, and later the Moors who invaded Spain in 711 A.D. occupying it until 1492, and in the process, lifting Europe out of their Dark Ages (Van Sertima, 1992/2008), were Black and not white, is so overwhelmingly conclusive that Euro-centric archeologists and historians have gone to great lengths to *prove* otherwise. Chandler (1992/2008), summarizing this same point, notes that, "the black Moors have been subject to the same treatment as have other African or African-influenced cultures—the Olmec, the Egyptian, the Harappan of the Indus Valley—for the same reasons" (p. 151). For example, the conclusion that the ancient stone and clay portraits (mentioned above) found in Central America, identified as indisputably African and "Negroid" in characteristics, and therefore presented as evidence for the ancient African presence in America, has been dismissed by Euro-centric historians, and is thus explained as the result *not* of a long period of African and South American contact, but the result of the random creativity of pre-Columbian artists. Von Wuthenau (1992/2002) views this proposition as "absurd" noting that, "nobody can 'invent' a Negroid face if he has not seen one" (p. 83), and the many artists that were simultaneously creating them cannot possibly be an example of a flowering of *random* convergence. What is more, these African portraits have been found in the elite tombs of ancient Central America strategically placed there to ensure the deceased were not alone "in their trip to the underworld" and "it is nonsense to believe that they would create somebody the dead never knew or could not recognize as a member of the community" (von Wuthenau, 1992/2002, p. 83).

Other mainstream archeologists, aiming for greater historical accuracy while maintaining the accepted Euro-centrism, have been forced to acknowledge the historical *fact* that African travelers made it to the Americas thousands of years ago, long before Columbus *and* the emergence of Christ, and have therefore strived to downplay its significance by arguing that while Africans did come to the Americas long before Europe's very late (late compared to other regions of the world, such as the Egypt of antiquity) age of exploration, they did so "carrying another man's cultural baggage" and therefore as the slaves and menial mercenary workers of Phoenicians, Greeks and Romans (Van Sertima, 1976/2003, p. 30). From this perspective, the African, "before and after Columbus," is a "beggar in the wilderness of history…the eternal and immutable slave" (Van Sertima, 1976/2003, p. 30).

Another argument made is that there is no way a group of shipwrecked foreigners, in this case Africans, could have such transformational influences (outlined above) without a substantial army to back them up, which might be an argument against the possibility of indoctrination during these early encounters, but it does not provide significant argumentation against the possibility of diffusion—the form of cultural transmission that occurred in the pre-Columbian South American world, as demonstrated above. This might be explained, in part, by the fact that the empire that grew out of the African influence was a truly South American empire, an Aztec Empire. The later competing European empires beginning with Spain, on the other hand, were decidedly *foreign* powers *in* the Americas designed to subjugate these distant lands and peoples to enrich the motherland. There was little genuine cultural exchange here, the Spanish practiced cold, calculated physical and cultural domination and wealth extraction leading to an epidemic of Mayan impoverishment and oppression so intense and complete its victims in the capitalist present are still deep within its grasp, although not without substantial resistance (further explored in Chapter Nine).

The attack on historical accuracy, underscored here and in Chapter One, has been an integral aspect of the colonization process since Cortez's conquest of the Aztec empire, which manifested itself as a form of cultural genocide, but would not have been possible without the unintended genocide brought on by the infectious diseases the Europeans unknowingly carried with them. After a series of devastating epidemics, the Catholic Church, to ensure the destruction of the Aztecs as a distinct human group, destroyed their cultural materials, such as thousands of Mayan books thereby obliterating the ancient knowledge of the Aztec including their Indigenous forms of literacy and alphabet. The intended consequence has been historical amnesia. For example, the Indigenous Mexican people, according to Van Sertima (1976/2003), tend to be somewhat unaware of the extent and details of their own ancient history with African merchants and nobility. This cover-up and active subjugation of knowledge has not been limited to the initial colonization process but has continued in the modern era. For example, in 1975 the Smithsonian reported on evidence of prehistoric Negro skulls found at Pecos Pueblo in New Mexico and two ancient skeletons "of an African morphological type with an African ritual dentition" (Jordan, 1992/2002, p. 102) discovered in the Virgin Islands. However, it has been reported that since then, "the Smithsonian has…disavowed the implications of pre-Columbian contact originally drawn from these remains, and further investigation of these skeletons by other researchers has not been permitted" (Jordan, 1992/2002, p. 103). We might note that such examples—examples that might be described as overt Eurocentric conspiracy—are not nearly as frequent as the Eurocentrism that manifests itself as the result of the normalization and naturalization of white supremacy.

Educators must be particularly cautious here because if they are not engaged in the never-ending process of self-reflection, they will be at risk for perpetuating the white supremacy that is everywhere all the time.

Implications for Critical Pedagogy

If our critical pedagogies are to take as their place of departure the concrete context in which they are situated, then the analyses presented in this chapter are of particular importance. The hierarchies indicative of the ancient and modern worlds, from Greece and Rome to South and Central America, owe much of their internal universalistic structure to Black Africa. This *evidence-based* reading of the world, situated in the context of contemporary global-capitalism, is particularly counter-hegemonic because it challenges the white supremacist assumptions the legitimacy of its ruling class and their social arrangements are based on. The story of human history that emerges from our counter-hegemonic perspective is one based much more on collaborative diffusion and exchange than on competition and antagonism. This ancient model of diffusionism challenges those of European descent to take a much more humbler approach to world history and give homage to the African and Native North American roots of the philosophical perspectives and interpretive frameworks they benefit from—starting with the universal democracy of the Iroquois (see Chapter One) and the scientific method of ancient Egypt (see Chapter Twelve), both of which have spread to much of the planet, including Europe, the Americas, and elsewhere.

While the history presented here and in Chapter One is, by implication, counter-hegemonic, and, therefore, controversial in mainstream academia, as critical pedagogues, we should make it one of our primary objectives to challenge this tendency. That is, it would serve us well to treat engaging with the subjugated knowledges of ancient Africa and Native North American indigeneity, for example, not as a *radical* endeavor, but as the practice of rationally expanding our epistemological parameters and therefore conducive to the ideals of justice and equality that our modern (Native American-influenced) democracies are based on. This approach is designed to celebrate the multiple epistemological perspectives characteristic of all peoples and all backgrounds, and is therefore substantially more revolutionary than any one perspective by itself, such as the many critical pedagogies associated with critical theories.

This unified approach is not just a liberal attempt to *lend equal weight to all ideas*, as it were, but rather, it represents a conclusion we have arrived at after a thorough investigation of the evidence. What we have seen is that the history of the many peoples and epistemologies of the earth are not a series of *isolated histories* where each individual locale represents a distinct and unrelated march toward the same universal standard for advanced civilization. The history of humanity, according to science, on the other hand, is a complex story of convergence, passive diffusion, and compulsory diffusion (see Chapter One). Such historical understandings make crystal clear that the epistemologies of the worlds peoples are closely related and share long, complex relationships as ancient as human civilization itself. In completing these initial investigations of this larger study we are left with a much more African-influenced understanding of world history.

Again, this Afro-centrism should not be conceived of as controversial, and it should not make *white* people, or anyone else who relies on a wage to survive, uncomfortable (which is nearly all of humanity because capitalists are a very small minority of the world's population) because there is only one species, even if at the present moment those of European descent happen to be the current beneficiaries of hegemonic prejudice and oppression. For example, white people in the United States, and throughout much of the contemporary world, who currently possess racial privilege because of the long legacy of the racializing that accompanied the African trans-Atlantic genocidal slave trade and the genocide of ninety eight percent of all Native American peoples since 1492, can become change-agents by choosing to denounce racial privilege, working as labor organizers, and opposing all forms of undemocratic hierarchy. For schools, this means that the curriculum needs to be de-Euro-cenric-ized. The content presented in this volume is an example of one such attempt. Of course, as critical pedagogues, we encourage all educators and all students to be actively engaged in this work. Reformulating the curriculum should not just be the act of replacing the subject matter that is to be deposited by teachers into students, but should question the very basis of the knowledge-producing process. This is the task of the socially just educator because it is the responsibility of schools to provide a positive and nurturing environment for all students taking special care to ensure their self-esteems are not damaged in any way by the learning experience.

Our approach to critical praxis here is informed by a refusal to accept the mainstream proposition that one often hears in the parroted echo of the dominant discourse: *there will always be inequality and exploitation because it is human nature* rendering any struggle waged against such tendencies counterproductive. Our critical pedagogies, which consciously strive for universal democracy, however, are based on the evidence that overwhelmingly suggests that social hierarchy is not an inherited biological trait universal among the species (see Chapter Twelve). Inequality, where the few dominate the many, is not determined by genetics, but by the combined use of force, consent and divide and rule, and can therefore be resisted and transformed. This is the objective of critical pedagogy, and our collective histories offer many invaluable insights and sources of empowerment, as demonstrated thus far.

But our attention to detail does not end here. In our critical examinations of Euro-centric curriculum and the subsequent explorations of subjugated knowledges, we must continuously challenge ourselves and the students we work with to always bring to the fore the contexts such perspectives are constructed in. Similarly, Joe Kincheloe (2005), in his *Critical Constructivist Primer*, notes that critical constructivist educators are "concerned with the processes through which certain information becomes validated knowledge" as well as "the processes through which certain information was not deemed to be worthy or validated knowledge" (p. 3). In the end then, to reiterate, from this critical pedagogical perspective, the goal "is not to transmit a body of validated truths to students for memorization," but rather, "engaging students in the knowledge production process" (Kincheloe, 2005, p. 3). Teachers who are successful at this show a great capacity to create the conditions where students can spark their own epistemological curiosities (Freire, 2005) which tends to be marked by the creation of a classroom "where students' personal experience intersects with academic knowledges" (Kincheloe, 2005, p. 4). Kincheloe (2005) offers some insight into what this might look like in practice noting that "in their search for ways to produce democratic and evocative knowledges, critical constructivists become detectives of new ways of seeing and constructing the world" (p. 4). Put another way, critical scholars, dedicated to not only understanding the world, but contributing to uplifting its democratic imperatives, tend to be perpetually searching for new interpretative frameworks (philosophies) or "ways of seeing" that can better serve these ends.

CHAPTER THREE

The Menominee: Sovereignty and Education in a Changing World

This chapter examines the complexities of Native American sovereignty, from a Menominee leadership perspective, focusing primarily on the contemporary context. The chapter that follows began as a series of recorded discussions conducted in the traditional ceremonial way. Because this chapter is based on the oral knowledge of the Menominee people from the perspective of their current elected Chairman, Lisa Waukau, you will not find as many references to scholarly sources as there are in the chapters before and after this one. Stylistically, we mostly speak in the third person, referring to *the Menominee*, but will occasionally speak in the first person, such as, *as Indigenous people we* (even though Curry is white), employed to signify emphasis. In this discussion, we look at the era of termination (for the Menominee it was 1961) and reinstatement (1973), and the complex ways in which they impacted the Menominee, and the ongoing recovery process that continues into the present. Currently the Menominee Indian Tribe of Wisconsin has a population of approximately eight thousand six hundred enrolled tribal citizens. Highlighted throughout this chapter is the role education has played in the efforts to strengthen the Menominee Nation, which, in short, deals directly with issues of sovereignty and self-determination. Because this chapter is written from the perspective of Menominee tribal leadership, it is able to showcase the intricate power dynamics at play between Indigenous Sovereigns and the United States and among Indigenous Sovereigns.

* * *

The issue of sovereignty addresses the right and responsibility of distinct human groups *to be* and *exist* as such. The process of colonization has taken, as a central focus, an attack on the philosophy informing Native American sovereignty through many tactics such as the compulsory assimilation of the boarding school project, the termination of Indigenous tribal status, the decimation of Indigenous economies through the occupation of traditional land bases, the slaughter of entire communities through warfare and massacre, and the creation of a nation of "white" men willing, out of economic necessity and prejudice, to do this counter-democratic work (Malott 2008). Because of the relative success of these efforts, Native American sovereignty and nationhood have experienced serious attrition.

However, as a result of the social upheaval and radicalization of the majoritarian *white* working class engendered by the Great Depression of 1929, the United States federal government began adopting social programs and Keynesian economics to the extent that "the traditional social mechanism" began "moving again" but without subverting the central relationship between the capitalist class and those relegated to the status of worker (Zinn 1997, p. 205). Consequently, Native America benefited tremendously from this atmosphere of change and social responsibility, especially during Lynden B. Johnson's (LBJ) presidency (1963–1969) and his *War on Poverty* social programs. Much of the chapter that follows is about that period in American history when North America's Indigenous peoples were able to begin rebuilding what they had lost through Europe's violent conquest and colonization of the Americas.

When engaging the following discussions keep in mind the contemporary "rhetoric of recovery" (Kincheloe 2009) of the conservative Christian fundamentalists that argue that Obama's stimulus plan is an example of socialism and therefore a direct assault on America and its most cherished values. In their paternalistic discourse conservatives argue that social programs, from Obama's plan to LBJ's *War on Poverty,* do not help people, but foster a state of dependency that prevents the recipients from realizing their full potential within a social universe that assumes that there exists social and economic equality leaving individual drive and intellect as the only *real* variables determining who grows up to be capitalists and who grows up to be wage earners.

One of many structural issues *not* mentioned is that capitalism is designed to perpetually expand in a competitive quest for wealth, which materially, contrary to dominant discourse, can only be produced through labor power, which has led an ever growing proportion of the world's human population, divorced from the means of production, the land, despite widespread working class resistance, exploited and impoverished. One of the primary mechanisms through which this unequal relationship has been maintained has not been through the use of force, but through the control of ideas, or the manufacture of consent, which the schools have traditionally played a major role (and can therefore also be employed to challenge oppression and human suffering).

For years critical scholars have pointed to the ways the school systems are designed to reproduce these class hierarchies. That is, upper middle class schools tend to engage students in considerably more higher order thinking and problem solving activities than in working class schools. The schools where the vast majorities attend are overwhelmingly designed *not* to produce actively engaged managers, but passive laborers who know how to follow directions and be externally commanded. Within the dominant discourse there is a malicious and deceptive tendency to use this socially constructed ignorance as biological and therefore genetic evidence to support class hierarchies and paternalistic policies.

Conservatives' paternalism stems from a thinly veiled racism that assumes that poor people are too stupid to know what is best for them. *It's like raising children*, conservatives frequently reason, *if you do everything for them, you will raise liberals*. As you observe below, the *War on Poverty*, in Indian Country, was not debilitating, but provided an opportunity for people to begin building a future without poverty, and was therefore an exciting time filled with hope and real progress toward cultural rejuvenation and economic independence.

Once again there is widespread optimism and hope in Indian country due to the election of America's first democratic Black President who has already legislated vast resources to *stimulate* what we might call *people's acceptance of capitalism and the basic structures of power*. In other words, there is anticipation that a new *War on Poverty* will, once again, offer Indigenous Nations resources that can be put to work, strengthening and advancing their independence, and in the process, challenge the paternalistic assumptions of contemporary conservatism that have treated Indigenous people as *naughty little children* who have to be told, for example, that *gambling is immoral*.

It is also important to keep in mind that the mainstream, corporate media defines the social universe of political perspectives dichotomously between liberals/democrats and conservatives/republicans effectively limiting the range of debate so narrowly that the Democratic liberalism of Obama is portrayed as socialism and the far left. Within this social universe subjugated knowledges, such as the many complex insights from Indigeneity, are either lumped together with countless other *special interest groups*, or simply ignored as if they did not exist.

As a result, when Indigenous philosophy is centrally included in philosophical and social foundations of education courses, it is unfortunately not uncommon for students with Native backgrounds in such classes to make comments such as, "being from aboriginal descent, I found that what was explored in this course and in Malott's (2008) *A Call to Action* opened my eyes to a world I have never had the opportunity to explore." The present chapter is therefore intended to offer both Native and non-Native students alike a window into issues of Indigenous sovereignty from a Menominee leadership perspective. The significance of the present discussion for future and current educators can be organized into three major categories:

- Knowing the experiences of students and how they think
- Engaging curricular reform from an Indigenous perspective
- Understanding the complex and contradictory ways colonialism has and continues to shape the goals and outcomes of institutions of education

* * *

Menominee Land Base: The Heart of the Nation

The Menominee Indian Tribe of Wisconsin has roughly two hundred and thirty four thousand acres of ancestral land, which they have continuously occupied for the last five thousand years rendering them unique amongst the five hundred or so federally recognized tribes in the United States. During the treaty period Menominee leaders made sure the land base was kept in tact. In 1854 the Menominee Reservation was created. That is the gift the old leaders left the Nation. However, on June 17, 1954 Congress ratified Public Law 108, which, in Indian Country, is known as the "Termination Bill" that President Eisenhower (1953–1961) signed into law. This act paved the way for an experiment in assimilation that materialized for the Menominee on the third of July 1959 when Governor Nelson signed a law rendering Menominee County Wisconsin's seventy-second county. The terrible disaster that ensued is discussed within the sub-sections below. Between 1961 and 1973 federal supervision of the tribe was terminated. Summarizing this history The Menominee Indian Tribe of Wisconsin (http://www.menominee-nsn.gov/), in considerable detail, note:

> On April 30, 1961 the Menominee Termination Plan was submitted to the Secretary of Interior. In 1962 the Menominee Council of Chiefs was organized as a non-profit organization ideally for the purpose of preserving the name "Menominee Indian Tribe of Wisconsin" which was technically abolished during termination. A petition was signed by 780 Menominees requesting the repeal of the Menominee Termination in 1964.
>
> In May 1968 the Tribe had filed suit regarding the hunting and fishing rights of tribal members. The U.S. Supreme Court ruled in the Tribe's favor establishing that when termination was effective it did not relinquish their right to hunt and fish Menominee Tribe vs. United States, 391 U.S. 404 (1968). When the Termination Plan was implemented the enrolled members became shareholders in the created Menominee Enterprises, Inc. which became known as M.E.I. The M.E.I. Board of Trustees consisted of seven (7) members; three (3) of whom were non-members. In 1968, the M.E.I. entered into the "Lakes of Menominee," project referred to now as Legend Lake.

In spite of many barriers, the Menominee persisted with their goal in restoring the land to trust status. On April 20, 1972, Wisconsin Senators Proximire and Nelson introduced Senate Bill No. 3514 in response to the Menominee's ambition to seek reversal of termination. With the dedication & persistence of Tribal members and a coalition of supporters the Menominee Restoration Act was signed into law on December 22, 1973 by President Nixon after two and one-half years of congressional testimony the Restoration Act was passed. It provided for the federal recognition of the Menominee Indian Tribe of Wisconsin thereby returning the nation to trust status and sovereign immunity through the development of the Menominee Indian Tribe of Wisconsin Constitution and Bylaws.

The sovereign immunity of the Tribe is retained through Article XVIII of the Constitution and Bylaws which allows suit to be brought against the Tribe in Menominee Tribal Court by those subject to the Tribe's jurisdiction. Suit may be brought against the Tribe to enforce an ordinance of the Tribe, a provision of the Menominee Constitution, or a provision of the Indian Civil Rights Act.

It is this history that explains why the Menominee tend to hold Nixon in such high regard. In this context he is viewed as one of the most progressive presidents as far as Indian self-determination and sovereignty are concerned. It is said that Nixon's primary motivation for ending termination for many tribes such as the Menominee was the positive influence of a Native American coach, Wallace "Chief" Newman, whom he had in college. Coach Newman, it should be noted, was not really a "Chief," but earned that nickname by his white colleagues because he was of Native American ancestry. Reflecting on what he had learned from Coach Newman, Nixon consistently commented that he internalized from him *a never say die spirit*. Nixon saw this quality of *indomitable spirit* as *what our nation's young people need today*. Nixon's support for Native American sovereignty is quite remarkable given the long record of anti-Indian policy within the Republican Party. The Menominee have therefore benefited from some very powerful friends. However, this is not the case with all of the tribes.

For example, there are two tribes right next to the Menominee that received land from the Menominee after being displaced through the process of European colonization and the intensification of intra-tribal warfare it engendered. The Oneida, one of the Six Nations, originally from New York, is one of those tribes who received a large chunk of land by Green Bay, Wisconsin. The Oneida took ownership from the Menominee in the 1820s and began selling the land in the 1860s taking advantage of the General Allotment Act of 1887, designed to break up the holding of land in common by Native Nations.

In other words, the U.S. Congress passed the Act to divide reservations into parcels of land to be distributed among their Indigenous occupants, "160 acres to each family head, 80 acres to single persons and orphans over eighteen years, and 40 acres to single persons under eighteen" (Adams, 1995, p. 17). Allottees were granted U.S. citizenship. The intended result was to dissolve traditional communal ways of cultural organization. "Full-blooded Indians" were granted a privileged land granting status resulting in the erosion of cultural conceptions of "Indianness" and tribal membership intended to divide and thus conquer the targeted group (Churchill 2003). Finally, "leftover" land, the very basis of traditional Native culture, was sold to white settlers. As a result, the land became fractionated. It is therefore not uncommon for Indian people to hold titles for extremely small fractions of land. For example, it is not unheard of in Indian country for people to hold land titles that amount to no more than one-foot by one-foot squares. This fractionation has become a horrible nightmare in Indian country.

The other tribe who received Menominee land, the Stockbridge Muncee, whose reservation is connected to the Menominee Reservation, are also from the North East, and like the Oneida, they too allotted out all of their land. The nightmare of land fractionation resides, in part, in the fact that once a tribe sells a part of their land base, it is extremely hard to have that land put back into trust as part of whatever said tribal nation. The Muncee, for example, have recently been engaged in this very struggle. Part of the land they sold after Allotment became a golf course. The Muncee bought that land back in the 1990s and brought in slot machines. Shawano Country, Wisconsin recently intervened resulting in the Supreme Court ruling that the land was not theirs anymore because they had sold it in the 1880s, a period of nearly one hundred years, rendering it no longer eligible to be held in trust by the tribe. Because these land dispute issues are held at the federal level, the membership of the Supreme Court is directly relevant for Indian peoples. It is no wonder that the Supreme Court is closely watched in Indian Country.

Again, as a result of selling much of their land after Allotment, the Oneida's Wisconsin reservation is speckled with small enclaves or villages, such as Hobart. The Oneida have been actively buying back as much of this land as possible. Whenever a piece of real estate becomes available they buy it back. This is a source of genuine angst for these villages. That is, when tribes, such as the Oneida, buy back land, it is taken off the tax role, which chips away at the tax base of little towns such as Hobart. This is therefore one of the primary concerns, from the settler-state perspective, with Indians having money and buying back land. This is why Indian gaming makes the government so nervous. If your tribe has a large profitable casino, you buy influence, lawyers, public relations firms, and, ultimately, your land back. The dominant society thought they had that market closed—that is, a monopoly on the usage of these services. The legal system and media outlets are the tools of hegemony—not intended to be employed counter-hegemonically, especially not by Indians. The argument that casinos are bad or somehow immoral is only a smokescreen; the real objection is Indians having money. Within the discourse of welfare reform and economic independence, which is based on the assumption that oppression does not exist so all people have an equal, un-manipulated opportunity to reach their full potential, policy makers cannot afford to be honest about Indian gaming.

Economic development issues, such as gaming, the black hole of tribal governments, dominate the political backdrop. It is the economic development department in tribal governments that never seems to accomplish anything, that is, nothing ever gets developed. The only thing that has been successful in the contemporary era are the casinos, which we place a one hundred percent tax on. Consequently, for many Nations, gaming pays for entire tribal governments. In other words, after the expenses and capital expenditures, all of the profits come back to the tribal government. If casinos have been almost the only source of economic activity in Indian country, why would the Washington elites be so anti-gaming and portray it as dirty and corrupt? Again, the answer seems to reside in the continuing attempts to incorporate reservation land into the taxable land base of the United States.

Indian gaming therefore has more oversight and is scrutinized more than gaming in Las Vegas or Atlantic City. In other words, we have more layers of eyes on our operations than anyone else. The standard paternalistic justification is that this oversight serves as a safeguard against organized crime infiltrating Indian gaming. It is still viewed as dirty and frowned upon even though it does not pollute, it is not strip mining, storing dangerous uranium, or housing dangerous criminals in prisons, which the government has had a more favorable attitude toward in Indian country. This is so contradictory that it suggests a fear of Indians becoming too powerful or successful.

When the Menominee applied for off-reservation gaming to the federal government, we had to guarantee that we would not give out per capita payments to our people. This paternalistic approach can be traced to the Protestant work ethic that is based on the belief that money comes from hard work and hard work will bring you closer to God. Of course the charge is hypocritical given the massive transfers of wealth through inheritances and investments that pay non-laboring shareholders. It is interesting to note the silence regarding the Catholic using bingo for at least fifty years to support their schools and churches. Some of the Catholic schools go as far as mandating that parents volunteer twice a month to help run the bingo operations. In fact it was the Catholic Church who gave the Menominee the most trouble when they were submitting their paperwork for off-reservation gaming. Kempthorn was never honest about his nonsupport of Indian gaming. There is a suspicion in Indian country that perhaps he is *in the back packet*, as it were, of Las Vegas gamers, such as Steve Win, Jim Grand, and Donald Trump. Las Vegas, from the perspective of a competing capitalist, absolutely despises Indian gaming—this much is certain.

Another reason why gaming is the perfect economic development initiative for Indigenous Nations is because Indian resources and land have so many restrictions placed on them. For example, all of the land within reservations is held in trust. Try to get a mortgage for land that is held in trust. It is virtually impossible. The purpose and value of property in a capitalist system is that it can be mortgaged by a bank. If you default on your mortgage, the bank takes possession of the land. Land that is held in trust cannot be taken by a bank, and you cannot get dollars on it to do any economic development.

The Menominee, for example, have worked with their Associated Bank in Shawano for thirty years. We went to them for one point three million dollars to finish a water project. To receive the loan, the bank wants us to waive our sovereign immunity, which we are not willing to do because if we default on the loan, they can take us into any court of their choosing. They would never come into our tribal court because they do not think they would get a fair trial, just as we do not believe we would receive an objective judgment in their system. The Menominee, with a flawless track record of paying loans back, is not *sub prime*. However, the reliability and trustworthiness of Indigenous peoples has never *really* been the issue. It has been about acquiring land and resources, which requires the dissolution of Native American sovereignty.

However, all hope is not lost. For example, the election of the United States' first African American president from the Democratic Party, Barack Obama, has generated widespread celebration and optimism among Native Americas' leaders because it is anticipated that if he can last eight years he will elect more liberal-leaning, fair Justices than were sworn in during the Reagan and Bush years. Consequently, the Menominee, among other First Nations, are waiting to take issues, such as off-reservation gaming disputes, to court until new Justices are appointed because of the fear of being ruled against by conservative, prejudiced, anti-Indigenous gaming Justices.

It is therefore always a highly strenuous endeavor when issues of sovereignty are being considered in the courts. For example, there was a case in the North Western region of the United States where a police officer was chasing a suspect, presumed to be dangerous, across a reservation. A sixteen-year-old young man was crossing the reservation perpendicular to the chase and happened to be at the wrong place at the wrong time, was T-boned by the police car and killed. The wealthy father of the boy who was killed sued the tribe. The tribe, rather than settling, which they should have done, argued they were immune because they have sovereign immunity. Because this was not an appropriate or judicial time to pull the *sovereign immunity* card, the case will go to the Supreme Court and there is a chance that all Native Nations will have their sovereignty further degraded. There is a sentiment among some Indigenous leaders that, at times, Indian peoples hide behind their sovereignty. In short, when a tribe takes an issue to court, they have to be extremely cognizant of how it will impact the sovereignty of Indian Country in general. It seems apparent, based on the historical record, that there are courts waiting for cases that will degrade Indigenous sovereignty.

Education Before European Influence

What we might call traditional, non-Western forms of Menominee social reproduction, or education, were highly formalized. When children were born, both boys and girls belonged to the grandmothers, who gave them baby names and taught them about who they were, their history, and who their relatives and relations are and were—many of the things related to issues of identity, which they needed to know to live in Menominee society. This continued to age seven or eight when the grandfathers assumed the primary responsibilities of socialization and education. This transition was signified by the replacement of baby names with adult names.

Grandfathers would continue the children's education ensuring they had everything they needed to survive, which included not only hunting, fishing, and gathering knowledges, but the knowledge of making war and when it is appropriate as well. These skills required children to learn about the physical world, which includes the physical sciences, encompassing vast knowledges about plants, animals, their relationships, and the natural laws governing the life system. To effectively engage the physical world a person needs knowledge of self and psychology, situated in the larger context of understanding that humans are not the masters of the universe, the Western perspective, but rather just one small part of it. Children would therefore be taught in the affective domain, that is, feelings, emotions, and everything related to communication and citizenship.

The result, to this day, is that much of Indian Country is purposefully underdeveloped. When spirituality, or a cosmology of interconnectedness, is at the center of social life, non-human life forms are not viewed as they are just to serve the short-term self-centered needs of people, but have an inherent right to exist, and therefore respected. In other words, through ceremony, children learn to respect the trees, for example, and therefore learn not to act irresponsibly and eliminate the whole forest. Rather, you maintain a balance, taking what you need without becoming a destructive force. Because Western science Euro-centrically rejects this non-empirical spirituality, modern civilization has become hyper-imbalanced threatening the very existence of the life cycle and therefore life itself.

Herein lies the central difference between Western and Indigenous worldviews or philosophies. That is, the Western mindset believes that the world can be controlled. Indigenous peoples know that the world cannot be controlled—it can only be respected or disrespected, and if disrespected, there will be *hell to pay*, as it were. The Earth has her own laws that people cannot alter, and such attempts will only lead to failure, this is certain. The Earth renews herself every year. Winter comes and brings snow, acting as a blanket so the Earth can rest and renew itself. When people cover the earth with concrete and buildings, she cannot properly rest and renew leading to imbalance. This lesson is a hard lesson for the Westerner to accept. It requires humility and a sense of respect and responsibility Western science has arrogantly ignored. From an Indigenous perspective, this is the great challenge of our time, of humanity.

In short, traditional Menominee society socialized its citizens to know about the vast richness and complexities of the world and how to live within it. These knowledge systems included very sophisticated and successful scaffolding techniques and strategies and explain why Indian peoples were able to survive on this continent through very difficult times, including an ice age and a rapidly changing environment. Before the arrival of Europeans, who brought devastating diseases and warfare, there were very large populations of Indigenous peoples in the Americas, as many as thirty million or more just in North America, which was possible because of these systems of knowledge and social reproduction. The fact that Native peoples still exist, whose populations have been reduced by as much as ninety eight percent of their pre-Columbian numbers, is testament to the brilliance of their keen observations.

An example of an ancient Menominee learning strategy that continues today is the use of games, such as La Crosse, which is designed to develop the mind and the body in harmony as one. It was designed as a *little war* to prepare children for real warfare—it is dangerous, that is why it is a club sport. La Crosse is a good example of the experiential nature of Menominee education. In other words, many of the important lessons were not things you were told, but knowledge you constructed through experiences that were set up, such as La Crosse. Under this system you learn as much from your mistakes as you do from your successes. It was a very different education system than the American or Western model. Because the Menominee system of social reproduction, in many ways, continues to exist, it is argued that the reason why many Menominee students do not do well in the American education system is because it is not based on experiential learning, but on telling and regurgitating.

La Crosse is preoperational in another sense. Because of the intensity of the sport, the players suffer, and the suffering is for the people. You find this same relationship in Christianity where Jesus suffered for his people so they would be better. When the game is over, people come and they touch those men who have suffered, and in the process, cleansed their minds, bodies and spirits. Touching these men gives you strength and it gives you life. This prepares the men and the community for the wars that are out there that they will have to fight. It is a lot of really cool symbolism. Each season is supposed to begin after the first thunder in the spring when the sun is shining and the wind is blowing and the players are running up and down the field, their hair flying.

As you engage the remainder of this chapter, be cognizant of the ways traditional Menominee approaches to knowledge production have consistently informed the struggle for sovereignty in the contemporary era. In other words, be aware of how the present is not abandoned by recent Menominee leadership by romantically evoking the past, but rather, is drawn on ontologically for its effectiveness as a way of negotiating difficult situations such as surviving as a sovereign nation with an intact land base in a hostile and aggressive environment. Central to these discussions is the role education has played, which we focus on in the contemporary era.

MENOMINEE-CONTROLLED EDUCATION

A New Beginning: Menominee Head Start

For the purposes of this discussion we argue that the beginning of post-colonization Indigenous self-determination came with John Collier's leadership of the Bureau of Indian Affairs (BIA) in the 1930s. His tenure differed from those who came before him primarily through his disdain for the governments' paternalistic attitude toward Indian peoples and the exploitative nature of the Boarding Schools' large-scale athletic programs and the nature of the whole experience. Collier, while critical of how these compulsory schools were run, did not close them because he believed they were still needed for orphans and for those who lived in isolated areas, such as many regions within the two million acre Pine Ridge Reservation. These isolated children therefore did not have access to Western education, which is a requirement for surviving in the system, as it currently exists. There are still boarding schools, such as Flandrew in South Dakota, where the Menominee, for example, send around twelve children every year—children who come from difficult family situations and need special attention. The primary difference, however, is that these decisions are not externally imposed, but come from within the Menominee community itself.

Menominee-controlled education evolved from the need for daycare, which Johnson's *War on Poverty* supported through The Office of Economic Opportunity and Operation Head Start, which was just one of many, many programs that were offered. The Menominee Head Start, started in 1965 by two sisters-in-law,

Dolores Boyd and Marlene Keshena, was one of the first ones in the country. Head Start was Lady Bird Johnson's little project. Dolores took Head Start and ran with it. She quickly outgrew the space she had and began searching for a larger facility, and eventually took over the old government school building. As a result they had a huge Head Start program with over 200 children at its height, which was one of the most successful programs in Indian country, because, in part it received a lot of good technical support and was run by energetic, hard working leaders. It was the resources that the government was willing to invest in America that fueled the excitement of the times. Eventually these programs became too rigidly controlled by layers of rules and regulations and in the process the creative spirit that gave them life was snuffed out and killed.

Before that, however, the leaders invested a lot in training, sending Menominee teachers all over the country to workshops and conferences, and brought many leading experts in early childhood education to the Reservation for professional development. Some of the *Volunteers in Service to America* (VISTA) workers who came in to do trainings were retired priests and other well-educated professionals. LBJ started VISTA, which was a domestic version of the Peace Corps that was required because of severe need within Indian country at the time. Government administrators would therefore frequently bring people in to review and learn from the Menominee Head Start who served children from infancy (three months) until they were four years old and off to Kindergarten, which is different from the way it is today, but they started with the infants.

Dolores would hire people who knew people and send them out to aggressively beat the bushes and get kids into the program. It was forward thinking—that is, it was based on the idea that early experiences with formalized knowledge production lay the foundation for later success in Western schooling, which Piaget theorized as scaffolding. The children were therefore exposed to a wide array of experiential learning, from field trips to pumpkin patches to trips in the woods. In the early days of the program most people on the Reservation did not yet have running water, so the staff would also ensure that the children were bathed.

Many children also received dental care for the first time as a result of the Head Start initiative, which was one of the most pressing concerns due to the introduction of processed sugars and food preservatives that are highly corrosive to the teeth's protective enamel. Because the teeth are linked to the ears through the nasal cavities, untreated tooth decay leads to inner ear infections, and ultimately, to significant delays in learning and language development, which is rampant throughout Indian country and correlated to poverty more generally. Head Start therefore was part of shifting the paradigm for Indian children so they received better healthcare and nutrition. Raw vegetables, for example, were a staple of the program, as were eggs and protein for breakfast.

Making positive strides in these areas of early childhood development it was an exciting time in Indian country in general and on the Menominee Indian Reservation in particular—it was a beehive of activity and energy. This is what Johnson brought to Indian country, the *War on Poverty*, which is what we are hoping will come back. Johnson, from our Menominee point of view, was a fascinating man. He came into office in 1963 and did not waste any time getting to work, which suggests that he knew exactly what he wanted to do from the very beginning of his administration. Unlike Truman who never thought that he would be President and therefore had to settle into the job, Johnson did not flounder around because he spent his entire life preparing for that moment to make the most of it. In retrospect, it was a great time to be an Indian person.

The Menominee had come from so far behind as a result of the ravages of Termination, which was ushered in by Truman after WWII in 1945 (Castile 1998). That Termination was fundamentally devastating cannot be overstated—it destroyed the whole fabric of our Indigenous Nation. It was like the Nationhood was broken by this one singular act of Termination, which occurred during the spring month of April in 1961. It broke our hearts. The story of the Mother Earth told us that we are the Menominee, the people of the wild rice, because everywhere we went wild rice would follow us, sustaining us, for thousands of years.

After Termination, however, the wild rice quit growing. We have been working to regenerate the rice ever since. Tragically, however, we have not been successful. This is a national embarrassment—being the people of the wild rice who are not able to grow it—and is therefore rarely shared outside the inner circle of the Nation. What does this say about us? Yes, we grow small patches here and there, but it speaks of what we have done to our Earth that we can no longer grow it as once was. Pollution knows no borders; what defense can tiny reserves in Indian country muster, situated in a sea of industrial imbalance? Seeking an answer to why wild rice can no longer be sown, employing all of the tools available, we have conducted water studies and many other environmental impact projects. Finding a solution suitable for the environment as it currently exists has led us to search for a hybrid of the wild rice that will grow for us.

Being able to produce wild rice serves a fundamental symbolic need for the Menominee. The inability to grow the rice has therefore affected the people spiritually because it signifies an imbalance in the life cycle, which impacts everything and everyone. Another similarly out-of-balance symbol for the Menominee are the sturgeon. The Menominee used to harvest sturgeon on their migration path each year, which included a multi day feast and festival celebrating and honoring the earth's life cycle. This educative ritual, which included naming ceremonies and dancing, ended in the early 1800s when the sturgeon's migration path was blocked due to the river being damned below our territory. We have been battling every since to enable the sturgeon to come home to Lake Winnebago. Again, these things, together, have hurt the psyche of the Nation.

In the *old days* we could travel all over the state of Wisconsin hunting, fishing, and sustaining our people. Once we were confined to a much smaller land base on a reservation that was no longer possible. However, our ability to adapt to that drastic economic change and survive has been the hallmark of our people. For us it has not been resisting change, but taking change and making it fit our needs. The *War on Poverty*, for example, was not designed to work the way it worked on Indian reservations. What it provided Indigenous people the opportunity to do was to take their innate knowledge, their traditional knowledge, and begin reconfiguring it and making it more applicable.

What came out of that for the Menominee and other tribes was an energy and attitude that said, "This is our opportunity to do these things on our own." In the realm of education it led to Indian parents taking action against having their children taught Western values in the dominant society school districts where Menominee children suffered between fifty and sixty percent drop out rates, were disproportionately placed in special education, and even physically abused. The Menominee, as discussed below, eventually established their own school system, which is based on a hybrid of dominant society (State of Wisconsin content standards and NCLB) and traditional Menominee content.

Collier and Self Determination

As a result of the paradigm shift that has began to move away from the paternalistic attitude toward Native Americans, a number of pieces of legislation have been enacted that reflect this spirit of self-determination such as the Indian Education Act of 1972 and the Tribally controlled School Act of 1988 (Malott 2008). However, the transition has been anything but smooth. Economic issues have been at the heart of the struggle. It has been a financial battle. That is, when the Menominee separated from the school district directly next to their reservation, many teachers lost their jobs. Consequently, they fought the Menominee for the right to educate their children because each Menominee who went to school there brought the school a certain amount of money each year. Again, this movement toward Indian control began in 1933 with John Collier as Commissioner of Indian Affairs under Franklin D. Roosevelt during the activist-era of the New Deal.

Collier was able to push through Congress a version of the New Deal for Indians with the Indian Reorganization Act of 1934, which, it is argued, disrupted the Allotment Act in an effort to end the further deterioration of Indigenous land bases and laid the foundation for Indian-controlled government and self-determination, a stark turn from the policy of cultural genocide through variants of compulsory assimilation policies of Protestant missionaries, such as forced Americanization through boarding schools and the break up of communally held land (Castile 1998; Daily 2004; Malott 2008).

Collier's vision of self-determination, however, generated fierce opposition. Cloaked in the Christian fundamentalist *rhetoric of recovery* (Kincheloe 2009) Gustavus Elmer Emanuel Lindquist, as "itinerant representative of the ecumenical Home Missions Council of the Federal Council of Churches" (Daily 2004, p. 3), responded by embracing the radical assimilationist crusade, which he had apposed as a gradual assimilationist before Collier. Summarizing Lindquist's pre-Collier, Protestant Missionary position David W. Daily (2004) in his *Battle for the BIA* notes that:

> …Missionaries supported the BIA's expanding programs by promoting the doctrine of Indian wardship. According to this doctrine, Indians were wards of the state not yet capable of supporting themselves in a cutthroat capitalist economy. So they required, according to Protestant leaders, the paternal hand of the BIA to help them assimilate gradually and minimize the loss of Indian properties. In their support for gradualism, missionaries like Lindquist provided strong backing for the BIA against those who wanted a more rapid, sink-or-swim approach to assimilation. Often called radical assimilationists, or "abolitionists" because of their desire to abolish the BIA, these more aggressive reformers believed the BIA intentionally thwarted the Indians' assimilation out of narrow institutional self-interests. Missionaries, though, defended the BIA, arguing that Native tribes needed a special federal agency to maintain trust protections over Indian lands and to administer health, education, and welfare services while the Indians made the slow and arduous journey into self-supporting citizenship. (pp. 4–5)

However, after Collier assumed control over the BIA and challenged its relationship with Missionaries, Lindquist led Protestants in a campaign against the BIA, arguing it was a form of domination by creating a state of Indigenous dependency. Subsequently, Lindquist played a significant role in situating "Protestant organizations like the Home Missions Council at the forefront of the termination movement of the 1950s" (Daily 2004, p. 5). It is therefore not saying too much that Collier and Lindquist were as close to being polar opposites as one could imagine. Lindquist, for example, was raised in a stable family whereas Collier came from a broken home whose parents divorced and then both his father and mother committed suicide. They had such different upbringings and then they both wound up at the Bureau of Indian Affairs battling for the souls of Indian people.

While at the BIA, Lindquist met some very interesting people, such as Carlos Montezuma, who believed that the BIA should be eradicated so Indian tribes, as Nations, can go forward in this country without the overwhelming burden of the BIA. The idea is that Indian tribes would truly be small Nations within the contiguous forty-eight receiving no financial support of any kind from the United States government—that is, the relationship between Indian Nations and the U.S. as wards of the state would be dissolved. Lindquist, however, can be described as a radical assimilationist, who believed that Indians should be slowly assimilated into the Euro-capitalist dominant society. Lindquist therefore found himself deeply involved in the anti-dancing movement, at which time Collier emerged as the Indian's savior. Lindquist's position was based on his own experiences as a Swedish immigrant who spoke his own language and English. However, unlike Native Americans, Lindquist looked like everybody else in the society he wanted to assimilate into. He also held a similar Western philosophy and worldview as the dominant society. He was also able to go back to Sweden frequently and marry a Swede. Lindquist did not seem to appreciate the complexities and painfulness of non-whites being assimilated into a white society that is informed by socially constructed racial hierarchies. This is what they wanted for Indian people, a very painful process, which people like Lindquist did not understand because, for him, a white man, the process was painless—his life was smooth.

Collier's life, on the other hand, was not smooth; it was filled with pain and loss. From an Indigenous perspective, the painful view from the bottom of the false hierarchy, Collier's experiences offer a possible way to understand why he demonstrated a greater sensitivity to the destructive process of assimilation. Collier was a tortured man. He was married three times and never developed a very close relationship with his children even though he lived in the same town. He went back to Indian country (Taos, New Mexico) during the final years of his life where he died. He began his career in Indian affairs in Taos and the surrounding Pueblos. For Collier it was also a mystical, or emotionally and physically intense, experience as they allowed him to participate in some of their sacred dances. When Collier took over the BIA, he despised what it was about with a deep bitter hatred, and therefore not only became the reformer known in Indian country as the savior of the Indians, but the longest serving administrator, twelve years. It is amazing that anybody could last that long in the BIA's administration because of the political intensity of being the mediator between the federal government and the Nations of Native North America. Collier served during Roosevelt's four terms in office, resigning shortly before the President's death during his thirteenth year in office.

Pratt was also a radical assimilationist as the architect of the Boarding Schools. His philosophy was *kill the savage, save the man*, which was emblazed across the front gates of Carlisle Boarding School in Pennsylvania, the first of one hundred and twenty nine compulsory boarding schools operating in the United States between 1880 and 1980, leading to eighty seven such institutions of assimilation in Canada (Malott 2008). However, Pratt's background was not in education, he was a military man, an Indian fighter, who believed that in two or three generations of forced removal and Western training in far-away boarding schools, Native Americans, as distinct cultural groups, would be gone. In short, evict them from their land base and they would survive, but there is no way to know, it is not quantifiable or measurable.

Collier was an interesting man because he believed in Native American culture (art) as an economic development initiative. In other words, he saw the money that could be made though developing a commercial tourism market for *authentic Indian-made art* to sustain Indigenous self-determination. He had the vision, which might have been inspired by the extensive time he spent at the Pueblos in New Mexico—a reasonable speculation because of the jewelry and pottery craftsmanship displayed and sold in Santa Fe at the old town market.

Today it is the Powwow circuit that provides the venue or market for Indian peoples across the United States to make a living as performers and craftsman. Dolores Boyd, before she became involved with Menominee Head Start, as discussed above, ran a small store she called "The Tepee," which is not a Menominee term it is Lakota. Boyd therefore marketed her business to white tourists exploiting their stereotypical image of *the Indian*. Similarly, Joe Kincheloe (2005) notes that, "if they are to survive, subjugated groups develop an understanding of those who control them" (p. 144). Outside liberal observers might scoff at Boyd, and others like her, charging her with *selling out*. However, as a savvy entrepreneur, Boyd subversively supplied her *tourist trap* with many arts and crafts that were not made by *real Indians* close to an imagined primitive past, but were rather inexpensively *made in Japan*. She and her sisters would sit and scrape the "made in Japan" stickers off the products while laughing and speaking Menominee. It was an example of what Gerald Vizenor (1994) termed *survivance* (survival and resistance).

However, Dolores and her husband would also purchase hundreds of traditional woodlands baskets, deer skin moccasins, and bead work in the spring that Menominee people wove, sewed, and threaded in their homes throughout the long winter months. Nowadays, however, with television and the ability to travel, you do not see as much of that anymore. It was a different kind of life. Dolores was a single mother with five children for many years. She ran The Tepee out of a stand she rented from a good friend of hers every summer, which was located on one of the Menominee's sacred sites where Sturgeon festivals were held and where they had signed a treaty. That is what Indian people do with what we get from the government, be it economic development initiatives or education: we take it and redesign it into an Indian-directed activity as, again, a form of *survivance*.

Again, Indigenous people, including the Menominee, were able to take advantage of this *new deal* away from paternalism. Our tribal council has always been educationally minded supporting the idea that education is the key to success. That is, the smarter each tribal member is, the better off he or she will be and the better off the tribe, as a whole, will be. Dedication and commitment to that idea has been a constant throughout our history.

The movement toward the emergence of the Menominee Indian School District began with the need to transport Menominee children ten to twenty miles each way to school everyday. The people went to the tribal council and said, "our children need a bus, many of them have to hitch hike to school everyday. Lets take some of our money and hire a bus. There happened to be an old man with an old bus. He took his old bus, fastened little seats in it. Everyday he would ride the kids to Shawano to go to school. It was a big deal to go back and forth because it was expensive, so he would sit in a tavern all day drinking while the children were in school learning. After school at the end of the day he would go pick up all the Indian kids at the high school and drive them back *drunk*. The girls would scream all the way home because they were absolutely terrified. The boys thought it was the greatest thing. He would be racing trains, running over dogs, and screeching to halts where he would drop them off. These things would go on everyday all year. We might say that was the education for Indian children, it was very exciting. These are the stories that you hear from people who are now in their eighties—the products of Collier.

Knowledge Production and Sovereignty

Having control over our schools has placed the Menominee to take a more aggressive stance on monitoring knowledge production issues. The following sub-section first examines the importance of the Menominee writing their own history. Evidence for this need is drawn from the Euro-centric ways in which anthrolopogists have portrayed the Menominee and other subjugated peoples. The latter part of this section draws attention to the benefits of research collaborations the Menominee School District have approved and participated in.

* * *

George and Louise Spindler (1971, 1984) began fieldwork with the Menominee in 1948 as cultural anthropologists. They wrote about our songs, our culture, our social groupings, everything that was very personal for our tribe and put it right out there in anthropology land. Much of this work is not very complimentary coming from a Western perspective. For example, the Spindler's (1971) first book, *Dreamers Without Power* was interpreted as a direct insult to Menominee culture because the Menominee were historically known and consulted by other tribes because they were powerful dreamers who could see into the future. Consequently, the Menominee were highly respected for their ability to construct valid and reliable knowledge this way. In 1984 they republished the book as *Dreamers With Power*.

One of the primary thrusts of their work is how Indian society became diluted and marginalized. They conducted studies on traditional people versus Christian Menominee informed by a romantic image of the noble savage. They appreciated and respected the Rousseau model that argued that Indians were corrupted because they did not stay children of nature, as they should have. It is the false idea that Indians are relics in a museum. Anthropology, at that time, reflected this approach. The renowned anthropologist Margaret Mead, for example, would not even study Indian people because she did not believe them to be a model worth studying anymore.

These anthropologists did not appreciate complexity and societies in flux—or why they were in flux. In other words, Indian society is a dynamic, ever-changing system—like any system. If it does not change, it becomes stagnant and dies. Many Western-trained anthropologists were not able to step outside their own value-systems and engage in the objective, scientific work they claimed to be engaging in. This has been one of the major criticisms of notions of objectivity—it allows the researcher to leave the influence of their own internalized, unchallenged schemas unexplored. Consequently, the biases researchers bring to *the field* tend to be reproduced as *subjects*, seeking approval or positive reinforcement, will frequently attempt to provide field workers with the story or data they think they want, even if it is untrue.

Unfortunately, for the tribe, this is where it usually ends. That is, researchers, after collecting their data, return to their institutions, publish their reports and analyses, and the tribe never sees what has been published. As a result, the Menominee, for example, has never critiqued the Spindler's (or anyone else's) work. The tribes should therefore be more proactive. If we do not want anyone writing about our history, then we have a responsibility to write it ourselves. Again, because this is about having control and power over how we are perceived and how we perceive ourselves, it is directly connected to our sovereignty and independence.

When tribes allow this to happen they suffer. It is important who writes your history. The people who have direct experience with whatever events should be considered as the primary experts. Allowing outsiders to write our history has not proven to be a good thing. When something false is published about a tribe, it's implications are compounded. It becomes a source and the false idea gets perpetuated and solidified as fact. For example, Schoolcraft is sometimes cited as a credible source for the history of Indigenous peoples in North America, but he was not a trained historian, he was a traveler who wrote travel logs. His work paints a picture that suggests all Menominee were drunks and had alcohol problems, but the reality, from a Menominee perspective, is that the vast majority did not drink. Because most of the texts produced about the Menominee by outsiders are wrong, we do not allow people to write about us. It is therefore the responsibility of those who care about their history as Indigenous people to write their own history.

This is part of how we protect our sovereignty, that is, culturally and politically. Our council of elders monitors what is written about us and encourages Menominee to take the lead in these endeavors providing them with the means, the tools, and the authority to do it. This requires placing tremendous emphasis on the importance of education because historians have to be created through rigorous training. The tribe also needs to develop, from within, specialists who can review studies to determine if they are based on good science and have value to our Nation. A related function is determining if proposed studies hold any potential usefulness in advancing the goals of the tribe.

* * *

Having our own district has enabled us to benefit from approving research studies in our schools proposed by academics and PhD students from such institutions as the University of Wisconsin, for example. Today, if someone wants to study the Menominee, they have to present their research proposal to a council of elders. Before Collier's push for Indigenous self-determination, people could write whatever they wanted about Native Americans. The researchers of one of these studies came with a science project they wanted to incorporate into the tribal school curriculum, which we approved. One of the researchers, a PhD student, found that Menominee children, from a very young age, had a strong science background in the natural world. They knew animals, habitat, seasonal activities of the plants and animals. In other words, they had very specialized knowledge about ecosystems. As a result, these children from reservation schools, for the first three years of testing, did very well in science. Their success in school remained consistent until they got into high school.

This shift is attributed to the method of teaching, which transforms in high school from experiential, hands-on, seasonal based approaches to science to decontextualized, theoretical models. Not only do the grades and test scores plummet in high school, but the interest in science also experiences serious attrition. Recent test scores have shown that as many as 81% of ninth graders at Menominee High School are failing biology. Blaming the students, in this context, is irresponsible—we have to examine the whole program, curriculum *and* pedagogy. Employing qualitative research methodologies the researchers therefore tracked the teaching styles and techniques from kindergarten through grade eight. Again, they found in the pre-high school grades the content is organized around the seasons making for richly contextualized instruction. Students are taken outside during each season for hands-on experience with the concepts in the curriculum.

In the spring, for example, the children would be taken into the forest to do maple sugaring, a central part of Menominee culture and tradition economy. There was an entire curriculum designed around sugaring, which includes vast bodies of ancillary knowledge, such as how to find the trees, get to the trees, and the knowledge of how to extract the material from the trees and cook it to produce the maple syrup. After all of that science and culture, the final step involves the knowledge of marketing and selling the product, which are economic development initiatives that are intimately connected to a Nation's sovereignty and ability to be independent.

In the fall the curriculum is structured around the wild rice harvest. The whole process and structure of the curriculum would be the same as the sugaring, but it would be for wild rice. Students would learn how to find where the best lakes were going to most likely be, and in the process, learn about geography and cultural identity and its connection to physical place/land. The winter brought more science and culture through an ice-fishing centered curriculum. The subject matter not only included knowledge of fish species, but techniques for checking temperatures and the thickness of ice as well. Finally, the summer curriculum engages students in a quest for berries and documenting the health of deer and other wild life for the fall hunt. As a result of this season-centered curriculum, children become agile scientists. Again, however, this passion to know vanishes by grade nine.

What this suggests is that the adolescent science curriculum needs to be reformed based on the tribal K-8 school model. It seems as though this is the way not only Native children should learn science but all children could benefit from this approach because it teaches to respect the Earth, and not to selfishly abuse it for short-term gain. It is foolish to teach it any other way, which is not an ethnocentric conclusion, but one that acknowledges the intimate, dynamic, ever-changing relationship between the physical and the theoretical, which becomes distorted when variables are reduced too far into the abstract (Kincheloe 2005). One of the major barriers to these initiatives is that traditional philosophy and the knowledge it produces is not valued in the Euro-centric context of the United States and Canada. It seems clear that teachers and policy makers still need to learn that every culture has valuable knowledge that can contribute to the Enlightenment values of democracy and peace, which education is supposed to advance, otherwise schooling would receive very little popular support.

Again, to understand why the K-8 model outlined above is so effective among Indian youth is because it resembles the way they learn about the natural world in their home cultural context. That is, the grandparents tend to be a child's first science teacher taking them out into the woods on a regular basis to learn about all the plants and animals, such as all the different trees and the gifts they give to people. As a result, the researchers found that Menominee children, although using different terminology, know as much science as the children in mainstream, dominant society schools in Shawano, WI.

Higher Education

Consequently, there has also emerged a trend in tribally controlled institutions of higher education and graduate studies. The Menominee, for example, have a community college that opened in 1993, which started out with two-year programs, and now offer four-year plans in some areas of study. It makes all the difference to Menominee youth. Children that would never have dreamt of going to college now go to school. The growth, of course, is incremental. People who would have gone off to college and lasted, at best, a semester, now go to the community college. They may still only last one semester, but unlike before, it is much easier for them to return. The difference is that with the community college in the community they are now able to pay off their bills after leaving at the end of their first semester, come back for a year, leave to pay those bills off, then come back and finish the course of study. A percentage of those graduates then go to a four-year school like the University of Wisconsin.

* * *

What these discussions suggest is that the continuing struggle for Native American Nations is designing effective strategies for putting Indigenous sovereignty to work correcting the errors of the past. There is no doubt that this is an indispensable task, however, as suggested above, it is not an easy *or* straightforward task. We might therefore observe that there is *no* manual or *one size that fits all* approach. While federal policies, such as *Allotment* and *Termination*, have been written using universal language that sets the political atmosphere for relationship between tribes and the government, each tribe has their own history and context that shapes the nature of policy implementation.

Considerations for Teachers in an Increasingly Diverse World

Something that future and current educators should be intimately aware of is the importance of the lived experiences of their students, which are always steeped in culture and class. This means that teachers learn to appreciate and respect student knowledge. However, because teachers, more often than not, do not share the same cultural and ethnic background with the students in their classes, it is not always easy for teachers to understand the experiences of their students. In practice this has manifested itself in many of the teachers that have worked in the Menominee Indian School District, who have been the worlds' worst listeners. They go into the classroom with the attitude, "I'm here to teach, and by God, that's what I'm going to do. I start in September, finish in May, and I'll get through the entire curriculum no matter what."

This rigidity refuses to follow the student-led side trips that veteran teachers know are the paths that lead to real growth and contextualixed knowledge production because they are grounded in the ways children understand the world mediated by their home culture, television, music, and everything else they experience. Some of the best English teachers at Menominee High School include in their curriculum, the work of renowned thinkers students identify with, such as the late rapper Tupac Shakur who was raised in the revolutionary environment of the Black Panther Party, which embraced both righteous resistance and egotistical power grabs. Studying Tupac gives students the permission to write and communicate in ways that traditional texts, such as *Romeo and Juliet*, are rarely able to.

One of the primary reasons thinkers like Tupac are so successful at unlocking and disarming marginalized students' insecurities is because he is recognized as one of them embodying the same complexities, contradictions, and brilliance that emerge from the competing drives of surviving and resisting in an age of hyper-materialism and vast inequalities. Students would say, "look what he wrote. He was brilliant. A genius poet of his time." This is the world of today, it is not the world presented in the *how to teach* books written in the 1920s. If you are unable to stay current on the times, you should probably rethink your profession. Teachers, throughout the United States, who understand these issues tend to be the teachers that are successful at sparking within their students a passion to know and the self-directed discipline that is a necessary attribute for becoming a life-long learner actively engaging new texts and challenging their own thinking and practice.

In the long run, this educational outcome is what is really important for the longevity of the Nation. That is, without an educated citizenry endowed with the capacity to read both the word and the world and thus make informed decisions about policy and practice, the future of the Nation as a sovereign entity becomes more tenuous and susceptible to outside manipulation. Again, it requires that teachers not only listen, but also hear and engage with student knowledge. Unlike teachers who are in the middle of their lives, the very young and the very old are closer to the creator and therefore have valuable lessons to teach us, if we are able to listen.

Conclusion: The Battle Continues

At stake in Indian politics in the twenty-first century are still the hearts and minds of Indian people. Along with gaming, tobacco is one of the most contested contemporary Native American economic development issues. For example, we can look at the Cherokee case, which concluded that Indians could produce tobacco products and distribute them throughout the country. The Cherokee were very successful in the tobacco trade putting their inventiveness to work.

The Seneca, in Western New York, have also recently had state taxes imposed on them for their tobacco products. These cases are clear violations of the United States Constitution, which plainly states, "Indians not taxed," acknowledging the sovereign immunity of Indigenous nations. In cases of international trade, the Six Nations, for example, have reserves in both Canada and the United States. There was a law written before the invention of semi trucks that guaranteed Iroquois citizens the right to transport as much tobacco across the border as they could carry. However, they are being taxed, which the Seneca are able to challenge because they have resources from gaming.

Many attacks against Native Americans are couched in terms of fairness. That is, it is argued that Indigenous Nations have an unfair business advantage because they are not supposed to be taxed. However, what is not mentioned is that in business school students are taught that successful capitalists are the ones who find the *competitive advantage*. United States' foreign policy and trade agreements, such as The North American Free Trade Agreement (NAFTA), especially since World War II, have been designed specifically to give U.S. corporations an unfair business advantage in the global economy. Many U.S. corporations therefore enjoy near complete monopoly over many of the markets in the Western hemisphere, especially in agricultural production and utilities. Situated in this context, it is difficult to take seriously the argument, posed oftentimes by Las Vegas corporate gamers, that Indigenous Nations have a monopoly over the gaming industry. More likely is that non-Indigenous gamers want Indians out of their way, so they themselves can enjoy complete control over the Casino industry.

From an Indigenous perspective, these are survival issues. That is, in order to remain sovereign and strong, nations need an economic foundation. The Oneida offer Native Nations a contemporary model to consider because of their success. For years they ended per capital payments and invested their revenue in business ventures with the goal of diversifying their investment portfolio in the traditional business sense. For example, the Oneida are not only involved in gaming, but they also own a bank, a software company, lots of off-reservation property, herds of buffalo, an organic farm, a chain of tribal smoke shops, and so on. Consequently, the Oneida Tribe is the largest employer in Brown County Wisconsin. They are also investing in the education of their children through an extensive scholarship program.

From a tribal government perspective, whose responsibility is the welfare of their people, owning a diverse array of businesses is only worthwhile if they employ their own people. Otherwise, the wealth generated does not go back to the tribe. Right now the Menominee employs people on their reservation in various industries, from education to timber, but there are no stores on the reservation, so people take their money into the surrounding towns. From a tribal government perspective, that is lost revenue that could be used to build up the economic independence and sovereignty of the Nation. The government has intervened against us by limiting our access to certain markets, such as the Internet. At the same time, the federal government has *not* intervened when Indians are unfairly taxed, such as alcohol taxes. Indians, institutionally, seem to be set up to fail. While arts and crafts have had their place in Indian self-determination, by overemphasizing it as an economic development initiative, the federal government has been less than helpful. Arts and crafts, as noted above, is season, work intensive, and far from sufficient to sustain a Nation's economy.

Another indicator suggesting that the U.S. federal government is not wholeheartedly concerned about the longevity of Native American Nationhood is the location of reservations. Reservations are always in the least productive, most remote locations. Situated on these unwanted small scraps of land Indians are expected to make a living through the creation of a sustainable economy. If this were not daunting enough, America's Indigenous peoples must do it with the trauma of having recently experienced (or currently experiencing) physical, biological, and cultural genocide (Malott 2008). Then, of course, after having all of our best land seized from us through the treaty process, we are told that we now have an *unfair advantage.*

From an Indigenous perspective, all we ever wanted was our sovereignty. That is what we want. The federal government has us overburdened with rules and regulations. It makes it hard to survive. We just do not want our basic right to exist interfered with. We have been fighting for it for the last two hundred and thirty three years. We have never given up on it. We act like sovereign people; we live our lives as sovereign people. That is all we want; without any strings attached. The federal government has been telling us what to do for over two hundred years, and their direction has proven to be inferior to what we know is best for ourselves. Critical pedagogy is correct in its assertion that those most directly affected by given policies are the best architects of such endeavors. This conclusion informs the remainder of this volume.

CHAPTER FOUR

A Closer Look at Menominee Sovereignty: A Discussion between Sisters

Candy: Do you want to talk about how sovereignty evolved? How did Indians get sovereignty? Where did it come from?

Lisa: It came from the very early period—the American government utilized the English form of treaty making as a tool for dealing with foreign nations and when you are dealing with a foreign nation, you are engaging on a nation-to-nation basis and that is where that comes from. That's the English model of treaty making.

Candy: So is that part of our Government based on English Law?

Lisa: Yeah, except they base theirs on Common Law and we base ours on Written Law. America's Written Law stayed that way as a nation-to-nation relationship until the 1870's when the Indian Wars took place. After the American Civil War, John Marshall reaffirmed them in the 1820's and 1830's.

Candy: In the Supreme Court?

Lisa: Right, and they defined the Indian Tribes as sound nations, though that was pretty much standard operating procedure until the 1870's and Indians kind of stayed out of the radar screen for the Americans because they were so involved in nation building and all of their little wars that they were in; wars of expansion and wars of imperialism that they were involved in. Americans really were imperialists.

Candy: It wasn't manifest destiny, it was imperialism, huh?

Lisa: It was indeed, but it was that manifest destiny that was a fancy phrase they used as a justification for taking whatever they wanted. If you look at some of their documents like the Monroe Doctrine of 1848, they clearly had a very imperialistic attitude. In it they claimed that nobody could have anything to say in the Western hemisphere but the American Government.

Candy: Yes.

Lisa: So that's pretty early. Then in the 1870's when the Civil War was over, the U.S. military was riding high and feeling very powerful with military people like Sherman as its leader.

Candy: And he hated Indians, right?

Lisa: Yes, he would say that *the only good Indian was a dead Indian*. He advocated what was called the Force Policy. It was based on the false belief that Indians would only respond to the force of a gun. That was his attitude. It was Sherman who was behind those terrible massacres. Did you ever see the movie Samurai where Tom Cruise keeps having those flashbacks and nightmares? That was from the Sand Creek Massacre, which took place in the early 1870's where the Indians made comments about Custer being an arrogant fool. It was in 1876 when Custer was killed at the Little Big Horn, which opened the floodgates for the Force Policy. It was Grant, however, who struggled to have an alternative to the Force Policy being the Peace Policy.

Candy: And he didn't agree with it right? He was President after Lincoln right?

Lisa: He was President after Johnson. His head of the Indian service was Carl Schurz who was very, very liberal.

Candy: Grant was military, wasn't he a General during the Civil War? Why was his attitude so different from Sherman?

Lisa: Well that's an interesting perspective; an interesting idea to explore; why was he—I guess he just was. He was a mid-westerner; I don't know where Sherman was from. You know what is really ironic is that Sherman's middle name was Tucomsa Sherman. But Grant was just a small town boy from Ohio and wasn't real successful in business so he went to West Point. Lincoln came along and he did very well. He and Sherman were contemporaries. I think they were at West Point at the same time. He was just somebody that Lincoln could relate to. They always had mean things to say about that though. They said Ulysses Grant was a big drunk and stuff like that; it was terrible. Lincoln just didn't care what they said; they were always bad-mouthing Grant to

	Lincoln and Lincoln would say, "I don't care if he's a drunk and if he is I will send a case of whatever he drinks to the rest of my generals so they will have some courage and do what their supposed to do and get this job done." It was interesting. And then he put a man like Carl Schurz in there and Carl Schurz was really way before his time; he was a liberal. I think some people said he had a lot of socialistic tendencies but he and Grant are the one's that brought the Church in as a way of saving Indian people. So that's where you get that missionary zeal. It was real hard to get various groups of church people because the Indians weren't good pickings for missionary work. But he did get Quakers and Quakers have always been more humane toward Indians. And therein lies a Nixon connection.
Candy:	Nixon's Mother was a Quaker, right?
Lisa:	Yes, his Mother was a Quaker; his father wasn't but he went to services a lot of times. The Quakers were as honest as the day is long, you know. If they saw wrong they brought it up. In fact, in some of our treaties they were part of the process and they didn't allow the traders to sell their liquors and their wares and run credit up for Indian people.
Candy:	Grant was President during the Battle of Little Big Horn. That brought about a lot of changes in the approach of the government toward Indians because it was such a devastating loss to America.
Lisa:	Yeah, it happened the same year they were celebrating their 100th anniversary and it happened like a week before their big celebration. Boy were they ever mad because the news came out just days before the 4th of July celebration. They have never forgiven Indian people generally and the Lakota specifically. I don't think it was just an oversight that no American President ever went to Lakota Country until Bill Clinton. In fact, I was the Acting Chair and the press called me; the National Public Radio called and wanted to talk to the chairman, but of course she wasn't there. So I was the Acting Chair and I took the call and they wanted to know what I thought about Bill Clinton going to Lakota Country. I said, "I think it's only right" and "I think it's about high time that the American government get over the battle of the Little Big Horn." I said, "the government has treated the Lakota like dirt ever since the Battle of the Little Big Horn because they blew up their birthday party" and the reporter just got mad at me. He was quarreling with me. "No," I said, "you read your history because the Battle of the Little Big Horn took place just a week before that big birthday party and there was headlines all over the New York Times and they have been mad about it ever since. The Lakota people have been treated like dirt and they were only defending their homeland just like anybody else would and the American military were the intruders."

Candy: Who was this guy?

Lisa: His name was Gill Halstead and he still gets mad at me. He will call me up from time to time and I will not let him off the hook on that. He didn't run it on his radio show because they don't want to hear that. Sometimes they don't like the truth and sometimes the truth hurts them. But that all happened and it was very political. I think we should really look at the congressional record. I would like to look at that and see what they had to say about that. It was certainly there. After the Battle at Little big Horn it was open season on Indian people. We just had to hunker down and take all of their blows because they were in a power position and we weren't.

It's really hard to listen to these Americans go on and on about how good they are and how generous they are. We have another story to tell. The story we have to tell doesn't reflect their mythology. Our heroes aren't their heroes. You know Crazy Horse was a hero. He led a heroic life. He was born the same year that Custer was born. Custer was their hero, white peoples', but he's never been an Indian hero. It's two different stories.

Crazy Horse never let anyone ever take a picture of him. That was Crazy Horse, and he never sought the glory. And then you look over on the other side at the man who was born the same year he was and they kind of grew up together and led parallel lives and met at Little Big Horn. They were the very same age. Crazy Horse was the polar opposite of Custer, who was just a glory seeker. Crazy Horse died the worst death that he could and that was to be killed by his own people. It would have been better if he had died in battle because he was a warrior. That was taken from him too. The army shot him in the back. They paid Lakota people to do these things, the bad deeds.

Candy: So after that the approach of dealing with Native people was totally different. They were not treated as sovereign nations any more, right?

Lisa: No, they were not. Then that old policy of paternalism came back in force, which they like for some reason.

Lisa: But if we are talking about Custer, he had been recalled because they had an excess of military officers after the Civil War.

Candy: And they were looking for things to do with them?

Lisa: Looking and getting rid of them because a lot of them were career people and it's like after every war, what do you do with all these Generals that you promoted and now you have them on the payroll? How do you get rid of them? Custer was one of those post-war excesses, an unnecessary cost, which they had to get rid of. I don't know that he got court marshaled but his redemption was to be sent

	to the West and that's where he made his name as an Indian fighter. After the Battle of Little Big Horn they just destroyed Indians.
Candy:	Isn't that when the boarding schools came about?
Lisa:	Yes, we see the boarding schools come in the reservations. Everything for Indian people, it is end-all and be-all for Indian policy as the acculturation and the assimilation of the reservation. That's all reservations were supposed to do to assimilate Indian people, but it was just crazy. It never worked because it kept people of like genes in the same area. What it did do was it turned Indian reservations into Indian ghettos. That's when you see the boarding school system emerge. It's in the 1870's. So it was a real interesting and tragic time.
Candy:	The 1890s?
Lisa:	Yes, by the 1890s the Indians were nothing but a little after thought, that is, little beads and feathers. That's all. They passed all kinds of incredible laws. Indians couldn't even gather together and they would just do terrible things to them. They would take cattle to Indian reservations for them to slaughter and the tribes in the West would let all those cattle go and then they would have a war party. The men would gather and they would go out and hunt them down and kill them like they had the buffalo in years past. They stopped that. They passed a policy against that–against Indians gathering for social events. They were forbidden to gather unless they were working.

What is amazing is that our people survived in tact, more or less. So when you speak about Indians and reflect on what their strength is, it is our ability to hunker down and dig in our feet. We found that the best way to deal with the white man was to stay out of his radar screen. Our leaders in those times are the real heroes. They are the people that we should build statues up for because they are the only reason we exist as Indian people today. What a terrible thought to think that, "oh yeah, we're Indians but we don't remember anything about it. We used to have a lot of land some place you know." That would be a horrible thought, don't you think? |
Candy:	Yes.
Lisa:	And that's exactly what they wanted. It's that old melting pot theory.
Candy:	It did happen for many Indian people right? I mean they did dissolve. Some tribes just melted away, right?
Lisa:	Well, they died off or they were killed off. Many in the California region after gold was found on their property were just killed off like rats at a garbage dump. Total impunity; Colorado and California have a shameful history with Indian people. You know you hear them talk about themselves and they are always breaking their arms patting

	themselves on the back about how wonderful they are, but they are awful people; just awful people. Texas is another state with a similar dreadful history.
Candy:	Are there any Indians in Texas anymore?
Lisa:	No, they killed so many Indians with total impunity like you would go out and hunt an animal. These are the states that are always talking about how wonderful they are like California and Colorado, but some of those events that took place there at the turn of the century are incredible. Frank Baum, for example, was such an Indian hater. He wrote for some newspaper in the West there. His articles were just horrible against Indian people. "Just kill them all," he would repeatedly advocate. And so you kind of laugh about the Utah football, the Utah Youths, the team that just beat Alabama the other night; they just wanted to kill them all.
Candy:	Ok, all this horrible stuff went on; so how do we get to sovereignty?
Lisa:	Well then we just stayed and stayed and stayed. And we didn't die.
Candy:	And the church groups wouldn't let Sherman kill us off?
Lisa:	No, they became our champions. As time passed, and we still survived, we made it through till FDR came in. FDR's new deal was a new deal for Indian people too. He was our savior. They did the new deal for Indian people just like they did for everybody else. Part of the background story behind the New Deal for Indians was the outrage that resulted from a best selling novel exposing the century of dishonor against Native peoples. It was written by Helen Hunt Jackson, did you ever hear of that woman?
Candy:	No
Lisa:	It was just a total expose.
Candy:	On the government?
Lisa:	On government policy. She talked about how Indians had been beaten down and how awful Indian reservations were. So there were some people that spoke for Indians and she was one of them; that Helen Hunt Jackson. I think she won some big prizes but it was on the best selling list out there in New York City and the East. There were other events that took place.

For example, there was a man, Standing Bear, he was a chief, and his ten-year-old son had died. He wanted to take him back to his homeland to bury him on the soil. They made a big racket about that and it became a big story. He tried to take his boy home to bury him and the government was going to stop him and he wanted to go back home. All of a sudden the public got involved and it became a |

big front-page news story. People sided with that Standing Bear and his son. I think they went to court. I don't know how that Standing Bear case was resolved but I don't think he was ever allowed to go back home again. It was so bad for Indian people; that's when that ghostance religion began to spread throughout Indian Country; it came this far.

Candy: It scared the government, didn't it?

Lisa: It scared them.

Candy: Would you question why that would scare them? They held all the cards.

Lisa: Well, they had completely demonized Indian people. If you think back and did a study on who the villains in popular culture have been, it becomes obvious. Now it's the terrorists. But at the turn of the century it was Indians. The early movies of Indians were Westerns and they were all villains. The problem with demonizing people is you can't turn it on and off like a switch. Once they decided that Indians were not so bad then they couldn't undo all of the damage that they had done. People still suffer from it today. There is so little known about Indian people. It is really scary.

Candy: It's like Sam talking to the kids when she was student teaching; the Hispanics and African American kids; they had such a little understanding—real understanding about Native people.

Lisa: Exactly. How many millions of people were killed? They try to sell a story, Candy, there was 90 million people here.

Candy: 90 million?

Lisa: Yes, 90 million. In Middle America, South America, and North America; 90 million.

Candy: And Native people are now down to about two million?

Lisa: No, actually I think were closer to four million but read Frances Jennings. He does a wonderful story on the destruction of Indian people. It's that part of the myth that the Americans have sold; that there was nobody here, this was an empty land; there was nothing going on here. They like to believe that story.

Candy: Ok, we digressed, we got to the new deal; how did we get to sovereignty? The sovereignty was always there because of the treaties, right? So it started with Indian reorganization which was under FDR?

Lisa: Yes, under FDR and under the head of the Bureau of Indian Affairs, John Collier. It was unusual for somebody from Chicago. He was a Chicago social worker but he would travel in the West and he just fell

	in love with Indian people. He'd go to the pueblos and they did some tourist things and he just fell in love with them.
Candy:	Sort of like Joseph Campbell?
Lisa:	Much like Joseph Campbell and he saw the beauty of the culture and he saw that it was something worth saving. So if you mark over renaissance and Modern Indian Native history, it goes to 1934, we quote the Indian reorganization all of the time in our legal documents. Every lawyer who works in Indian Country; they better know their Indian Reorganization Act because it's from there we get all of our ability to be sovereign and negotiate.
Candy:	And so FDR didn't really know what he was doing?
Lisa:	No, but John Callier certainly did and he had no trouble getting it through.
Candy:	And so then it was Indian Reorganization.
Lisa:	Yes, and then it kind of came to a halt—and then remember we talked about WWII?
Candy:	Yes.
Lisa:	Because WWI pretty much changed the whole focus of government, they re-did government up until that point; WWII Washington D.C. was just a sleepy little burg, a little southern sleepy town and with WWII it became a metropolis—it became a city because so many people were there working; that's how huge an event—WWII as WWI wasn't. All he wanted, all he needed was our money; but WWII they needed a whole lot more.
Candy:	So then after WWII all bets were off, everything changed; including for Indians. Indians got smarter, they wised up.
Lisa:	Yes, in fact, the National Congress of American Indians came into existence during WWII, the last part of WWII. Hoover was trying to eliminate Indians and the trust responsibility to save money. The National Congress of American Indians immediately began to organize and George Knott was a founding member of the National Congress of American Indians. I went there one day to visit and I looked at that picture in there, George Knott was really proud.

Teaching Native America across the Curriculum

CHAPTER FIVE

The Social Studies and Epistemological Diversity

Highlighted here is the importance of the interconnectedness of all that is, and the interrelatedness of the histories of all peoples in the Americas. What is argued is not an "additive" approach where the dominant Eurocentric curriculum is supplemented with *Native American* content. Rather, what is advocated for is a restructuring of the study of the social from what is currently a Euro-centered perspective to one informed by the complex interrelatedness of all peoples situated in specific geographical contexts.

* * *

The social studies, or the study of the social, tends to be that one subject area that we think of when the issue of interdisciplinary curricular reform emerges, which is not surprising given the widely accepted understanding that it "contains an almost unbounded body of subject matter" (Thornton, 2005, p. 2). For traditional arrangements of social studies curriculum, content is based "on material already gathered under the rubric of a discipline, material authoritatively endorsed as knowledge" (Thornton, 2005, p. 2). While it is widely acknowledged that the phrase *the social studies* implies the inclusion of many disciplines and fields of inquiry, it is assumed that they will be "taught as a collection of separate courses in individual social sciences such as geography or economics" (Thornton, 2005, p. 3), again, from a traditional social studies instruction framework.

For example, Columbia University social studies professor, Stephen Thornton (2005), while acknowledging the debate over "what aims ought to be emphasized" and "what form the curriculum should take," presupposes the existence of U.S. nationalism arguing that "no responsible party seriously questions that social studies courses such as American History ought to be taught in American schools" (p. 4). Thornton (2005) uncritically defines *American History*, which he mentions is a course required by law in most states, as a "narrative of national progress" with special emphasis on "the Revolution and the Constitution, the conquest of the West, the Civil War and emancipation, industrialization, reform movements, and the United States as a world power" (p. 32). For Thornton (2005), the debate over the social studies, at its core, is between college historians who advocate using banking methods in schools and social studies instructors who argue that this approach "does not motivate students to learn the material" because its not connected "to some relevant purpose" (p. 33).

From this *liberal* to *progressive* social studies perspective the traditional *disciplinary boundaries* are *ignored* and content is arranged to meet the concrete needs of the settler society and the micro specificities of student lives. From a modern, Enlightenment-based social science paradigm, this *objective reality* can be *objectively known* and scientifically remedied through social engineering (Saxe, 1991; Thornton, 2005). Extending the progressive leanings embedded within this approach through critiquing fundamental assumptions informing the modern project, the post-modernism of critical constructivism challenges the conclusion of *scientific realism* that knowledge is something that objectively exists *out there* waiting discovery or mastery, arguing instead that the ideologies of our schemas are constructed socially in the minds of men and women.

Rather than viewing content as an entity that can be objectively known, the critical constructivism of Joe Kincheloe (2005) points to the ways in which power works to shape our understanding of *the facts*, that is, knowledge about ourselves in relationship with others and the rest of the material world. Language or discourse, from this paradigm, does not merely reflect *material reality* or *the truth*, but informs our actions *in* and *on* the world. For example, the knowledge constructed about the world, and the subsequent practice in that world, from the perspective of the oppressed, is going to be antagonistically related to the ideologies constructed by the oppressors. From here we can begin to understand why a ruling class would seek to restrict the meaning of language through propaganda. The complexity of the contemporary era can be understood as the product of the experience and practice of subjugation and oppression and the attempts to foster false consciousness within the oppressed populations through media outlets and schooling institutions (Malott, 2008). The study of the social therefore becomes integral in understanding the larger power-based historical and geographical contexts in which mathematical, scientific, and language arts knowledges are constructed. The social studies, based on this approach, can become an integrating entity unifying knowledge production en masse and challenging the Western scientific propensity to reduce, separate, and distort in the interest of the dominant capitalist class.

Kincheloe's (2005) focus on power and oppression within his critical constructivism is informed, in part, by an Indigenous perspective that understands that the social studies, irrespective of form, unifying and democratic *or* reductive and hierarchical, was constructed to be part of the process of Western colonization, that is, native national *dis*placement, foreign invading *re*placement, and hegemonic continuation. Underscoring where power lies and how it operates can lead to a social studies that is counter-hegemonic.

For example, from the perspective outlined in *A Call to Action* (Malott, 2008), *no responsible party* would question teaching the history of the Americas from a Native American perspective, thereby challenging the hegemony of the settler-state. An Indigenous social studies would situate the United States in the context of Indigenous democracy, the colonization of the Americas, and the genocide of America's First Nations. From this perspective settler-state social studies curriculum and instruction is understood as embodying the tension between the settler-community's ruling class and the settler community's working class marginalizing Indigeneity and the enslavement and genocide of millions of Africans in the process. The tension we refer to is the product of these two antagonistically related settler classes' historic struggle over the distribution of wealth extracted from lands violently denationalized from Indigenous Nations.

It is from this multi-perspective approach that we will continue to explore the social studies. As we proceed we will discover an increasingly complex concrete context from which to understand the theoretical context of social studies knowledge production.

Contextualizing the Social Studies

A central component of exploring the specificities of the development of the social studies, which began during the first decade of the twentieth century, is to set the stage, that is, construct a picture of the social and political landscape of the United States during that time. In our discussion we pay particular attention to those aspects that seem to have been the most influential in creating the need for a social studies. Leading social studies historian David Warren Saxe (1991) suggests that the roots of the social studies in the United States can be traced to the popularization of *social science* around the beginning of the twentieth century as the "ravages of urbanization and industrialization" (Saxe, 1991, p. 3) were becoming increasingly barbarous. The social sciences deterministically promised to uncover hidden truths of human sociability through the reason and unbiased rationality of the scientific method, which could then be put into practice as a panacea for the ills of modern society. The problem with gaining support from those in positions of power, as we will see in later chapters, was that the democratic conclusions of social science did not serve the interests of those ruling classes that profit from their position within capitalism and the price those who rely on a wage to survive—the working classes—are forced to pay, which has been mass exploitation and increasing suffering until the contradiction of production and consumption reaches its cyclical crisis.

However, conscious of the ways we risk essentializing Native North America here, we can cautiously observe that from an Indigenous perspective, modern industrial society in America was made possible by conquest and genocide, which Marx called *primitive accumulation*, and is therefore an imposition regardless of whether the rulers of the settler state are democratic or authoritarian. Summarizing the magnitude of the United States' "quest to expropriate native land," infamous Native Studies scholar Ward Churchill (2002) notes that, "between 1787 and 1930," in an unprecedented series of broken treaties and genocidal military invasions, "the federal government seized approximately ninety percent of all remaining Indian acreage" and in the process "has projected itself into the posture of a world power" (p. 113). Upon closer examination we notice that within fifteen to twenty years before the emergence of the social studies the United Sates government was militarily engaged with Native Nations in the appropriation of their traditional lands in the name of progress.

For example, in 1890 the U.S. Census admitted that the Native population of California had been reduced from 300,000 in 1800, considered far greater now, to less than 20,000 in 1890 largely due to massacres committed by white settlers and miners. Killing Native peoples was a viable, if not entirely savage, way to supplement a miners' income during the off-season when water levels and flow were not conducive to mining. Not only was Indigenous land mined for its metallic riches, but the seemingly endless stocks of wild salmon runs in the Pacific Northwest were heavily exploited to feed the growing industrialism on the Eastern seaboard. To secure access to this "resource" the United States engaged in a series of wars against the Native Peoples of the Pacific Northwest. As a result, between 1854 and 1855, the U.S. was able to sign nine treaties with more than seventeen thousand Native peoples relinquishing them of more than sixty four million acres, which now comprise the majority of the Pacific Northwest (Malott, 2008).

Again, as the size of the working class in Great Britain and the eastern United States exploded, the need for an inexpensive source of protein to fuel the wealth generating potential of this highly exploited and over-worked source of human labor power too increased. To profit from the creation of this new industrial market commercial fishing technology was developed in three primary areas: extraction, packaging and shipment. With an intercontinental railroad stretching from the east coast to the Columbia River realized, and therefore the availability of an efficient and reliable shipping method, and the development of a technique for sealing fish in airtight cans, the first salmon cannery was opened on the Columbia River in 1866 by Hapgood, Hume and Company (New England capitalists that were already involved in the Northwest timber industry). Technology was also developed for extracting the fish from the rivers. Initially, a variety of netting methods adapted from Native fishers were used such as gill nets, traps, and seines, but much larger in capacity due to the use of teams of work horses employed to literally drag the massive hauls of fish from the waters. However, a uniquely industrial capitalist device was developed, the fish wheel, and thus completely foreign to Native Northwest America, that worked to literally pump salmon from their runs faster than previously thought possible. Painting a picture of what this contraption looked like in full swing Robbins (1999) describes it as:

> ...An elaborate Ferris wheel-like structure powered by the current that scooped fish from the water. First used on the Columbia in 1879, the highly productive wheels (both stationary and mounted on scows) literally pumped salmon from the river; the giant Phelps wheel at The Dalles took 227,000 pounds of salmon from the river from May to July, 1894. And on a single spring day in 1913 the Suffer brothers' wheel no. 5 turned a record catch of 70,000 pounds. (p. 11)

At the height of operation it has been estimated that there were canneries on virtually every Oregon, and northwestern, coastal stream. By the late 1800s and early 1900s fish stocks had been noticeably diminished. Removing massive quantities of fish from streams and rivers was only one source of wild salmon depletion. The development of residential areas, continued logging practices, and the damming of major waterways had a tremendously detrimental impact on salmon habitat and ecosystems rendering recovery in some areas impossible (Lackey, Lach, & Duncan, 2006a). For example, with the construction of the hydroelectric Grand Coulee dam, one of many massive undertakings on the main stem of the Columbia River designed to meet the propaganda-induced and thus manufactured, electricity needs of an increasing settler population; over 1,100 miles of salmon spawning grounds were eliminated forever. What is more, increasing urban sprawl has meant not only encroachment on salmon habitat, but the increasing pollution from sewage, lumber mills and factories has left the oxygen levels in many waterways so low as to render them lifeless (Robbins, 1999). As a result, every species of salmon fish stocks, at one time thought to be limitless, are now severely endangered. For example, in the Columbia basin current salmon runs are approximately only 1.7% of their pre-Euro-American size. For Washington, Oregon, California, and Idaho, combined; the number is 5.2% of its original salmon population. In British

Columbia, however, the numbers, while far from acceptable, are substantially better than those within the contiguous 48, with salmon populations at 36.2% of their pre-contact numbers (Lackey, Lach, & Duncan, 2006b, p. 24).

The reductionist wealth-extracting conception of land that fueled this destruction has inevitably led to the areas' Tribal governments, on more than one occasion, taking the state to court based on articles written into treaties guaranteeing traditional fishing rights forever. For example, in the Treaty of Medicine Creek of 1854, Article III states that, "the right of taking fish, at all usual and accustomed grounds and stations, is further secured by said Indians..." (quoted in Blumm & Bodi, 1999, p. 178). While it has been argued that Native fishing rights have been illegally limited since the signing of treaties, such as Medicine Creek, it was not until fish stocks in the Pacific Northwest began to be dramatically reduced that we see major efforts to prevent Native peoples from fishing while simultaneously protecting the fishing practices of white settlers. In 1889, for example, after Washington achieved statehood, numerous laws were passed limiting Native fishing activities in western Washington Rivers in the name of conservation while ignoring white commercial fishing in the ocean and Puget Sound (Blumm & Bodi, 1999).

Not only did the industrial machine have its eyes set on the Pacific Northwest, but they also targeted the gold within the Black Hills, the Lakota Nation's most sacred place. It is within this context that the U.S. waged a thirty-year war against the Lakota people. However, the Lakota have not been the only Indigenous Nation in the region targeted for wealth extraction. For example, the U.S. also sought out the resources within the land base of the Navajo Nation that currently holds "an estimated 150 billion tons of low sulfur coal, about forty percent of 'U.S.' uranium reserves and significant deposits of oil, natural gas, gold, silver, copper and gypsum, among other minerals" (Churchill, 2003, p. 21). These resources have overwhelmingly tended to be "developed" by non-Native outsiders, who then in turn profit while the local Indigenous community is left with the often deadly environmental bill and no form of economic livelihood. As alluded to above, the Lakota also possess similarly endowed reservation lands. Because of the wealth extracted from their territories, Native Americans should be the wealthiest people in the United States, but instead, they are the poorest and most oppressed according to every imaginable social indicator, such as life expectancy, education, and income, for example (Churchill 2003).

Highlighting the tactics that led to this sad chapter in American history is the Wounded Knee Massacre of 1890, which was committed by the U.S. 7th Cavalry. During the onslaught more than 300 unarmed Lakota were slaughtered, many of whom were women, children, the elderly, and non-combatant spiritual leaders and keepers of sacred knowledge (Churchill, 1995). Contributing to the genocide between 1800 and 1895 the great herds of bison, which provided the primary source of nutrition for many Native Americans of the Great Plains, the Lakota most notably, were reduced to near extinction. During "aboriginal times," it has been estimated, these herds were as great as sixty million strong. By the beginning of the nineteenth century they had been reduced to forty million. The most dramatic decline occurred between 1800 and 1895 when the buffalo, reaching their nadir of less than one thousand, were brought to near extinction resulting in "…widespread starvation and the social and cultural collapse of many Plains tribes…(Thornton, 1987, p. 52).

Demonstrating the interconnectedness of the buffalo and the Lakota way of life, and in turn, Indigenous philosophy, traditional Lakota philosopher Joseph Marshall III (2001) in *The Lakota Way*, notes, "the bison was the greatest nomad on the plains and our association with and dependence on it turned us into nomads as well. As the bison went, so did we" (p. 211). It was understood by the U.S. army that the Plains Indians existence was intimately connected to that of the bison, and the extermination of the bison would advance the policy of Indian extermination, that is, genocide. Because the culture of the Lakota, for example, was so intimately connected to the bison, it can be argued that the destruction of the great herds was not only an act of physical genocide, but cultural genocide as well. For example, General William Tecumseh Sherman encouraged hundreds of white buffalo hunters and sportsmen to slaughter the great herds by the tens and hundreds of thousands as part of a systematic effort to tame "…the wild Indians by killing off their lifeline" (Marshall III, 2001, p. 217). Employing the graphic imagery necessary for comprehending the physical genocide just laid out, that is, the unfathomable magnitude of these crimes committed against humanity in the last five centuries by predominantly European colonizers and settlers, Ward Churchill (1997) notes:

> The people had died in their millions of being hacked apart with axes and swords, burned alive and trampled under horses, hunted as game and fed to dogs, shot, beaten, stabbed, scalped for bounty, hanged on meat hooks and thrown over the sides of ships at sea, worked to death as slave laborers, intentionally starved and frozen to death during a multitude of forced marches and internments, and, in an unknown number of instances, deliberately infected with epidemic diseases. Today, every one of these practices is continued, when deemed expedient by the settler population(s)…(p. 1)

Drawing on the perspective offered by Native activist/poet John Trudell and the work of radical Chicano activist/scholar Rodolfo Acuña (1988) in *Occupied America: A History of Chicanos* Churchill (2003) has consistently situated the analysis of physical genocide embedded within the above quote in a larger context by describing "the moment predator washed up on American shores" as the beginning of predation, that is, *the act of plundering and preying*. We might also refer to the effects of physical genocide as perdition—*complete and irreparable loss and ruin*. The completeness and irreparability of the loss and ruin has been all but total for many Indigenous societies. In the annals of the traditional history and social studies curricula this destructive march is romantically referred to as *westward expansion* and *manifest destiny*.

From a traditional Native American paradigmatic perspective, the idea that the *westward expansion* of industrialism represents the will of God disregards the unwavering, deterministic, spiritual law that says that if the water is poisoned and the earth is fouled, people will suffer. *Manifest destiny* therefore represents a spiritual contradiction, and, as such, can only ever exist through negative means such as force, coercion, deception, and manipulation. Native American philosophy, to be sure, understands the intimate interconnection between all that exists rendering the damage done to any part or subset harmful to the whole. It is a deceivingly simple concept. Comprehending the constantly shifting interconnectedness of all that exists, is, by definition, beyond the capacity of any one single entity, and living this awareness is a life-long occupation. As we continue with our exploration of the historical context that gave way to the social studies, it is worth restating, from an Indigenous perspective, that the social studies can be understood as the Western-based content area that is most centrally implicated in the manufacture of society and social stability on Indigenous land, yet dismissive of the spiritual centeredness indicative of indigeneity.

Progressive historian Howard Zinn (1997) describes the era in which the social studies emerged as the time when "the permanent characteristics of the United States in the twentieth century were being hardened" (p. 178). Zinn (1997) points to "the growing power of corporations" (Zinn, p. 178) and the conservative tendencies of trade unions as those features of the economic infrastructure of the United States that continue to hold political sway. The Great Depression posed a serious threat to this corporate dominance because it radicalized the settler population who were increasingly unwilling to have the losses of financial risk-taking be externalized to them, as is the case now with the "bail out."

Before the Great Depression capital was relatively unregulated and mobile allowing the business class to serve as a sort of defacto *virtual parliament* who *vote* on government policies through *capital flight* (Chomsky, 2008). Because of the *instability* or *crisis in confidence* created by an increasingly militant and critical working class, the ruling class felt it necessary to respond to the public will and concede to some social democratic policies. The Bretton Woods system established in 1944 represented these concessions by imposing restrictions or regulations on the mobility of capital. These safeguards against the abuses of capitalist power were dismantled in 1971 giving way to the neoliberal era that views the mobility of capital not as the primary source of economic coercion but as a *right* and simultaneously views that the *humans rights* underscored in the United Nations Declaration of Human Rights, such as education, health, and satisfying employment, as *preposterous* and nothing more than *myths*. As a result, an increasing emphasis has been placed on the manufacture of consent through the propaganda system because the settler and immigrant population has retained significant elements of its former democratically radical self.

Focusing our attention here on this solidification of corporate dominance, and therefore the hegemonization of the labor-capital relationship, we can situate these tendencies, as noted above, within the context of settler-state encroachment on, and occupation of, the traditional territories of Native American Nations. In other words, only by gaining access and control of the land, which, again, Marx referred to as primitive accumulation, could the process of plunder firmly take hold and fully engage its driving force, which is the quest for wealth *by any means necessary* (Malott, 2008). Within the settler-state society before Bretton Woods the radicalization among the population was most strikingly demonstrated within this atmosphere of increasingly violent authoritarianism by the Industrial Workers of the World (IWW). From their birth the IWW was dedicated to the revolutionary emancipation of the working class from a highly concentrated and unregulated capitalist class. The IWW believed, somewhat romantically perhaps, and without the help of Karl Marx, that if they seized control of the means of production, the workers of the world ultimately would be in a position to democratically redistribute the collective fruits of labor, that is, wealth and political power. The aim of the IWW was therefore to organize all workers under "One Big Union" across all lines of difference, including national, linguistic, racial, gender, and skill-level, employing the strike as the primary tool to shift power from the elite few to the restless many thereby delivering the final blow to capitalism as a viable economic system (Loewen, 1995; Smith, 1984; Zinn, 1997).

The *bosses*, on the other hand, were fully committed to ensuring that the IWW was not successful and that the basic relationship between labor and capital remained intact. Not only did individual corporations hire their own private militias to battle and murder the leaders of organized labor, but the federal government also played a decisive role against the working class revolution by institutionalizing a permanent federal policing agency, the Bureau of Investigation (BoI). The BoI would later be renamed the Federal Bureau of Investigation (FBI) in an effort to escape the controversy that emerged from their war against the IWW, which included such tactics as bombing, killing, falsely arresting and imprisoning, and manufacturing and disseminating disinformation. Spearheaded by Attorney General Charles S. Bonaparte the BoI was established in 1906 on a departmental order despite fierce opposition from Congress, to their credit (Malott & Peña, 2004).

Again, this development led to a long legacy of U.S. government-led domestic terrorism against its own population, which effectively neutralized the IWW. For example, there is overwhelming evidence that conclusively demonstrates that the BoI systematically orchestrated "an 'anarchist' bombing campaign aimed at various corporate and governmental facilities" leaving the scenes scattered with "anarchist leaflets" intended to set up the IWW for prosecution and simultaneously erode public sympathy for the counter-hegemonic organization (Churchill & Vander Wall, 1990, p. 21). IWW leaders were repeatedly falsely arrested on charges ranging from murder to inciting resistance resulting in punishments as severe as execution to lengthy prison sentences and costly fines leading to the eventual bankruptcy and dissolution of the IWW itself. While this use of force is a significant aspect of the nation's history, the ideological assault whose primary battleground has been in the country's public schools, has had the most long-lasting and devastating implications on democracy and the likelihood of the realization of the social justice envisioned by the IWW and many others.

Before we continue documenting the specific characteristics and manifestations of this ideological assault, it is worth pausing a moment to expand on the significance of hegemony since Bretton Woods. Chomsky (2008) argues that in the nineteenth century "the public had not been much of a problem" rendering it relatively easy for "the virtual parliament" to transfer "the severe costs" to the "general population" (p. 3)—that is, privatizing profits/surplus value/unpaid labor hours and socializing, through a system of taxation, the costs, such as mass compulsory education/indoctrination, an imperial army to pave the way for capitalist expansion/reproduction, and the necessary infrastructure to transport commodities and support the population. Because Bretton Woods weakened capitalism's stranglehold over workers by restricting the movement of capital, it was never intended to be permanent. Required was therefore a renewed and intensified system of mass indoctrination to foment the required internalization of oppression and limit the democratic habits of mind nourished by the crisis in confidence that would be engendered by The Great Depression and the way it highlighted the antagonistic relationship between labor and capital in stark contrast.

The Early Years of the Social Studies

Operating in this context of controversy progressive educator John Dewey was interested in establishing a model of education that could effectively resolve the social problems that stemmed from industrialization. Dewey and his colleagues, such as George Counts, advocated for curricular reforms focusing on the history curriculum, which they argued was out-of-date, decontextualized, and inherently incapable of providing students with the higher order critical thinking skills needed to address the major issues of the day. The struggle became over the purpose and focus of the social studies. Dewey (1916/1966) saw education as a neutral vehicle through which particular societies reproduced themselves noting that "the conception of education as a social process and function has no definite meaning until we define the kind of society we have in mind" (p. 97).

Commenting on the concrete context of American society around the beginning of the twentieth century Dewey (1919/1966) observes that "the present economic conditions," which he defines as a class-based society, are reproduced through a system where those relegated to the status of *worker* are "made merely tools for the higher culture of others" (p. 98) resulting in an education system focused on the manufacture of patriotism and authoritarian discipline. However, Dewey argues that it is not enough to ensure that education is not "actively used as an instrument to make easier the exploitation of one class by another" (p. 98). Education must also foster "respect" for "the fuller, freer, and more fruitful association and intercourse of all human beings with one another" as a democratic "disposition of the mind" (Dewey, 1919/1966, p. 98).

Careful not to romanticize, we must acknowledge that Dewey's (1919/1966) democratic "ideal" was situated within the theoretical context of the hierarchies of civilizations paradigm which was based on the Darwinian observation that the natural order represents a continuing development where "some species die out," and in turn, "the life process continues in increasingly complex forms" assumed to be "better adapted to utilize the obstacles against which they struggled" (p. 2). Dewey (1919/1966) then defines his use of "life" here as "the whole range of experience, individual and racial" (p. 2). As a result, Dewey (1919/1966) suggests that "race" is a well defined property, and in the process, supports the European construct that more adapted *races* replace less adapted *races* in a natural linear progression, which depends on education as "the means of this social continuity of life" and without it "the most civilized group will relapse into barbarism and then into savagery" (pp. 2–4).

Because Dewey arguably represents the more democratic end of the political continuum in which we find the institutionalized manifestation of the social studies as a distinct subject and therefore part of the standard curriculum, we can safely conclude that it was never intended to foster the development of the democratic citizen endowed with the sensitivities conducive to challenging or disrupting the violent process of Native American conquest whose completion roughly coincides with the beginning of the social studies, as noted above. Dewey, to be sure, was born in 1859, so he grew up during the United State's last major *Indian Wars*, as underscored above. By the time the great Lakota leader and medicine man/philosopher, Sitting Bull, was murdered, Dewey was thirty-one years old and an established scholar. Yet, rather than challenge the imperialistic tendencies of *westward expansion*, Dewey apologetically argued that more adapted *races* make redundant less adapted ones.

While it does not seem to be too far of a stretch to say that Dewey saw the existence of a colonial state situated on occupied lands as evidence of European supremacy, he did, nevertheless, understand the importance of non-exploitative social arrangements as a necessary component of a democratic society. Because industrial capitalism is based on the domination of one class over another, Dewey's proposal for a democratic social studies was met with fierce opposition by the educational supporters of big business and the ruling elite who advocated for a model of social education that was based on the assumption that the curriculum should be constructed to fit the indoctrinating needs of business and nationalism following the strict disciplinary reductionism of subject matter.

This traditional model of education was based on the idea that education resources should be tightly controlled to ensure the regimentation of knowledge production and the development of habits and dispositions conducive to the needs of business, which persisted despite widespread professional opposition that saw the schools as lacking in practical democratic value. While many teacher educators and the "social studies insurgents," such as Dewey, "believed that the traditional program of education was wrong and needed redirection," policy makers and other power brokers tended to paint a picture of a well-functioning system that was leading to much progress "being made in many areas of education" (Saxe, 1991, p. 115). While the history of this struggle over the purpose and function of public education has continued to develop with many important and nuanced manifestations and alliances, further historical discussions will be outlined below in the context of making comparisons with the contemporary era.

The Social Studies Today

In the contemporary era the social studies continues to take on the characteristics of a contested terrain where the competing interests of *multicultural/multi-perspective* labor and a manufactured *monocultural/single perspective* capitalist class battle, in increasingly complex and contradictory ways, to define the official purpose of the field and what it looks like in practice. For example, the National Council for the Social Studies (NCSS) defines the social studies as:

> …The integrated study of the social sciences and humanities to promote civic competence. Within the school program, social studies provides coordinated systematic

study drawing upon such disciplines as anthropology, archeology, economics, geography, history, law, philosophy, political science, psychology, religion, and sociology, as well as appropriate content from the humanities, mathematics, and natural sciences. The primary purpose of social studies is to help young people develop the ability to make informed and reasoned decisions for the public good as citizens of a culturally diverse, democratic society in an interdependent world. (www.socialstudies.org/standards/introduction)

NCSS, which is the primary professional organization of the social studies, is clearly in concert with the view that the primary function of the social studies, more than any other subject, is to facilitate the development of citizenship, or *civic competence*. Emphasis is therefore placed by NCSS on what is considered to be the necessary *knowledge, skills and attitudes* most conducive to the *ideas and values of our democratic republic* represented in the interdisciplinary approach underscored above. Ultimately, NCSS, like Dewey in earlier years, presupposes an unproblematized nationalism, that is, *civic competence*, unconscious of the stolen Native American geography upon which the settler states are built. In short, NCSS offers a liberal, democratic social education designed to foster highly educated citizens. It is important to keep in mind that social studies educators do tend to be actively engaged with, and informed by, NCSS, even though the organization has no real executive power at the level of state or federal policy. For example, NCSS membership can offer curriculum recommendations, pass resolutions against war, and remove social justice language from their literature, as they have done, because the implications, through the actions of the membership, are arguably more than symbolic.

We can therefore conclude that the approach to the social studies offered by NCSS has real implications in the social studies terrain. Before we continue with these considerations, it is worth pausing and restating that NCSS advances an approach to the social studies that is traditional because it does not consider the central role power plays in the legitimation process. At the same time, we can place this model on the liberal end of the traditional social studies continuum because it endorses an equal access approach to the hierarchies of capitalism. In other words, what is theoretically supported is a form of capitalist rule that governs without prejudice or bigotry rejecting the practice of oppressing some groups more than others in favor of a system that exploits all equally.

In the elementary grades this accommodative social studies is based on the "expanding environments" *social education* model that is not directly connected to the academic disciplines of the social studies that are stressed in the secondary grades (Thornton, 2005, p. 13). The expanding environments approach looks broadly at the role geography plays in shaping culture and human society. Summarizing this position Thornton (2005) notes that, "defenders of expanding environments in the primary grades have noted that although children may be familiar with concepts such as shelter, they are unable to explain why, say, different kinds of shelter might be used in different kinds of physical environments" (p. 13). Providing a thorough example of what this expanding environments model might look like in practice, JoyAnn Hauge Morin's (2003) *Social Studies Instruction Incorporating the Language Arts* offers "example social studies units, activities, and recommended content for elementary grades one through six" that are "based on the general curriculum standards set forth by the National Council for the Social Studies" (p. xi).

A common theme throughout the volume is the celebration of a depoliticized cultural diversity represented in activities such as stories from around the world told through the perspective of animals. The goal of these primary grade lessons, beyond the acquisition of language arts skills, is to develop an appreciation of cultural diversity. However, the primary grade social studies curriculum also includes a focus on the development of a basic understanding of relational thinking using the example of the family, which is developed in later grades to the community, state, nation, and finally the world with increasingly focused disciplinary emphases. This content standard could be used to engage those in the early grades in thinking about the historic relationships between cultures tapping into what some have argued is the inherent sense of fairness found within young children.

While the debate over what the specific content of the standards should include or not include makes it easy to lose sight of the larger picture, not all contemporary social studies teachers and teacher educators fall victim to this tendency as evidenced by their positions against the standards movement. For example, critical social studies scholar and educator, Wayne Ross (2000), has consistently held that "curriculum standards, as they are presently pursued, promote standardized school knowledge, divert attention from teachers' roles in curriculum development, and skew the discourse of curriculum reform away from issues of equity" (p. 204). Ross's qualifier, "as they are presently pursued," is elaborated on in an essay coauthored with social studies educators Sandra Mathison and Kevin D. Vinson (Mathison, Ross & Vinson, 2006) where the team distinguishes between dominant approaches to standards that promote a passive engagement with subject matter through rote memorization, and learning standards that are designed to foster an active and critical engagement with content and knowledge production through an emphasis on skills and pedagogy.

Similarly, *Rethinking Schools* scholar and social studies teacher Bill Bigelow (2003) argues that the efforts to standardize curriculum, pedagogy, and assessment have been an attempt to "silence dissident voices" (p. 232), which is an attack on what Kincheloe (2005) describes as the "epistemological bazaar." The importance of this bazaar can be found within the role it plays in providing the life-giving nourishment for the manifestation of a critical democracy that is informed by the values of environmental responsibility, interconnectedness, social justice, freedom, equality, happiness, and fun to be practiced now so future unborn generations will be able to benefit from the natural world. Another *Rethinking Schools* activist-educator, Linda McNeil (2003), responding to these standardization trends and their implications for reading comprehension, argues that the centralization movement has led to teaching to the test and that "the kind of test prep frequently done to raise test scores may actually hamper student's ability to learn to read for meaning outside the test setting" (p. 218). This is, in large part, explained by the tendency to "ignore" what McNeil (2003) identifies as "a broad and sophisticated research base on the teaching of reading" (p. 218) that has stressed the importance of understanding literature from multiple perspectives, including, and perhaps especially, *dissident voices*.

We can situate these educators within the context of a new social studies movement that is part of larger trends in critical pedagogy that are focused on pursuing radical, liberatory approaches to education. The emergence of the popularization of this movement can be identified as growing out of, and benefiting from, the struggles of the 1960s and 1970s, that resulted in the academic legitimation of subjugated knowledges/multiple perspectives represented in the emergence of sub-disciplines within the humanities and the sciences such as Environmental Studies and Ecology, Native Studies, Chicano Studies, African Studies, Women's and Gender Studies, Marxism and labor studies, and Peace Studies, to name a few. Making this point Merry Merryfield and Binaya Subedi (2006), in "Decolonizing the Mind for World-Centered Global Education," note that it was "not until the civil rights movement of the 1960s" that the social studies began to noticeably "include content" from "African Americans, Asian Americans, Latinos, Native Americans, new immigrants, and other groups on the margins of economic and political power in the U.S." (p. 283).

Threatened by this grassroots move toward democratic participation and curricular inclusion, advocates of the traditional approach/the ruling class interests of the rich responded during the 1980s arguing that an emphasis on cultural diversity led to the *ghettoization* of the curriculum, and in turn, falling test scores in schools and ethnic divisiveness in society. Conservatives called for a return to *the basics* and the reemphasis of a common, compulsory, patriotic culture, that, they argued, *unifies* rather than *divides*. The standards movement and No Child Left Behind (NCLB) dominated the schooling context during this time serving as an easy target for progressive educators dedicated to the promises of equality and multicultural justice of the 1960s and 1970s and the increasing need for Marxist analysis demanded by neoliberal capitalism.

However, there is currently widespread anticipation that this conservative backlash is coming to a close symbolized by the election of Barrack Obama November 4th 2008 to be the next President of the United States of America, and the country's first African American president. Obama received sixty three million votes, or fifty two percent of those who voted, by appealing to a general sense of economic justice that is widespread throughout society and to the multicultural sensibilities of today's youth with promises of *real change*, such as ending both the war in Iraq and the test-driven focus of NCLB and redistributing wealth more equally among the population by providing tax relief for working people while simultaneously increasing the taxation of the rich. Obama has also consistently pledged to pursue this path of peace, which is what people want, by promising to listen to not only other world leaders previously ignored and demonized by the U.S., such as President Hugo Chavez of Venezuela, but the people of the United States, which we hope will prove to represent the beginning of the United States' acknowledgment of democratic ideals in the contemporary era.

However, it is also true that Obama achieved what he achieved by distancing himself from affirmative action, the Reverend Jeremiah Wright, and aligning himself with the bankers, which were necessary moves to gain the support of capital and it's media. It is important to note that much of the enthusiasm over an Obama presidency overlooks the simple fact that the position of U.S. President is not a kingship. While the power of the presidency has greatly increased during the Bush years, the framers of the Constitution nevertheless sought to ensure that the Commander in Chief was not too powerful indicated by Congress' ability to veto the President's vetoes. The President's main functions are to validate all of the laws passed by Congress and to lead the armed forces. While the President can propose legislation, only the Congress can pass them, again, rendering the power of the executive branch limited. This brings us to a very serious issue.

That is, because much of the population is riding high on the hopes and aspirations of the presidency of the nation's first Black President, there is great risk of even deeper cynicism and hopelessness that existed during the Bush years if those dreams are not realized by the Obama cabinet. The selection of Rahm Emanuel, who made millions as an investment banker, as Obama's Chief of Staff is an indication of more of the same. Emanuel voted for NAFT, welfare reform, and The PATRIOT ACT. However, these points, which indicate that Obama represents the interests of the ruling elite, are obvious and no surprise to most working people. That is, while many oppressed people, overcome with joy over the fist African American president-elect, are well aware that the grass roots struggle for justice must continue in earnest. At the same time, Noam Chomsky (2008) brings attention to the *fact* that during the past sixty years real income for working people has grown twice as fast under Democrats as compared to Republicans. In other words, while the election of Obama and the Democratic Party did not subvert the basic relationships of power, it most likely will lead to real benefits for those who rely on a wage to survive, and a more positive socio-political environment to engage in cross-racial class struggle and social justice work.

The challenge for critical pedagogues is therefore to connect with community organizations and not lose sight of what millions of Americans have themselves acknowledged what they have in common with each other, which the Obama victory has trumpeted for the world to hear—symbolically *and* actually. He demonstrated that over sixty three million American citizens are roughly of the same mind when it comes to democratic values such as freedom from economic oppression and embracing diversity. Obama was right in his acceptance speech that the victory is not his, but ours, because it is only an actively engaged citizenry that can create the lasting change that so many long for.

However, if democratization *does* begin to happen within the Obama presidency, which, in a limited way, is likely (noted above), as it is happening among the larger population, it will and is signifying a return to the Native American democratic philosophy of peace, equality, and freedom that have become American traditions within the settler state. Part of the critical pedagogical challenge is therefore to be part of the process of bringing public attention to the Indigenous roots of not just American democracy, but of contemporary modern democracy more generally (Lyons & Mohawk, 1992). That is, as we move forward with peace and democracy at the forefront of our minds, it would be wise to look to the original source of these insights for guidance and inspiration, which a growing number of today's white settler youth are doing on their own according to many Native American leaders such as University of Buffalo professor and Six Nations Chief Oren Lyons.

Again, because of the popularity of democratic ideals within the settler communities, it should be no surprise that the neo-liberal agenda has been the focus of widespread student resistance and lamented in the contemporary era by radical educators as culturally insensitive, white supremacist and a hegemonic tool designed to manufacture the necessary consent needed to continue to reproduce the hierarchical relationships indicative of capitalist society. Supposing Obama's administration follows through with what they have proposed in regards to education, which is a *real* possibility, and engages in the process of looking for new directions for curriculum and pedagogy, we must speak loudly and encourage the Secretary of Education to review *all* of the scholarly evidence, and be conscious that their lofty multicultural goals will not be realized without the contributions of not only multicultural education, but critical pedagogy as well, which has been gaining popularity in schools of education throughout the world. Within this context it is not surprising that new forms of radical social studies have found increasing appeal in recent times (although not without significant opposition).

For example, Joe Kincheloe's (2001) monumental critical constructivist-oriented social studies text, *Getting Beyond the Facts*, has been hugely popular in teacher education programs leading to multiple editions. In it Kincheloe (2001) advances a social studies education that "fights against the abuse of the poorest and most vulnerable people in the world and the tyranny of the most powerful. It explores the ethical requirements of citizenship in the globalized society of the twenty-first century with its sweatshops, dire poverty, disease, and famine in the midst of the greatest wealth created in human history" (p. 13). The philosophical influences informing Kincheloe's approach clearly include elements from indigeneity. For example, in laying the theoretical foundation for over eight hundred pages of *Getting Beyond the Facts*, Kincheloe (2001) informs his audience that "the social studies education envisioned" here "is grounded in an appreciation of the interconnectedness of all inhabitants on the planet," and in the process, developing "new concepts of citizenship and social action" (p. 13). This ontological position—that all entities in the natural world are intimately interconnected by an unwavering spiritual law that demands humans to be conscious of the destructive and irresponsible potential of our biological endowments that, gone unchecked, can lead to the break down of the life cycle (i.e. environmental devastation such as global warming) when all life is not respected—has been identified as a common theme among the vast diversity amongst Indigenous cultural traditions (Deloria, 1997; Grande, 2004; Kincheloe, 2005; Lyons & Mohawk, 1992; Malott, 2008).

Following this trend toward more critical approaches to the social studies, Malott and Pruyn (2006) have named what they understand to be the most effective or democratizing and engaging approach to the social studies as *Critical Multicultural Social Studies* (CMSS). In their theoretical exploration of CMSS Malott and Pruyn (2006) have stressed the central importance of Marx's conceptualization of capitalist society because of its ability to uncover the hidden structures of power built into today's class-based global social economy. Malott and Pruyn (2006) have taken the theoretical insights from Marx and other critical theorists and situated them in the life-affirming context of multicultural education (MCE) because one of humanity's greatest assets, our rich cultural diversity, has been under constant attack since at least 1492 when Columbus washed up on the shores of present day Haiti proclaiming that the Indigenous people would "make fine servants" and that "with fifty men we could subjugate them all" (quoted in Malott, 2008, p. 25). Malott and Pruyn (2006) define CMSS as "a student/community-based radical pedagogical approach that strives for the fomentation of social justice by and amongst students, community members and activists, teachers, administrators and our society at large via the social studies and history"

(p. 166). In our original exploration of CMSS we did not explicitly bring to the fore the philosophical insights of indigeneity. What follows is therefore a revised CMSS strengthened by the democratic tendencies of traditional Native American sociability/philosophy.

CMSS AND THE INDIGENOUS CHALLENGE

We can begin here with the argument on *natural law* previously mentioned. Oren Lyons summarizes this position by pointing to what he identifies as *the* spiritual center that is at the heart of what we can name *natural democracy* or a democratic practice that is lived in concert with the laws of ecology and living systems that demands respect for the world's interconnected ecosystems. We might call this an *eco-Marxist CMSS*. Scholars of Native Studies such as Four Arrows (2008) argue that indigeneity is in fact gaining popularity in critical circles. For example, Four Arrows (2008) comments that, "in spite of rigorous efforts by a number of academics to discredit genuine accomplishments and potential contributions of indigenous worldviews and philosophy, many others have endorsed the relevance of them for a healthful future" (p. 494).

In his discussion Four Arrows (2008) provides a much broader historical context demonstrating that indigeneity is not only gaining mainstream acceptance in the contemporary era, but points to some of the Founding Fathers of the United States as early evidence of European American leaders who saw the lived practice of Native American philosophy as representing "the ideals of democracy" (p. 496). For example, Four Arrows (2008) looks specifically at Thomas Paine's observation that the human misery and suffering indicative of European civilization was the result of a "flawed" conception of "land ownership," which stood in stark contrast to "the native way of equally distributing land" (p. 496). These differences in social arrangements stem from antagonistically related values. From the European perspective, the accumulation of wealth and property serves as the driving force. For indigeneity, on the other hand, widespread happiness, fairness, and peace serve as guiding principles.

Because the roots of American democracy are fundamentally indigenous to America's First Nations, we can conclude that for a social studies education to truly be a CMSS, it must advocate for a form of citizenship that is grounded in the previously mentioned Indigenous values of peace, equality, and freedom as central and non-negotiable. However, while this move must certainly be embraced widely throughout the settler states of North America, we must also proceed cautiously aware of the implications of the Euro-centric civil to savage scale on the hierarchical structure of white consciousness, which stands as a major barrier for white people to be able to openly engage with indigeneity without bias, prejudice, or romanticization. In other words, from a Euro-centric perspective, which currently exists as the *non*-perspective, or *just how it is*, following the insights from indigeneity represents a move backwards away from progress and a retreat back into savagery and barbarism. This is the essence of the white imagination. Unless this implicit white supremacy is addressed, the retardation of democracy will persist and the Earth's interconnected life cycles will continue to suffer. These dynamics therefore lead to a wide array of contradictions when white people make attempts to work with Indigenous peoples and learn from indigenous philosophy. Commenting on her own engagement with indigeneity as a white woman situated in the context of these challenges, Shirley Steinberg (2008) offers the following reflections:

> In my work, in my writing, I try to incorporate Indigeneity within all of it, but I wonder sometimes if I am still tokenizing it. How authentic can I be? To give one example, I had an Indigenous artist do a book cover for me. Of course, I love the book and the artwork, and I am very happy about how the whole project turned out, but is my use of that book cover still exploiting Indigenous talent? Is it fetishizing it? Where can we as white invader colonists step back and not be fetishizing or tokenizing indigeneity in our attempts at engaging in critical solidarity? (p. 185)

A place of departure for addressing Steinberg's challenges might be to simply acknowledge that contemporary democracy was a gift from North America's Indigenous Nations and confederacies, and the most appropriate way to honor that gift is to practice it and pursue the path of peace and wellness. That path requires unity, but not a Euro-centric neo-liberal unity that demands people sacrifice themselves to appease the basic structures of power, but a unity grounded in the celebration of humanity's most special attribute, our rich cultural diversity.

CHAPTER SIX

Indigenous Children and the Social Studies: A Menominee Case Study

The Following chapter examines the example of Lisa Waukau in her role as a veteran social studies educator at Menominee Indian Middle School. Waukau's practices are explored because of the reputation they have earned her on the Menominee Indian Reservation as a *master teacher* who intimately knows the concrete and theoretical contexts of Menominee children. Her reputation as a caring and effective teacher has, in part, resulted in her repeated nomination to the office of tribal Chairperson. Her example is also showcased because it is applicable to Indigenous peoples more generally. In this chapter, we review the observations of this Native American teacher about what she calls Menominee Indian English (MIE) and Standard English in relation to her students. Furthermore, she will share what she does in her classroom to help her students. We begin with an overview of the Menominee Indian Reservation, the Menominee Indian School District and a biography on Native American teacher Lisa Waukau.

* * *

In a context unfortunately marked by high drop out rates and low student engagement, it is an extraordinarily impressive achievement that, in her role as an educator, Lisa Waukau's students consistently did their homework and turned it in. They came to her class every day and arrived on time. She had no discipline problems and she rarely gave detentions. Students worried about their grades in her class and studied for tests. When she would call home, parents would listen. Again, we are not talking about a teacher in a *successful* middle class community, but a teacher on an Indian reservation with *at-risk* students. Teacher folklore claims that if you can teach on a Reservation, you can teach anywhere. According to the inclusion teachers that have worked with the students in her classroom, Lisa Waukau is nothing short of a master teacher.

Children on the Menominee Indian Reservation

Menominee children are similar to other Native American children where there has been extended contact with the white world. Menominee people certainly exhibit a large degree of acculturation and assimilation. There are some important statistics and demographics to keep in mind in regard to Menominee Children. Note the following information from:

- The school *Attendance Rate* in Menominee is 82% which is the lowest in the state of Wisconsin.
- The *Third Grade Reading Test* results show 14% of the students in the Menominee Indian School District (MISD) score in the *substandard* category. This is the highest percentage in the state even when compared to Milwaukee City schools.
- MISD high school students score on average 17.7 on the ACT, which is the lowest in the state where the average composite score is 22. (WisKids Count 2000)

There are a number of good indicators of the poverty level and social problems in a community that we can examine. It is valuable to look at the following indicators because they give insight into the problems facing this particular community:

- The *Free/Reduced Lunch Rate* in MISD is 75%, which means the majority of children are under the poverty level.
- The *Percent of Children in Single Parent Households* in Menominee County/reservation is 57% and this is second only to the city of Milwaukee.
- The *Highest Rate of Births to Mothers Under the Age of 18* is in Menominee county/reservation.
- The *Lowest Medium Income* in Wisconsin is noted in Menominee County/reservation at $22,500. This statistic is true even with the advent of the Menominee Tribal Casino on the reservation.
- The second highest rate in the state of Wisconsin of *Juveniles in Correctional Institutions* is in Menominee County/reservation. (WisKids Count 2000)

It should also be noted that these demographics and statistics are not unique to the Menominee as other Native American communities suffer from similar trends. Because termination transformed the Menominee Reservation into a county, which still exists despite reinstatement, Menominee County and the Menominee Indian

Reservation are separate political entities that exist within the same physical space or territory. MISD is a public school system and so reports on their students are generated yearly and sent to the state of Wisconsin. This situation is unique and does not exist for other Native American communities. It should be noted that we have seen definite improvements in all the demographics quoted above.

Menominee Indian School District

The Menominee Indian School District (MISD) was started in 1976 and it is one of the few public Native American schools. It was started because many tribal members were displeased about the treatment of their children in the surrounding schools. There was a very high drop out rate as a result and so many parents thought their children would receive a better education on their own reservation. This caused a great deal of heated discussion among tribal members because there was a strong contingent that believed a white education was important.

There was also a long debate over whether the school should be a Bureau of Indian Affairs school or a public school. In the end, the community decided that MISD would be funded by the state of Wisconsin. It is a K-12 school district, which observes all mandated state laws and regulations. The district provides services for approximately 1100 students. There are approximately 100 teachers and 15 percent are Native Americans. The support staff is primarily Native American.

It is interesting that Menominee language is taught in grades K -8 and it is optional at the high school level. Students may decide to take Menominee Language to fulfill their foreign language requirement for college. Students at the high school level are required to take a year of Menominee and Native American history that the school board has mandated for the last 30 years. Menominee culture is always taught in conjunction with learning traditional singing because the two are so intertwined. Students participate in special projects to learn how to gather wild rice and play traditional lacrosse. The art department offers classes in traditional arts and crafts that includes learning how to bead.

Lisa Waukau: Tribal Leader & Social Studies Teacher

Lisa Waukau exhibits a strong work ethic that she credits to her mother. She recognizes her stepfather, who was a traditional Menominee, as a major influence for her love of her culture. In the following story Lisa reflects on the impact her early childhood years had on her thinking:

> I remember as a small child, if I had gotten hurt and was feeling bad my father would say, "Don't cry, you will be getting your stumpage soon." Stumpage is a fairly uncommon word for a very small child, but I knew that I would be getting some *sunyin* or money very soon. (Stumpage is the government word for payment for use of the trees off the stump that belonged to me and every other enrolled Menominee.)
>
> When I started kindergarten an old lady in my parent's grocery store told me, "Study those white man's books and you could grow up to be the depot agent." The person in charge of the lumber mill's train depot was to this old lady the most important job a person could aspire to.

Like those who taught her as a young child, Lisa too lives what she teaches her high school social studies students. She served on the Menominee Tribal legislature for nine years, which is almost a fulltime job in itself, and now serves as Tribal Chairman, taking a temporary leave of absence from teaching to fulfill her duties. Being the Chairman of the tribe is synonymous to being the President of the United States because the Menominee Tribe is a sovereign nation. Needless to say, Lisa is well respected on the reservation as demonstrated by her election to the tribal legislature multiple times. In at least two of the elections Lisa received the highest number of votes of all the candidates (Menominee Tribal News February, 1995, 1998, 2001). She also served as the Tribal vice-chairman and secretary. Lisa graduated from the University of Wisconsin—Green Bay with a major in history and she was the first one in her family to receive a college degree in the early 1970s. She received her teaching certification in elementary education through the University of Wisconsin-Madison Teacher Corp Program in 1979. She has taught at MISD for the last 25 years and at the high school as a social studies teacher for the last 22 years.

There are a number of accomplishments on the legislature of which Waukau is particularly proud. She was instrumental in the development of burial insurance for tribal members, which is a godsend for poor people. This is one of the benefits from the profits of the casino that she thinks is important for all tribal members whether they live on the reservation or not. But what she is most proud of is the development and writing of the Language and Culture Code for the reservation. Because of her persistence, it is now tribal law. The Tribe funds the ongoing work of the Language Commission, which oversees the code. The law had the unexpected effect of elevating the elders/native speakers to positions of rightful authority and respect. This code allows the elders and traditional Menominees to oversee the preservation of the Menominee Language and also limit the kinds of outside studies that can be done on reservation. Lisa also currently serves as president of the Menominee Tribal School board. She was selected by the Menominee Tribal Legislature along with four other members to oversee the running of the Bureau of Indian Affairs (BIA) K-8 school. The school provides an education for approximately 230 students using a more traditional approach than the public school.

The Evolution of *Rezonics*

Lisa was originally a history major in her undergraduate studies and she is an expert on Native American history and Menominee history. As a result, she has spent a lot of time reflecting on the impact the Menominee language has had on her students as they struggled to learn in her social studies classes. Her students have had difficulty with writing and vocabulary. It seems to Waukau that at times English is like a foreign language to her students. The following is analysis of how Menominee Indian English (MIE) has evolved through the years.

The Menominee came into very early contact with the Europeans by way of the French and the Jesuit missionaries in the 1630s. The French very quickly saw that saving the souls of the Great Lakes tribes was not going to be their primary foreign policy focus. It was commerce. Fur hats were all the rage in Europe at the time and the Great Lakes provided a plethora of *free for the taking* beaver pelts. Commerce rapidly overtook missionary work and within a decade the fur trade became a huge moneymaker for France. Consequently, conversion of the Menominee to Catholicism quickly became a sidelined afterthought. Integral to the fur trade were the Native entrepreneurs, as they knew the land, the animals, and how to find them.

Language, of course, is the key to any business venture. The Menominee learned French and the French learned Menominee. In fact, today many Menominee people have French surnames, which is further evidence of the interrelationships between the French and Menominee (Menominee Indian Historical Review). The language interaction was based primarily on commercial usage. The Menominees were hardly the only tribe in the Great Lakes involved in this market economy. Actually, most tribes in the region wanted access to the trade items the French brought to the region.

By virtue of their larger population, the Ojibwa people became major players in the trade networks and their language became the "lingua franca" of the Great Lakes. Thus, it was in the Menominee nation's interest to be fluent in the Ojibwa language as well as French. By the 1700s, the Menominee people were tri-lingual. We still see the after effects of this development in traditional Menominee language speakers. For example, the late Mani Boyd, a traditional Menominee, could converse easily in the Menominee and Ojibwa languages (Spindler and Spindler 1984).

After the French lost the Great Lakes to the British in the French and Indian War of 1763, the British forced their way into the fur trade economy (Borneman 2007). Consequently, the English language was introduced into the Great Lakes region. This added yet another language that the Menominee had to learn in order to remain competitive with their neighboring tribes. By the time the English had significant economic influence in the Great Lakes, the Menominee spoken language had a large number of additions from the French and English to accommodate the commercial needs of the people.

Let us fast forward to the 1800s because we again find major upheavals that affected the Menominee language and culture. This time period encompassed the Menominee Treaty Period from 1817–1856 and the subsequent Reservation Era (Spindler and Spindler 1984). The Reservation Era started with the 1854 treaty, which reserved the Wolf River Region for the Menominee for perpetuity. Once the Menominee Nation was settled and confined to the Wolf River Region, the U.S. Federal Government vigorously attacked the Menominee language in an attempt to complete the Americanization of the Native people. Native language was seen as a connection to the old and primitive ways and the government therefore wanted to obliterate all remnants of Menominee culture. The government believed that the acculturation and assimilation of Native Americans would obliterate the Menominee and other Native Americans as distinct cultural groups—cultural genocide (Malott 2008). The ultimate goal was to gain access to all Native resources and to extract their wealth generating potential.

Toward these ends, in the 1870s the government began to look at boarding schools as the most expeditious way to civilize the "savage" Indian (Adams 1995; Malott 2008). Education was seen as the way to attack Native language and culture. Consequently in 1879, Captain Richard Pratt established the famous Carlisle Indian School in Pennsylvania, which had a major impact on thousands of Native American children. Many Indian children were taken from their tribes and families at very young ages. Some children as young as five years old were taken to boarding schools and they were kept there through young adulthood. During this long absence from home, many children forgot their language, which provided a significant generational split within the Tribe. Tragically, there existed children who in some cases could not converse with their grandparents. And, that was precisely the goal of the Americanization policy. Summarizing the seriousness of the boarding school project Churchill (2004) notes:

> …Of all the malignancies embodied in twentieth-century U.S./Canadian Indian policy, the schools were arguable the worst. The profundity of their destructive effects upon native people, both individually and collectively, not only in the immediacy of their operational existence but in the aftermath as well, was and remains by any reasonable

estimation incalculable. Ultimately, neither the nature nor the magnitude of the genocide suffered by Native North Americans can be truly appreciated unless the impact of the residential schools is understood. (p. xlv)

Put another way, a policy or practice can be said to be an act of cultural genocide if it is "aimed at destroying the specific characteristics by which a target group is defined, or defines itself, thereby forcing them to become something else" (Lemkin, 1944, quoted in Churchill, 2004, p. 6). It is worth noting that the choice to engage in cultural genocide (i.e., boarding schools) was ultimately an economic one because it was estimated by the U.S. government that it was more expensive to physically kill "Indians" than to "educate" the "Indian" out of native peoples (Adams, 1995). Consequently, between 1880 and 1980 there were 129 Indian boarding schools operating within the United States and 87 in Canada. As a result, roughly between the late 1800s and the mid-1900s more than half of all Native American children had been removed from their homes to be forced to act and think like white children (Churchill, 2004) and therefore become something other than what they formerly were through the boarding school project.

This compulsory assimilation was put into practice in the classroom by beating Native children over the head with ideas like the U.S. and Canadian governments and white society in general represented everything good and civilized and that "Indian" ways were shameful and savage. The "unhappy history" (colonization and genocide) of Indigenous peoples was rarely discussed, and if it was, it was to be contrasted with the superior future that is now within their grasp, thanks to the generous gift of "Western civilization" (Churchill 2004).

In addition to manipulating the curriculum, Native American children were *whitestreamed* by severely controlling their actions and very closely monitoring their behavior. The "teachers" accomplished their objectives through a number of means: changing the children's dress and hairstyles from their individualized traditional tribal attire to institutionalized military-style uniforms; destroying all of the cultural materials they brought with them from their home communities; banning all cultural practices and severely punishing "students" for engaging in their Indigenous cultures such as speaking their native tongues, even outside of "class"; and by only allowing English to be spoken while spending the majority of one's time toiling in boarding school factories.

In 2001 the Truth Commission on Genocide in Canada found that mainstream churches and government were directly responsible for the deaths of at least fifty thousand children as a result of this process of compulsory assimilation. The list of crimes these institutions were found to be guilty of includes murder through beating, poisoning, hanging, starvation, strangulation, medical experimentation, and forced sterilization (Smith, 2005). The report also found that

"...clergy, police and business and government officials were involved in maintaining pedophile rings using children from residential schools" (Smith, 2005, p. 40). Indigenous children were so thoroughly dehumanized and commodified through the predatory process of value production that they became frequent victims of sexual predators, who flocked to boarding schools under the false titles of "priest" and "teacher." In other words, while cultural genocide both damages the soul and deters the mind from reaching enlightenment, physical and sexual abuse provide the final attack on one's sense of self, giving way to the creation of a slave.

It was an openly expressed policy among Indian boarding schools that the students would contribute to the funding of their own cultural destruction through their collective labor power expended at "school." Some girls toiled in sweatshops sewing linens and garments while others worked in laundries or bakeries producing an abundance of food sold to the surrounding white communities while they themselves were malnourished. The labor power of boys was put to the task of turning out commercial items in wood, metal, and leather shops. Churchill (2004) cited a 1928 U.S. investigating commission that determined that most of what went on at Indian boarding schools would be illegal in most settler-communities because of child labor laws. Native American children were forced to work long hours often for no wages at all, but in some instances were "paid" between one and three cents an hour as an "incentive." These "wages" were often put in a fund and then typically mismanaged and squandered by the BIA (Bureau of Indian Affairs).

It should therefore not be surprising that many Native children resisted this abuse and forced assimilation. Summarizing the frequency and ways Native American children fought back, Churchill (2004) notes:

> ...Native children were not merely the passive victims of all that was being done to them. Virtually without exception, survivor narratives include accounts of subversion, both individual and collective, most commonly involving such activities as 'stealing' and/or foraging food, possessing other 'contraband,' persistence in the speaking of native languages and running away. In many—perhaps most—residential schools, such activities were so common and sustained as to comprise outright 'cultures of resistance.' (p. 51)

This was therefore a chaotic time for Native people (Adams 1995). In addition to the generational divide that emerged between those were "whitestreamed, and those adults who were not, there were divisions between those Native American people who continued to embrace their traditional religion and those Native people who became Christians. We also saw divisions between those Native Americans who had not intermarried with the whites and those who had. There were also differences between those Native people who saw the white way as the only way and those who wanted to maintain the traditional ways. Within this environment and upheaval, as noted above, the government had free rein to attempt to re-make Indian nations into their own images (Adams 1995).

However, the government did not account for the degree of passive resistance they would face from Indian people. The leadership on the Menominee Reservation was resentful of the high handedness with which they were treated by the government. Even though education was embraced to a certain extent, it was never embraced to the extent that many immigrants did as they fought their way out of poverty and into the American dream. Menominee people and other Native Americans as a rule have a huge distrust on educational institutions (Adams 1995).

Menominee people did verbalize an acceptance of what they considered the white man's education and only accepted it up to a point. The Menominee people would not allow the white man's education to conflict with Menominee values. Today this resentment can be seen in the low school attendance rate on the reservation. Most Menominee people would say that education was important. However, activities associated with Menominee culture, for example, tend to be considered more important, and when things come up, children are often allowed to stay home from school.

In order to survive as a distinct cultural group—a Native Nation—in this context of cultural genocide has required not only culturally conscious parents, but also cleaver leaders. In other words, the Menominee leadership had to develop ways to effectively interact with the myriad of bureaucrats and bureaucracy that was the hallmark of an Indian agency. The successful tribal leader was not the one that had a diploma, but the one who could get what was needed for the people from the Indian agent in charge of the Reservation. Therefore, to be successful the tribal leader had to be efficient in *bureauspeak*. Bureauspeak can be defined as how the white Indian agents talked and the government language they used.

Menominee people had a very bureaucratic worldview because of this. Their English word bank was limited and so the people were basically on our own with the rest of the language. The English language was seldom seen and even more rarely heard. What evolved was what we call *Rezonics*. We see this as a blending of the stilted English we acquired and our own Menominee language.

REZONICS AND EDUCATION

Lisa Waukau has always been captivated by the variations of Menominee language her students used in her classroom and how it related to their learning. Teaching in this context it is important to understand that culture and language are not static entities, but dynamic and evolving, especially in the environment of colonization documented above. What is more, contrary to the sentiments of mainstream language conservatives seeking to limit Indian culture, *Rezonics* is not English slang invented by Indigenous youth as a tactic to exclude their elders. Much of the *Rezonics* vocabulary has been around for several generations and everybody on the Reservation knows their meaning and uses them *correctly*. Even long term non-Indian teachers at Reservation schools are able to understand *Rezonics*. The following are examples of *Rezonics* that are commonly heard in schools and in the reservation communities:

- *Sook*: I am just kidding
- *Wa Now:* I can hardly believe that
- *Skotas*: give me a light
- *Sunyin*: money
- *Skunk dat*: no, I don't believe I will do that
- *Yiie*: that is pretty difficult to believe

These examples are variations and shortening of Menominee language words and are very economical in their usage. Adults and students alike will use these words in their every day verbal interactions. At the beginning of each school year, Waukau teaches a unit on the development of language in her Native history course. Students will go through word lists that are Indigenous to the reservation. These words are not something they picked up off cable television, which virtually all students have access to from their satellite dishes. They will do their best to spell them and determine the root words. They need to determine whether it is Menominee or a shortening of an English word. Afterwards, the class will put the words on the word wall with their definitions in Standard English. Waukau allows her students to freely use the words when they are doing group work or if they are in discussions.

However, they cannot use any of the non-Standard English words during guided writing. The rationale is that these students must understand and use formal English in school and the work world they are preparing to enter to be successful. Because dialectical differences in colonizer/colonized societies are politically used by the dominant society as evidence of inferiority, dialectically marginalized students benefit from learning the standard syntax assisting them in not only surviving within the world that exists, but also transforming it by advocating for the rightful legitimacy of their Indigenous languages. Waukau therefore believes that her students need to hear Standard English and use it as much as possible. Lisa hopes that there will be carry over usage as they become more comfortable with the formal English. Because it is known that *Rezonics* is the shared *primary language* of her and her students, Waukau is very careful in her class presentations to model Standard English.

Dialectal differences also make it difficult for students to ask questions syntactically. If students cannot ask questions syntactically, their ability to learn is significantly reduced because they cannot identify what they do not know nor can they systematically access what they do know. Lisa argues that some of this difficulty comes from the leftover vestiges of the Menominee language. The following examples of *Rezonics* and their English translations are indicative of student conversations written in poetry as part of a social studies lesson:

- *Rist yaz giz*: Hey you guys!
- *Rya going ta Shawano or what*: Are you going to town?
- *Do ya got jing*: Do you have any money?
- *Yaas already*: Yes?
- *Let's gizzo den*: Let's go, then

- *Dats swearing dough*
- *Noo eye dough know wah!*
- *I don't know what ta say*: I don't know what to say
- *What cha dooing howzit*: How are you doing?
- *Gimmie some moolah*: Give me some money
- *Later den*: See you later

Students are not humiliated or denigrated for the use of Rezonics (Menominee Indian English) in the school environment. However, teachers like Ms Waukau explain to their students why they must be able to use Standard English. It is the language in which their textbooks are written and in which all their standardized tests are written. In other words, it is the language required to be successful in the world outside the reservation.

Language, Poverty & Native American Children

According to Joos (1967), every language, including English, has five registers:

1. *Frozen*: Language that is always the same, including prayers, poems, and published or written text in general
2. *Formal*: The standard sentence syntax and word choice of work and school
3. *Consultative*: Formal register used in conversation
4. *Casual*: Language between friends characterized by a 400–800-word vocabulary
5. *Intimate*: Language between lovers or twins

Montano-Harmon (1991) found that minority students and poor children do not have access to the *formal* register in their homes and tend to have difficulty using the formal register. From these findings it should not be surprising that Menominee children who live on the reservation predominately speak in the casual and intimate registers. A distinction in language usage must therefore be made for them as they enter school. Ruby Payne (1998) postulated that children from generational poverty, as opposed to situational poverty, do not speak in the formal register. She defined generational poverty as being poor for at least two generations and indicates that it is more devastating than situational poverty. Payne (1998) estimated that approximately 260,000 Native American children live in generational poverty today.

Even though it might be argued that Payne's (1998) analysis of these data support a deficit model ontology, where *Rezonics* is viewed as inferior to *formal* English, it still stands that schools serving Native youth could best meet their learning needs by providing them with the cultural capital of standard English while simultaneously celebrating their own cultural traditions situated in a larger social/historical context of colonization, survival, and resistance. Again, the use of the formal register or Standard English is required on tests, in schools, and on the job. Because many minority and poor children do not have that formal vocabulary or the knowledge of the formal sentence structure and syntax, they are at a major disadvantage in the Euro-centric schools and larger society.

Indian Children & Standard English

In today's world more than two-thirds of Native American young people speak American Indian English and it is the only Indian related language that they know (Leap, 1993). Furthermore, Leap postulates that they will learn their rules of grammar and speech from their ancestral language traditions. This is certainly important knowledge for teachers of all native children to recognize and to take into consideration in their teaching.

John Satterlee, who was an early educator on the Menominee Reservation, taught in what was known as Crow Settlement. Interestingly, he taught in both English and Menominee, which was long before the bilingual approach to education was implemented. He obviously was a man before his time. Satterlee had his students memorize poetry and recite it because it had a rhythmic quality to it. He knew that the first sound we hear is the heartbeat from our mothers, which is why we like the rhythm of poetry.

Phillips (1970), in her studies of Native American Children on the Warm Springs Indian Reservation, found a number of things that should be of note to teachers. Although this study was completed a number of years ago, I believe it is still relevant today for children who are not Native speakers. One of the interesting observations from her study was that Indian children do not participate verbally in classroom interactions because the social conditions are different from the reservation community. Secondly, educators cannot assume because Indian children are not Native speakers that they have "assimilated all of the sociolinguistic rules underlying interaction in classrooms and other non-Indian social situations where English is spoken" (p. 392). This is a relevant observation because so many Indian children are what would be considered non-Native speakers today and they struggle with learning to read and reading comprehension.

Other Strategies and Techniques

Through the years Ms Waukau's teaching style has changed. As a beginning teacher, she was very teacher-centered. Lisa felt she had to be somewhat authoritarian because she had students who were difficult to manage and she believed classroom management was critical in teaching her students. Waukau believed that even if she had the most well developed knowledge base, but could not keep her students' attention, it would all be for naught. She maintained control in her classroom by her wits and a sharp tongue. Students would not dare cross her for fear of what she would say and the embarrassment it would cause them. Native people, like people in general, do not like to be publicly humiliated. She became a legend for this control and seniors told freshmen not to upset her. The principal always gave her the largest classes and the most difficult study halls because he knew she could maintain control of the students.

As Lisa matured and became more comfortable with what she was doing, she began to exam her approach. She began making a conscious effort not to use her sharp tongue to correct students knowing students are nevertheless aware of it. Her preference today is to be more student-centered. In her upper level classes where she has some of the brightest students, she will turn more control over to them and they *thrive*. However, Waukau continues to employ teacher-centered pedagogy with classes who struggle academically and consequently, with behavior. Lisa prefers being student centered but she knows that given the needs of the student population that this is not always possible.

Knowing her students is fundamental in determining appropriate pedagogical strategies. At the beginning of each new school year Lisa does informal evaluations of student word usage during class discussions to determine the level of concrete thinking versus abstract thinking. Waukau believes that there is a relationship between the ability of her students to use Standard English and abstract thinking. Reading the first week essays that usually reference summer vacation activities or family biographies also augments this evaluation. The questions in the first exam are clearly divided between concrete and abstract questioning. By this time, she has a clear idea of who needs learning strategies to move them to becoming more abstract thinkers.

The monitoring of student development, however, is an ongoing strategy employed throughout the academic year. That is, Lisa makes a point of reviewing concrete thinkers' schedulers on a daily basis. Students at MIHS are required to carry their daily planners to class. She will also check their data usage and organization in order to see how accurately they are visually transporting data. She will pay close attention to them during guided reading. If they are struggling here, then she will incorporate more cognitive strategies. These strategies will include such techniques as sketching mental models and discussing visual analogies.

Another problem area she sees in her students is the ability to ask questions and take essay tests. She has very lively discussions with her students in class and her students feel free to verbally interact in her classroom. However, they have a difficult time phrasing questions syntactically and in answering questions in writing. Self-regulated behavior is important in all children, but it is especially important for at-risk children. Ms Waukau incorporates rubrics into all major assignments. She also helps them monitor their learning. After every major test students must evaluate why they missed the questions they missed. This can be a time consuming activity depending on how many answers the students got wrong. But this activity forces them to analyze whether they answered questions too quickly or if they did not study enough.

To help students improve their test-taking skills Waukau uses informal storytelling as an important strategy. She does this in order to give them retrieval cues and something they can relate to on a personal level. Lisa is forever searching for funny or interesting stories to incorporate into her curriculum because background knowledge is so critical to children and learning. Storytelling can help children develop their background knowledge through vicarious experiences. Because Native American children so often live in poverty and in isolated areas resulting in limited experiences, we must provide these experiences in other ways. The use of informal stories is a wonderful way to accomplish this goal. Summarizing this point Waukau notes that,

> This is a short, to the point way of teaching a difficult concept to my students. I like this and find it effective because it allows me to translate an abstract idea to the concrete very quickly and gives students a system to hold and retain the information.

The following guideline, developed by Lisa over more than twenty years of practice, are believed to be fundamental to keep in mind when using storytelling in the classroom:

- Access prior knowledge before you tell a story
- Make a word wall and put the vocabulary on the word wall prior to telling the story
- Make sure you are hitting the standards before you start the story
- Tell the story: pick short ones that you can elaborate on if the situation presents itself
- Try to keep stories to around five minutes. Base stories on fact and add fiction
- A follow-up activity is to have students sketch a mental model based on the story

The following is one of the stories Ms Waukau shares with her students to peak their interest and to hold their attention, and simultaneously teach them about their history in a way that affirms their identity non-Euro-centrically. That is, she provides them with examples of the critical consciousness of their historical leaders as lessons for being Menominee or Indigenous in the context of colonialist occupation:

> It was a beautiful October and the year was 1811 when the word spread that the great Tucumthe was planning to visit the Menominee and it was a time the young people of the Tribe would always remember. You may know him as Tecumseh. Imagine this man, the greatest warrior of his time, was coming to visit the Menominee.
>
> The young men could barely contain their excitement and the young women could not understand why. He was after all, just a man not even from our tribe. So what that he was coming from so far away. One girl was heard to comment, "He isn't exactly the sun in my cornfield." And a young man retorted, "Well, when Tucumthe speaks, his enemies tremble. How many people do you know that can do that?"
>
> But, the big question was why is this hero of the battles in the Ohio Valley coming to visit the Menominee? It must be important for him to come all this way. Menominee bands from all over were coming to meet Tecumthe in a Grand Council and soon the main band was hosting people from all over at the little village at the mouth of the Menominee River called Minikani. They wanted a chance to see, to hear, and to touch the great Tecumseh.
>
> Finally he arrived in his flotilla of canoes and excitement was in the air as he disembarked. There he was: tall, muscular and handsome and not very old and he looked every bit the son of a great chief. Our Chief Tomow greeted the visitor along with all the other band chiefs and they escorted our visitors to the Council Lodge where they smoked kinnikik, exchanged gifts, and prayed that the creator god would look kindly on their gathering and hear their good words.
>
> Finally, Tucumthe rose to speak to our council of chiefs: "Brothers, I wish you to listen to me well so that you understand why I have come all the way from where the sun comes up to speak to this grand council. Brothers, the Americans have made treaty after treaty with the red man and have broken every one. He kills our women

and children and takes our lands and then hides behind his army. He gets our old chiefs drunk with his strong whiskey and convinces them to sell land that does not even belong to them. Those who sell the land must be punished and they shall suffer for their conduct.

But, my Chiefs, as I stand before your wise council, I humbly ask that you and your warriors join the Shawnee in our fight, not against those old chiefs who sell the land, but against those Americans who swindle those old men with their strong drink and cheap presents. Brothers, I say that if you choose not to join us now, who will come to your aid when the American wants to cut down your mighty forests to fence their land and when their broad roads pass over the graves of fathers. Soon, brothers, you too will be driven from your Native lands as leaves before the winter storms. Stand with me brothers in our Great War confederacy. Fight with me to reclaim all the lands the creator gave his red children. Many of us may die in this noble cause. And we must all die sometime and isn't it better to die defending your families than to live like paupers. If it is your time to die, be not like those cowards whose hearts are filled with fear of death, but sing your death songs, my chiefs, and die like a hero going home. Confederacy or extermination is your only choice, my brothers. Which do you choose?"

When he sat down, it was so quiet you could almost hear a leaf falling in the forest, and then the council exploded with clapping and hoops and tomahawks were flying in the air. Even the wise old chiefs could not hold back the young warriors. And so the Menominee made ready for war.

REACTIONS FROM COLLEAGUES AND FORMER STUDENTS

A former student of Lisa's, Shannon, who went on to become an elementary teacher on the reservation wrote a letter to her former teacher. What she wrote encapsulates much of what her current students said about her in focus groups, as well as her colleagues. Note the following excerpts from this letter:

> The most influential teacher in my life was my high school history teacher. To this day I have an enormous amount of respect for her. She lived her life with dignity and dedication to the community she served and she still does.
>
> Ms Waukau was a fun teacher. She wanted to get to know the students on a personal level. She always started her classes with a "gossip session," chatting with everyone in a large group setting. I always remember her standing in front of the room and saying to us, "So tell me some gossip..."
>
> Teaching at MIHS is a tough job. Teaching is a tough career, but when you add dozens of hormone-charged, street smart, socio-economically disadvantaged teenagers to the equation, only the strongest teachers survive! Ms Waukau was as strong as they come. From the moment we walked through the door on day one, however, she laid down the law, and beware anyone who dared to cross the boundary lines she set. It was classroom management, mixed with the personal relationship that she

established with her students that made her class so fun. We were able and willing to learn...

As times change, so does the make-up of the classroom. More and more children with special needs are included in the regular classroom. We interviewed a number of the inclusion teachers who work and worked with Lisa in the past to see what their observations were. One of the teachers observed that Ms Waukau is a "master teacher and that she is always trying something. Her lessons are never the same from year to year; they change with the times and with her students." All of the inclusion teachers noted that they respected her a great deal, her students respected her and that she was respected in the community. One of the teachers noted that she wanted to be just like her.

They observed that she has well-defined parameters in her classroom and students know exactly what is expected of them. One of the teachers remembered a day Lisa walked into her classroom and asked the students, "Do I give you too much homework?"

They all raised their hands. She said to them, "No, I don't, I should give you more." This particular teacher observed that, "Lisa knows what counts in life and that kids have to work. Her lesson very structured and laid out very well. She knew how to bring humor to her class and she always told them funny stories."

Lessons in the Classroom

A particularly important time period in Native American history, as noted above, was the boarding school era. During this time children were forcibly taken from their families and placed in boarding school located far from home. In a lesson on the impact of the boarding schools on Native Americans, Ms Waukau introduced the lesson by having her students design their own schools for children of the recent tsunami who had to come live on the reservation. The students were divided into groups and they were told to develop everything they thought a school should have to meet the needs of these new students. Students were enthusiastic about the assignment with some of the students even coming in during their free time to work on their schools.

After the activity was completed, Ms Waukau lectured the students on why the government implemented the boarding school approach and how they hoped to "civilize" the Menominee. She discussed the cost of housing Native children in these government schools. Students analyzed the amount of money the government spent on food for the children at Carlisle, the most well-known boarding school. The students discovered that the money spent on food for the children was well below the average cost being spent in other schools at the time. They discovered that the children were given very little protein and a great deal of starchy foods. The students made connections between the high diabetes rate among the Menominee today and the starchy diets of their ancestors. This can be an emotional lesson for the students as indicated by their responses:

> *It is sad the way they were treated and lied to.*
>
> *I finally understand how the boarding schools affected each Native American's lives by cutting their hair and not being able to speak their language.*
>
> *I feel bad that Native land was stolen from us and we now live on reservations.*
>
> *I hate the fact we get treated badly and still today we get treated the same way.*

Conclusion

We would like to close with a poem that Ms Waukau's students wrote, which summarizes why we need an appreciation, an understanding, and a respect for our children's heritage.

> Menominee Indians are the bomb
> We write and talk like Menoms
> Other people think we talk funny
> But they can't see
> They don't know me
> We say yah
> They say yes
> We're all different, is my guess

CHAPTER SEVEN

Native American Philosophy and Western Science *with Andrew Gilbert*

Indigenous cosmology provides another perspective on the nature of the universe and the beginning of time separate and distinct from those offered by Western science. The following chapter explores these differences in the context of science education considering possibilities for curricular reform. This essay also addresses the connections between the biological contexts of human genetic endowments and dispositions; the social context of human society; and the ways science and indigeneity can assist in bridging the gaps between theory and practice.

* * *

Within this chapter we focus on the social context that existed during Europe's scientific revolution paying particular attention to the spark that ignited a new democratic revolution in Europe—a spark made possible by the living example and inspirational influence of Native North American social arrangements. In our discussion we attempt to trace the primary scientific concepts central to our analysis to their respective locations of origin, from ancient Egypt, Greece, to Native America. Central to our investigation here is the fact that, in Europe, there were always two Enlightenments and therefore two approaches to science—the boss' science on one hand and science for democratic liberation against divine-right tyranny on the other. The study that follows begins during Europe's scientific revolution and ends in the contemporary era. We conclude this chapter arguing that a renewed democratic science of responsibility is needed now more than ever given the current state of the planet—ecologically *and* socially. Within this discussion we point to contemporary democratic scientists as examples of the many possible paths a *liberation science for democratic independence* (LSDI—explained in the final section of this chapter) can lead to.

EUROPE'S SCIENTIFIC REVOLUTION AND THE COLONIZATION OF THE AMERICAS

The current hegemonic role of the boss' Eurocentric version of science is underscored by the simple fact that there is almost a *universal* tendency within modern, Western science education to identify the thinkers that "led" to "a revolution in thinking about our physical world" to European sources (Good, 2005, p. 1). The ideas that tend to be associated with the key figures are as follows: Copernicus (1473–1543), for example, is credited with displacing the Earth as the center of the universe; Galileo (1564–1642) is said to have laid the foundation for the "experimental method and modern science" (Good, 2005, p. 2); Newton's (1642–1727) contribution is said to lay in having advanced the work of his European scientific forefathers resulting in the foundation of modern mechanical physics dedicated to uncovering the laws of the universe; finally, Darwin (1809–1882) is said to have made paradigm-shifting discoveries after employing the scientific method in biology, concluding that through the process of natural selection, those genetic traits most conducive to survival are passed on to future generations rendering the "God hypothesis" that invokes "supernatural causes" no longer "necessary" (Good, 2005, p. 4).

Professor Ron Good (2005), forty-year veteran of Science Education, summarizing the foundations of modern science, notes that "questioning authority... was a necessary condition for modern science to take hold and make progress in seventeenth century Europe" (p. ix). It is widely accepted in Western science education that it was Copernicus who was the first to propose a theory that replaced the Earth with the Sun as the center of the universe, "thereby demoting" the world of humans "to a far less exalted place in the whole scheme of things" (Good, 2005, p. 1), and in-turn, challenging Christian doctrine. However, the dangerous scientific knowledge informing Copernicus' astronomy, for example, did not represent new developments in the production of knowledge.

George Sarton (1959) draws attention to this point in a detailed summation of the evidence that suggests that the Greek astronomer Aristarchos (III– 1 B.C.), "put the center of the universe in the sun (instead of the Earth) and assumed the daily rotation of the Earth around its own axis" and therefore "had conceived what we call the Copernican universe, eighteen centuries before

Copernicus" (p. 57). Martin Bernal (1987) extends Sarton's (1959) conceptualization of Copernican influences beyond ancient Greece and into Egyptian antiquity. Bernal (1987) suggests that the special attention Copernicus and others of his time provided the sun can be attributed to the popularity of Hermetic Texts (mysticism and magic popular during late antiquity and again during Europe's Renaissance) that contain "repeated references to the special sanctity of the sun seen as the source of light and sometimes as the second god which governs the third god, the animate world and all its living creatures" (p. 155). For Bernal (1987) the connection of Copernicus to ancient Egypt can be identified in the fact that "the texts shared the Ancient Egyptian focus on the sun as the chief divinity and life-giving force" (p. 155).

Standing on the conceptual groundwork laid by Copernicus, it is said that Galileo Galilei found the strength to "question religious dogma" through the advancement of the mechanical philosophy of the universe that, rather than directed by God, is a series of interconnected machines. Galileo was persecuted for these ideas in 1633 by the Inquisition in Rome and sentenced to house arrest for life. Galileo, who lived in Southern Europe almost one hundred years after Columbus began colonizing the Americas, and in the process, committing the most horrendous acts of genocide in the name of Christianity, can be said to have been part of that very early scientific revolution, the Renaissance, which played an influential role in the radical Enlightenment that refused to accommodate, with varying levels of success, the religious ruling-class hierarchies of antiquity.

Galileo's *new science*, which, again, challenged theological dogma, accurately tends to be attributed to not only those who came before him, such as Copernicus, but also to the Thirty Years War that "devastated" and "brutalized" vast tracts of Germany and Bohemia between 1618 and 1648 (Israel 2006, 63). This war cost much of Europe, including Spain and Italy, an "unprecedented" amount of money and human life, and in the process, left unresolved the religious crisis between Protestantism and Catholicism (Israel 2006, 63). While this analysis is important, it only tells part of the story. That is, it speaks to what Galileo (and Descartes) was against—ruling-class religious dogmatism—but it does not address the source of what he was *for*, which can be summarized as "freedom of thought, and independence of the individual conscience" (Israel 2006, 64).

According to Galileo biographer and translator, Stillman Drake (1957), Galileo's dedication to freedom of thought manifested itself in his emerging humanism that translated into his refusal "to write in Latin" because "the readers he cultivated...lived outside the universities" (p. 2). In other words, Galileo was democratically interested in making knowledge available to the commoner. This imperative clearly broke with the hierarchy of religious idealism that views knowledge as emanating from within the mind based on the will of God. Highlighting this point Galileo Galilei (1610/1959) notes that "the nature of the human mind is such that unless it is stimulated by images of things acting upon it from without, all remembrances of them passes easily away" (p. 23). For the time and place, this was a radical statement challenging the social foundations of the monarchy. Equally impressive, Galileo made this observation in a letter to the Grand Duke of Tuscany seeking approval for his sun-centered ontology.

Alluding to the Indigenous influences within Galileo's praxis Drake (1959) notes that, "with the opening of the Renaissance...preoccupation with religious matters began to give way before the wonders of reported explorations and discoveries" (p. 8). In an effort to contextualize the democratic values outlined above we can look to the ways they spread to Europe from Native America through the process of cultural diffusion. From the very beginning Christopher Columbus, documented in his journal, alluded to the democratic values of the Indigenous peoples he encountered in the Americas, the Arawaks in the Caribbean basin. Consider:

> They exhibit great love toward all others in preference to themselves. They also give objects of great value for trifles....I did not find, as some of us had expected, any cannibals among them, but, on the contrary, men of great deference and kindness. (Columbus, quoted in Bigelow, 1998, p. 18)

In a similar reflection Columbus comments:

> They...brought us parrots and balls of cotton and spears and many other things, which they exchanged for the glass beads and hawks' bells. They willingly traded everything they owned...They do not bear arms, and do not know them, for I showed them a sword, they took it by the edge and cut themselves out of ignorance...They would make fine servants...With fifty men we could subjugate them all and make them do whatever we want. (quoted in Zinn, 1995, p. 1)

Providing further insight into the reductionist intentions informing the former African slave trader's "adventurous" pedagogy, Columbus boasts, "as soon as I arrived in the Indies, on the first island which I found, I took some of the Natives by force in order that they might learn and might give me information of whatever there is in these parts" (quoted in Zinn, 1995, p. 2). Contrary to popular opinion that paints Columbus as a noble sea traveler bringing civilization to the "new world," Columbus was ultimately interested in slaves, gold, and the extraction of wealth regardless of the human costs. Consequently, within only a few decades of his arrival Columbus' actions reduced what was once a bountiful and populated land to desolation. Commenting on the bewildering atrocities he had witnessed, documented in his book *History of the Indies*, Bartolomé de las Casas, Spanish missionary and former plantation owner gone staunch critic, offers a sobering account of what took place:

> ...Our work was to exasperate, ravage, kill, mangle and destroy...Thus husbands and wives were together only once every eight or ten months and when they met they were so exhausted and depressed on both sides...they ceased to procreate. As for the newborn, they died early because their mothers, overworked and famished, had no milk to nurse them, and for this reason, while I was in Cuba, 7000 children died in three months. Some mothers even drowned their babies from sheer desperation....In this way, husbands died in the mines, wives died at work, and children died from lack of milk...and in a short time this land which was so great, so powerful and fertile...was depopulated....My eyes have seen these acts so foreign to human nature, and now I tremble as I write....(quoted in Zinn, 1995, p. 7)

These crimes against humanity sanctioned by the Church as the will of God can be understood as part of the fuel that led some Euro-scientists to disregard or challenge monarchical authority because "major European thinkers had connected Indians with the idea of equality" (Mohawk, 1992, p. 69). Similarly, it has been argued that, "the colonization of the Americas and the engagement with her peoples...opened an intellectual floodgate that stimulated dramatic changes in the way Europeans viewed the world" (Lyons, 1992, p. 31). Lyons (1992) looks specifically to the French who, he contends, "more than colonists from other major countries, joined the Indians on the Indians' terms" (p. 27). The year this relationship really began to take hold, according to Lyons (1992), was 1608 when Champlain successfully established a trading settlement in Quebec. Outlining the diffusion that ensued Lyons comments:

> ...The Jesuits brought the stories about adventures with Indians to France in great detail and complexity. Some Jesuit writers elaborated on the theme of the 'noble savage,' and pointed to numerous advantages of Indian life, including examples of the freedom of the individual. In general, the Jesuit writings helped to inform a growing intellectual movement in France that would build upon the ideals of egalitarianism and the dignity of the individual. (p. 28)

The apparent fierce independence of Galileo can be understood, in part, within this context of European exposure to, and atrocities against, American Indigeneity. The ideas that have been associated with Galileo that are most relevant to our present discussion on individual freedom deal with "the concept of mental nature," which "underwent an important revision in the Galilean era" (Chomsky, 2002, p. 49).

Western Science, the Elusive Mind, and Indigeneity

Rather than being attributed to divine intervention, as suggested above, "the concept of mind was framed in terms of what was called the 'mechanical philosophy'" that was based on the assumption that "the natural world is a complex machine that could in principle be constructed by a skilled artesian" (Chomsky, 2002, p. 49). The mind-body dichotomy that Descartes is often critiqued for, as we have done in Chapter One, according to Chomsky (2002), represents a logical attempt to demonstrate that there is something unique about the mind unexplainable through mechanical philosophy.

Chomsky (2002) credits Newton with making the Mind-Body debate a moot point by demonstrating, to his own displeasure, that nothing in nature can be explained in mechanical terms. Newton achieved this through his "discovery of action at a distance," which Newton himself found to be "absurd" (Chomsky, 2002, p. 52) arguing that anyone who would accept it was not mentally fit, but was nevertheless forced to adopt it even though he had no means to explain it. The mind as a conscious, non-material entity could therefore not be explained by God *or* science and therefore remained (and has since) a great mystery—a common sentiment of Indigeneity. Again, Newton would have preferred to endorse a physics that presupposes a mechanical universe that's separate and distinct parts operate not according to their own mysterious free-will, but by their mechanical functions and the laws of mechanistic collusion. So distraught by his *absurd* discovery Newton is said to have spent the remainder of his life attempting to disprove it (Chomsky, 2002). Perhaps this can partially explain why Newton drastically transformed his attitude toward ancient Egypt, which began to mirror the rise of European colonial dominance and the hegemony of the Aryan Model of world history (see Chapter One).

Situating this phenomenon in the larger political context of seventeenth-century Europe Bernal (1987) comments that in Newton's "early work he followed his Cambridge Neo-Platonist teachers in their respect for" Egypt, "but the last decades of his life were spent trying to diminish Egypt's importance by bringing down the date of its foundation just before the Trojan War" (p. 27) around 1200 BC. Bernal (1987) argues that Newton's change of heart was not only due to a growing European white supremacist hegemony, but it was also based on the threat ancient Egypt posed to the mechanical "conception of physical order and its theological and political counterparts—a divinity with regular habits and the Whig constitutional monarchy" (p. 27). From this perspective, the politico-philosophical brilliance of ancient Egypt was their "pantheism," which challenged the dominance of mechanical philosophy by "implying an animate universe without need for a regulator or even a creator" (Bernal, 1987, p. 27).

In other words, Newton was in favor of a universe that operates according to knowable and predictable laws, which he knew did not represent absolute certainty—standing in stark contrast to this was the random, chaotic and independent nature of pantheism. Was Newton's belittling of ancient Egyptian accomplishments part of his attempt to save mechanical philosophy? The speculation is not unlikely, especially when we consider the larger context in which Newton was operating. Jonathan Israel (2002) situates the scientific community of Newton's age in an "atmosphere" marked by "constant threat of suppression emanating especially from the Church and the *parlements*" and his work, along with other English thinkers such as Locke and Bacon, was:

> ...Everywhere regarded, even among the most reactionary sections of the French Church, and by the Spanish and Portuguese Inquisition, as intellectually safe...innovative perhaps but entirely supportive of revealed religion, Providence, and the political and social order. (p. 516)

Highlighting his efforts not to offend Britain's Christian ruling elite with his natural science of motion that could be interpreted as displacing the hand of God Newton (1952/1987) reassures his readers that "God suffers nothing from the motion of bodies" while, at the same time, "bodies find no resistance from the omnipresence of God" (p. 370). As a result, Newton (1952/1987) leaves in tact the hegemonic notion that "the Supreme God exists necessarily; and by the same necessity he exists *always* and *everywhere*" (pp. 370–371) and, by implication, the ruling powers that claim to be the messengers of God's will. Perhaps shielded by the position of imperial superiority at that time of all things British, including hegemonic English thinkers, the publishing of David Hume's *A Treatise of Human Nature* (1888/2003) was not met with controversy or much attention at all for that matter. However, over time, his work has proven to be foundationally influential. In his *Treatise* Hume (1888/2003) recounts the implications of Newton's discovery noting that as a result, "the nature of mind" has become "obscure" and "uncertain" (p. 166) as it was and will forever remain. Making this point Hume (1888/2003) argues that "what is unknown, we must be contented to leave so" (p. 166). Hume (1888/2003) challenges the philosophers who claim that whatever exists can be known by suggesting that the answers to some questions lie beyond the capacities of human intellectual endowments. Consider his words:

> Certain philosophers...promise to diminish our ignorance; but I am afraid 'tis at the hazard of running us into contradictions, from which the subject is of itself exempted. These philosophers are the curious reasoners concerning the material or immaterial substances, in which they suppose our perceptions to inhere...This question we have found impossible to be answer'd with regard to matter and body: But

besides that in the case of the mind, it labours under all the same difficulties, 'tis burthen'd with some additional ones, which are peculiar to that subject...What possibility then of answering that question, *Whether perceptions inhere in a material or immaterial substance*, when we do not so much as understand the meaning of the question? (pp. 166–167)

We might say that Darwin became one of Hume's "curious reasoners" although this time interested in the evolutionary history of the ever-elusive human mind, and, as a result, refused to let well enough alone, as it were. Drawing on the brilliance of seventeenth century European philosophers and beyond, Darwin described the human ability to associate an extra-ordinary amount of sounds with ideas, that is, language, as the species' most *marvelous invention*, which he hoped would be "incorporated within the theory of evolution" (Chomsky, 2002, p. 47). While Darwin's observations remain relatively uncontested, Chomsky has advanced this theory of language describing it not as an invention, but rather an innate system that is part of the genetic code. However, like those who came before him, Darwin did not have a scientific explanation for the mind. That is not to say that Darwin did not have powerful insights regarding the mind. For example, Darwin (2007) argued that it was through humanity's "powers of intellect" that "articulate language has been evolved" which our "wonderful advancement has mainly depended" (p. 84). Indeed, following Galileo and others, Darwin (2007) recognized language as humanity's greatest invention, which he contextualizes in the following passage:

> Language—that wonderful engine which affixes signs to all sorts of objects and qualities, and excites trains of thought which would never arise from the mere impression of the senses, or if they did arise could not be followed out. The higher intellectual powers of man, such as those of ratiocination, abstraction, self-consciousness, &c., probably follow from the continued improvement and exercise of the other mental faculties. (p. 403)

Following the insights of Indigeneity (discussed below) we remain skeptical of any hierarchies, even Darwin's universalized human-centric intellectual scale alluded to in the above quote. That said Darwin's conclusion that humanity's genetically-determined intellectual endowments are responsible for our success as a species seems rather indisputable. So significant is this trait, and therefore "highly beneficial," Darwin (2007) reasons that the human mind, as it currently exists across the species, must have "been acquired through natural selection" (p. 404). The very notion that the human mind is not the result of a divine master plan, but the product of evolution, is perhaps the scientific straw that broke the clerical back of the institutionalized mainstream Church, that is, the Boss' religion.

Indeed, Darwin's popularization of the evolutionary approach to biology has proven to be one of the hardest scientific pills for establishment religion to swallow. Even the Western scientific community itself has often been too steeped in prejudice and anti-Blackness to be able to heed the full message within Darwin's work. For example, Charles S. Finch (2007) notes that, "as far back as 1871, in the infancy of modern evolutionary biology, Charles Darwin suggested that Africa should be the primary field of search for man's origins. Curiously, Darwin's heirs forgot or ignored this explicit hint and spent nearly two generations searching Europe and Asia for evidence of man's beginning" (p. 289). Darwin (2007) himself was acutely aware of the politically-motivated racialization of his own time, which his evidence-based theory of *The Descent of Man* was, in part, intended to challenge.

During the mid-1800s when Darwin was engaged in his studies it was commonly argued that "races were so distant from one another that interbreeding was impossible" (Zimmer, 2007, p. 226). Darwin, on the other hand, who, at his best, was truly a man of science, "considered many of the differences between peoples to be minor," so minor in fact that he did not "think natural selection had shaped them" and that our species is "variable" like "dogs or pigeons" (Zimmer, 2007, p. 227). Summarizing these conclusions he reached after years of rigorous academic, field-based study Darwin comments,

> The great variability of all external differences between the races of man...indicates that they cannot be of much importance; for if important, they would long ago have been either fixed and preserved, or eliminated. In this respect man resembles those forms, called by naturalists protean or polymorphic, which have remained extremely variable, owing, as it seems, to such variations being of an indifferent nature, and to their having thus escaped the action of natural selection. (p. 274)

Darwin's scientific habits of mind, at their best, clearly led him away from the false hierarchy of white supremacy and about as far from the so-called *social Darwinism* that attempts to inscribe the racial biases of conquest and capital on his work through the imposition of natural selection, which, to reiterate, was never considered a factor in determining human variability or race. In other words, while Darwin concluded that natural selection must be responsible for human intelligence, it is not related in any way to the socially constructed concept of race, rendering intellectual variability among the species completely random, as suggested by Descartes and others. From a critical constructivism perspective, it is incorrect to view the natural variance in human intelligence hierarchically, but rather, as indicative of multiple intelligences which constitutes but one factor in the existence of diverse epistemologies (Kincheloe, 2005).

These democratic implications of Darwin's work, with few exceptions, have been overshadowed by the oppressive and exclusionary ways in which the idea of evolution has been interpreted in regards to race. Another important factor that has pushed Darwin's social justice biology into obscurity is other aspects of his own work, which suggest that he, like Descartes and others before *and* after him, was only partially able to overcome the hierarchy of Euro-centricity. For example, while Darwin largely discounted the notion of race because it is not scientifically verifiable, he upheld the hierarchy of civilizations paradigm that can be interpreted as serving as an apology or justification for empire and the colonization of the Americas and much of the world. Arguing that more evolved civilizations and tribes have always subsumed less advanced ones Darwin (2007) notes that:

> Relics of extinct or forgotten tribes have been discovered throughout the civilized regions of the earth, on the wild plains of America, and on the isolated islands in the Pacific Ocean. At the present day civilized nations are everywhere supplanting barbarous nations, excepting where the climate opposes a deadly barrier; and they succeed mainly, though not exclusively, through their arts, which are the products of their intellect. It is, therefore, highly probable that with mankind the intellectual faculties have been mainly and gradually perfected through natural selection. (p. 202)

Deloria (1997) focuses on this "evolutionary prejudice" in *Red Earth, White Lies: Native Americans and the Myth of Scientific Fact* commenting that "tribal peoples," within this paradigm, have been "placed at the very bottom of the imaginary cultural evolutionary scale" (p. 49) that is based on the "belief that all peoples began as primitives and inevitably moved toward Western forms of organization" (p. 51). The intended result has been "tribal peoples" in mainstream settler-state societies, such as Canada and the United States, being reduced to "a marginal status as human beings" and denied their vast epistemological and ontological contributions to modern democracy and global society more generally.

Kincheloe (2005) argues that this bias is representative of a larger tendency within modern science noting that "with the birth of modernism and the scientific revolution, many premodern, Indigenous epistemologies, cosmologies, and ontologies were lost, ridiculed by European modernists as primitive" (p. 84) because they tend to view nature and the world not mechanistically, but as interconnected living systems, which, ironically, is the way contemporary Western science is heading attempting to finally catch up to the sophistication of Indigenous philosophy/science. Gregory Cajete (2000) contextualizes *Native science* as being "based on the perception gained from using the entire body of our senses in direct participation with the natural world" (p. 2) and defines it as "the collective heritage of human experience" arguing that at "its more essential form" (p. 3) it can be understood as:

> A map of natural reality drawn from the experience of thousands of human generations. It has given rise to the diversity of human technologies, even to the advent

of modern mechanistic science. In profound ways Native science can be said to be "inclusive" of modern science, although most Western scientists would go to great lengths to deny such inclusivity. (p. 3)

There are many who believe that science is solely a Western construction and that Indigenous science, if one exists, is merely a collection of myths and folklore that does not follow a rational systemic method of investigation to discover knowledge (Brayboy & Castagno, 2008; Cajete, 1999). This demonstrates the Western egocentrism that runs throughout its short history of scientific investigation. In reality, Indigenous ancestors "were very sensitive to in their relationships with the land. They systematically organized experiential information about cycles, seasons, connections, and strategies in to their cultures" (Goes in Center, 2001, p. 120). Conversely, the Western capitalist science worldview has expressly disconnected human experience and culture from the natural world as a means to control and conquer it (James, 2001a). This mindset was demonstrated when Europeans came to the Americas and subsequently saw the continent as something to conquer, where both the land and the inhabitants represented a material commodity that needed to be exploited (Hughes, 1983). In sharp contrast to the Western notions of exploitation through science, "Native science builds on our innate sense of nature's majesty, the core experience of spirituality" (Cajete, 2000, p. 98). This "sense of nature's majesty" is grounded in a philosophy of living and built on a foundation of community that reflects a way of life. Reflecting on this magnitude and consistency of the democratic ideals among "tribal peoples" in North America Oren Lyons (2007) concludes that "from what I know of all the people I have met and places I have traveled in Indian Country, they are all democratic" (p. vii), which is no casual statement given his long history of global activism as *Faithkeeper* of the *Onondaga Indian Nation.*

Again, to suggest that science and politics should *remain* separate is to ignore the rich and controversial history this tradition of knowledge production is immersed in, which is filled with examples of how science has never existed in a de-politicized vacuum—except in the *dis*-informative pages of the dominant curriculum. While it is true that scientists such as Darwin argued that humans are part and parcel of the evolutionary history of the natural world, which operates according to universal, objective laws that do not hold any intrinsic morals or ethics (McNally, 2001), human consciousness, however, is always mediated by ethically and morally informed culture rendering the schema through which we perceive the concrete *and* theoretical contexts highly malleable. In other words, if our socially-constructed schemas have not been formed in a way that renders us sensitive to the differences between the biological context of science and the socially constructed context of human culture, and imbued with the capacity to perceive the ways in which they interact, then we will be unable to develop the democratic habits of the *scientific mind*. As we have seen thus far, even the greatest of Europe's scientist philosophers from Descartes to Darwin have only managed to partially assimilate the objectivity indispensable for the development of the scientific mind.

What becomes clear here is that while there are verifiable truths in the standard account of history that positions science in general as serving one unified interest and therefore standing in firm opposition to the hierarchy of antiquity, it oversimplifies a much more complex situation. In other words, the mainstream story fails to acknowledge the multiple ways in which the hierarchy of antiquity successfully subverted many of the primary institutions engaged in the production of scientific knowledge thereby counter-revolutionizing science itself. It is therefore not surprising that the accommodationist texts of Newtonianism, for example, have largely overshadowed the revolutionary implications of his "absurd" discovery of the mysterious force of the mind for which he had no scientific explanation. Commenting on the lack of progress science has made in the past two hundred years in regards to understanding and explaining the creative nature of free will and choice Chomsky (2002) offers the following summary:

> …there has been little noticeable progress in addressing the…hard problems that seemed no less mysterious to Descartes, Newton, Locke, and other leading figures, including the free will that is "the noblest thing" we have, manifested most strikingly in normal language use, they believed, for reasons that we should not lightly dismiss…How remote the remaining mountain peaks may be, and even just where they are, one can only guess. (p. 60)

In other words, there is no *body of doctrine* now available that provides a scientific explanation of free will as some of the sixteenth century scientists predicted there would be (Chomsky, 2002). Rather, the mystery of *force at a distance* or *free will* remains cloaked in secrecy, which, in the seventeenth century, Hume argued would forever remain. From this account, it is clear that science, in the Western world, from at least the sixteenth century, has been a highly controversial and political undertaking persisting and intensifying in this vein into the present moment, underscored in considerable detail below. So what *was* truly new in Europe's age of scientific revolution? Our answer, so the evidence points, can be found within the irreverent attitudes and shameless independence exhibited by the likes of Galileo and others, that, before Euro-American contact, were non-existent, and, when rigorously observed, can lead to the democratic habits conducive to the development of the scientific mind.

Examining closely the socio-political context of Europe's age of Enlightenment Jonathan Israel paints a picture not of just one single European Enlightenment, but of two competing, antagonistically-related Enlightenments, as suggested and alluded to thus far. For the purposes of the following section we will refer to the coddling or hegemonic Enlightenment of the contemporary era as *Science for Capitalism* and today's Radical Enlightenment as *Liberation Science for Democratic Independence (LSDI)*. As we transition into our discussion of mind situated in the context of an LSDI we find Russell's (1945/1972) observation (mentioned in Chapter One) particularly useful:

> Science tells us what we can know, but what we can know is little, and if we forget how much we cannot know we become insensitive to many things of very great importance. (p. xiv)

Science *for* Capitalism *versus* Liberation Science for Democratic Independence (LSDI)

The Reductionism of Science Education

Over the years it has become increasingly clear that just about any time a teacher education class in North America (especially the Anglo-dominated regions) assumes as its conceptual framework critical pedagogy and is therefore centered around the idea that because teaching and learning are always situated in sociopolitical contexts, the practice and implementation of a neutral education, of whatever subject matter, is an ontological impossibility, at least one student (but usually a group) will always parrot the dominant society belief that *politics and social issues should be left for the social studies because you don't want to pollute and water-down the fact-based objectivity of math and science—there is just too much to learn in the hard sciences to try to cover the soft stuff too.*

This notion that critical approaches can get in the way of teaching science content seems to stem from both internal and external factors for the classroom science teacher. As for the internal barriers to LSDI, most North American teachers have not been trained, nor asked, to critically examine their own assumptions that sustain racist and hegemonic notions of white superiority (McIntosh, 1988). These uninvestigated hegemonic notions create internal barriers related to race and privilege for many white students and teachers. When they are faced with the stark reality of their privilege, many white students retreat to a position where they deny seeing race or color and that privilege does not exist. James and McVay (2009) demonstrated that when teachers decided to shed these traditionally held beliefs they were able to move beyond these deeply held notions and help students investigate history in more honest ways. It is far too common that teachers go through teacher education programs that do not challenge or confront their assumptions about schools as places of compliance, where future teachers are not asked to envision the democratic possibilities that exist within school contexts (Leafgren, 2008). In terms of science, if students are encouraged to see scientific understanding as the accumulation of disconnected pieces of previously discovered phenomena (which is also disconnected from culture and human experience) than it is commonsensical to believe that critically examining science as a subjective activity seems to stand in the way of memorizing science related trivia. In the context of science teacher education the willingness to embrace testing procedures, such as Praxis, within the content areas also further subjugates the notion of science as a political endeavor. In this regard, teacher education programs send clear signals as what counts as science knowledge, which solidifies the internal barriers to critical practice within future teachers.

Interestingly, the internal barriers to enacting LSDI are manifest within larger external issues related to science and science teacher education. Most often guidelines for teacher preparation are defined by content area specialists and are often quickly seen only through the lens of content proficiency. This quickly gets transferred to classroom teachers who envision their role solely as an effort to increase student scores on state proficiency exams. In addition, states have created a static body of science standards that bound the accepted range of science content for each grade level. Standards represent how Western science continues to conceptualize itself as a hierarchical categorization of nature. Standards further imply that there is actually a finite static body of previously discovered science truths to master and this depiction does not account for the contributions of those outside of the Western science tradition (Braboy & Castagno, 2008). This again is symptomatic of the Western science notion that demands the categorization and commodification of knowledge (James, 2001b). These external pressures work to discourage individuals from attempting revolutionary science approaches while simultaneously mapping the boundaries of scientific pursuits. In this way, any measure of critical approaches to science must be carried out under the protective cloak of larger standards and standardized assessment. We argue that this system of external checks on science teaching ensures that science in schools carries out capitalist science agendas of dominating and extracting wealth from the natural world as opposed to as a means for understanding our delicate relationship with the system of earth itself.

It is the long legacy of first Platonic Idealism and Aristotle's' obsessive categorization of *all knowledge* which laid the conceptual foundation for this modern manifestation of Cartesian reductionism, which persists despite Newton's scientific demolition of mechanical philosophy and the very question of material versus immaterial. In Chapter One we argued that the danger of Cartesian reductionism in education is the tendency to disconnect the production of knowledge from the social political arena in which it is situated. Conceiving the world as chopped up into areas of study or disciplines, such as the sciences on one hand, and politics on the other, is a central feature of how Western reductionistic and thus decontextualized education has manifested itself, which has served to reproduce and advance the hierarchical structure of power and privilege in the service of empire building for wealth extraction and the process of value production. For example, the technological engineering and computational feats that have advanced capital's ability to extract wealth and build empire is presented as an a-political sign of human progress because it is grounded in science and *science is objective*, according to the dominant paradigm—this is the ideological justification for the counter-revolutionary science of capital, which has always been far from achieving any respectable sense of objectivity as it is heavily burdened by bias and prejudice favoring wealth and privilege. If Galileo were alive today he would surely be displeased, although not surprised, with much of what has been done in the name of science, from the nuclear arms race, biological racism, to the very practice of science education.

The acquisition and usage of scientific knowledge that is conceived of not as a highly political undertaking, but as a matter of *getting more of it* suggesting that the learner engage passively with the curriculum and to therefore *use* rather than *produce* science. Wolff-Michael Roth and Angela Calabrese Barton (2004) in their critically important *Rethinking Scientific Literacy* summarize the dominant perspective noting that "because every citizen should have some level of scientific literacy, so the argument goes, the implications of such individualistic takes on scientific literacy are finding ways in which the individual comes to know more of the facts…of science" (p. 49).

Arguing against this reductionistic analysis based on the premise that "science and society" are two mutually exclusive "entities," Roth and Barton (2004) look to foundational advances in anthropology that clearly demonstrate that "science and society cannot be separate, but, as categories, are produced inside a more general, heterogeneous matrix of culture" (p. 50). In other words, all knowledge is produced in a social situation by social actors, and all social actors or citizens are informed by a particular cultural perspective that is either part of the dominant culture or, because of its hierarchal structure, is subjugated. Roth and Barton (2004) continue, documenting the ways in which scientists tend to view "science as pure" and therefore take special care to protect it from the "sullied" context of society "with its economic, ethico-moral, and political dimensions" (p. 50).

As demonstrated by our analysis of the Renaissance and the age of Enlightenment in Europe, science, in the Western context, has never held any special place in society, insulated from the highly subjective and prejudicial nature of the political domain. The result: A long legacy of white supremacist pseudo-scientific biology;

a war-mongering and hate-filled physics and chemistry; and an entire discipline motivated by market mechanisms and the cold calculations of profit-seekers.

Again, it is worth briefly revisiting Cartesian reductionism here because modern scientists continue to understand the act of learning or acquiring knowledge to be the passive and objective transmission of predetermined *facts* that occurs when we "detach" the "mind from the senses," as Descartes (1637/1994) argued was possible leading him to believe that he was able to "abstract my mind from the contemplation of [sensible or] imaginable objects, and apply it to those which, as disengaged from all matter, are purely intelligible" (p. 103). Challenging mainstream conceptions of science—what we have called *science for capitalism* or simply *the boss's science*—we observe that because humans are inherently social beings, everything we do, including learning, occurs in the highly political terrain of society—the *scientific mind* and the *political economy* can no more be disconnected from one another than can *the mind* and *the body*.

Not only is modern, dominant-society science based on the false dichotomy between the subjectivity of society on one hand, and the objectivity of pure thought and reason on the other, but it is too often based on other forms of hierarchy. The result contributes to the unscientific idea that the low levels of scientific literacy found within large numbers of people in what are typically described as *advanced industrial societies*, like the United States and Canada, are beyond remedy because the vast majority of humanity is "incapable of scientific literacy" (Roth & Barton, 2004, p. 49). From a critical, that is, a Native North American, theoretical perspective, on the other hand, "reason and sense," and the capacity to achieve scientific literacy, however conceived, are the most equally distributed attributes found throughout the species and, as such, are "found complete in each individual" (Descartes, 1637/1994, p. 3). Kincheloe's (2004) postformal cognitive theory is based on a similar conclusion, that "most students who don't suffer from brain disorders or severe emotional problems can (and do) engage in higher-order thinking" (p. 19). Ideas about learning and the practices they inform are therefore never objective and can thus be described as unavoidably and always situated in the politics of history. What we are beginning to lay the foundation for here is a *liberation science for democratic independence* (LSDI). To complete this chapter we must now carefully define exactly what we mean by *liberation science for democratic independence*.

The Science of an LSDI

Because we are seeking a *liberation science for democratic independence*, we are interested, first and foremost, with challenging the bias and prejudice that has plagued science since at least Newton—the reactionary politics presented as neutral and objective in capitalist schooling. This initial step requires a radical education, which, in the context of the highly controversial white-supremacist capitalism, is revolutionary—that is, it offers an antagonistically related interpretive framework, and thus, a shift in understanding. It therefore makes sense to begin briefly mention the approaches of other revolutionary change agents. For example, considering his experience-based insights on how to build a revolution, *Ché* Guevara, successful guerrilla leader of the Cuban Revolution, offers an appropriate place of departure for our discussion. In the following passage Guevara (1969) stresses the importance of education in fomenting mass insurrection, noting that "effort" be "directed at large concentrations of people in whom the revolutionary idea can be planted and nurtured, so that at a critical moment they can be mobilized and with the help of the armed forces contribute to a favorable balance on the side of the revolution." (p. 85) For Guevara (1969), in practice this looks like organizing "popular organizations of workers, professional people and peasants, who work at sowing the seed of revolution among their respective masses, explaining, providing revolutionary publications for reading, teaching the truth. Little by little, in this way, the masses will be won over" (p. 85).

While we most certainly challenge the prescriptive/banking orientation within Guevara's (1969) blueprint here, his overall idea of raising the critical consciousness of the underlying population, essentially, has been the task of critical pedagogy. While this work has been indispensable for democratic education, what is too often left unexplored is the science that seems to offer the most relevant insights for putting it into practice. Because we are talking about teaching and learning, from a scientific perspective, it would be wise to begin with an analysis of the mind, focusing, in part, on the mind's grammar, that is, language.

The conditions under which humans learn languages, from this perspective, speak to the inherent intelligent nature of the species, that is, the *human endowment*, which George Sarton (1952/1980), in a similar vein, describes as the "monogeneis of mankind," a conclusion he came to as a result of his analysis of the convergent tendency of "prehistoric science" (p. 6) the world over. Alluding to this point Chomsky (2002) notes that "the logical problem of language acquisition" resides in the fact that,

> ...Children acquiring this knowledge do not have that much data. In fact you can estimate the amount of data they have quite closely, and it's very limited; still, somehow children are reaching these states of knowledge which have apparently great complexity, and differentiation and diversity... Each child is capable of acquiring any such state... so it must be that the basic structure of language is essentially uniform and is coming from inside, not from outside. (p. 93)

Chomsky's linguistic analyses have focused on this *human essence*, which is the basis of what he calls *universal grammar*—the common root structure among all languages. While Chomsky (2002) maintains that his linguistic work, which is centered on human biology, should not be deemed any more controversial than questions concerning the internal state of the "dance language" of honeybees, for example, his contributions have been widely criticized for failing to take into account the highly political nature of the concrete contexts in which languages are acquired (Moraes, 1996; Macedo, Dendrinos & Gounari, 2003). Attempting to challenge the fundamental thesis behind Chomsky's *internalist* analysis Jerome Bruner (1990) in *Acts of Meaning* argues that, "...the child's acquisition of language requires far more assistance from and interaction with caregivers than Chomsky has suspected. Language is acquired not in the role of spectator but through use" (p. 70). However, perhaps Bruner's critiques are not entirely founded here. Chomsky (1988) does seem to acknowledge that the biological determinations of the language organ will only develop through practice—in a social context.

For example, situating the *creative aspect of language* in a concrete social context Chomsky (1988) notes that for its "rich capacities" to manifest themselves in their "own largely predetermined way...certain kinds of stimulating environments are necessary" (pp. 172–173). For Chomsky (1988) then "a good system of raising children puts them in a stimulating, loving environment in which their natural capacities will be able to flourish" (p. 173). Staying true to his *internalist* analysis Chomsky (1988) stresses that, "these capacities are not being taught. They are simply being allowed to function in the way in which they are designed to develop" (p. 173). Comparing what he characterizes as the ideal situation of natural development to the actual practice of schooling, Chomsky (1988) notes that, "what the schools actually do is often exactly the opposite. The school system is designed to teach obedience and conformity and prevent the child's natural capacities from developing" (p. 173). However, this is as far as Chomsky's linguistic analysis tends to venture into the realm of politics.

The perspectives offered by Chomsky's critics—especially those of the critical theoretical tradition—are therefore fundamentally important in situating biological insights in a larger social, historical, political context. However, before exploring the implications of the critical critiques leveled against Chomsky's *internalist* paradigm, we briefly explore the work of one of the relatively early influences of the critical approach to psychology, Lev Semyonovitch Vygotsky. In his theories concerning the development of thought and speech Vygotsky clearly broke with the tradition from which Chomsky comes—that is, the tradition of reductionistic theorizing that reduces the essence of humanity to its biological determinants disconnected from the social-historical context in which they are situated.

For example, in *Thought and Language* (first appearing in Russia in 1934), Vygotsky (1962) notes that, "verbal thought is not an innate, natural form of behavior but is determined by a historical-cultural process and has specific properties and laws that cannot be found in the natural forms of thought and speech" (p. 51). As a result, the "development of behavior" can be understood as being "governed" by "the historical development of human society" (Vygotsky, 1962, p. 51). In other words, Vygotsky downplays the notion that humans are endowed with a built-in language acquisition device that operates mechanistically without thought, and rather emphasizes the importance of "outside factors" such as "socialized speech" in the "development of logic" (Vygotsky, 1962, p. 51).

However, Vygotsky (1962) does not completely discount the biological in his social theory of learning commenting that children "'discover' the symbolic function of speech...not suddenly but gradually, through a series of 'molecular' changes" (p. 50). The philosophical perspective advanced here by Vygotsky is therefore based on an ontology and epistemology of complexity that brings to the fore the socially constructed nature of internalized schema. Vygotsky's approach to education therefore focused on the importance of context and culture in the intellectual development of children. At the center of his model was what he called the zone of proximal development (Vygotsky, 1978), which has been described as "an analytical tool for evaluation of school children's development in connection with schooling" based on the assumption that "development and instruction are socially embedded" (Hedegaard, 1990, p. 349).

His influence on the founders of critical pedagogy, such as Paulo Freire, who, like Vygotsky, places special emphasis on the interaction between the concrete and theoretical contexts, is made clear by Freire (2005) himself in *Teachers as Cultural Workers: Letters to Those Who Dare Teach* commenting that "it is undeniably important to read the works of...Vygotsky" because he understands "the relationship between reading and writing" as "processes that cannot be separated" and should thus be "organized" by educators "in such a way as to create the perception that they are needed for something" (pp. 43–45) because knowledge is not separate from the social worlds in which it emerges. Building on the work of Freire, Vygotsky, and others, Marcia Moraes (1996) observes that language is "ideological" because it is "socially constructed" rendering Chomsky's work shortsighted for neglecting the "ideological environment within the process of acquiring a language" which is fundamental in understanding the discursive role of speech for it "embraces cultural, historical, and political dimensions" (p. 8). Elaborating on this critique Bruner (1990) offers some contextualization, clearly influenced by Vygotsky's social-historical psychology:

> Because the lexico-grammatical speech of almost all children improves steadily during the early years of life, we too easily take it for granted that language acquisition is "autonomous." According to this dogma, part of the Chomskian heritage discussed earlier, language acquisition needs no motive other than itself, no particularly

specialized support from the environment, nothing except the unfolding of some sort of self-charged "bioprogram." (p. 89)

Six years after these observations Bruner (1996) concedes, in part, to Chomsky's analysis, reflecting that, "something in our genome makes us astonishingly adept at picking up the lexico-syntactic structure of any natural language" (p. 184). Bruner seems to have accepted Chomsky's assertion, which he has maintained through many years of ridicule, mentioned above, that his analysis should not be considered "controversial" or political.

However, Macedo, Dendrinos, and Gounari (2003), in their appropriately named *The Hegemony of English*, note that Chomsky's presentation of language as a "unitary innate system" that "relegates all variation to the random vagaries of performance" has been instrumental in influencing "the norm of monolingualism" (p. 51). In other words, by employing a form of essentializing reductionism that reduces the species to its common *language-organ* element, largely ignoring language differences because they are scientifically insignificant, Chomsky has failed to address the monumental political implications of language acquisition situated in its social context, and, as a result, has been susceptible to the oppressive politics of monolingual homogenization. Summarizing the social context of "linguistic function" Macedo, Dendrinos and Gounari (2003) note that

> Linguistic functions are not restricted to simple reflection or expression. Language actually shapes human existence in a dual way. For one, it affects the way humans are perceived through their speech. Secondly, individuals develop discourses that are formed through their identity in terms of class, race, gender, ethnicity, sexual orientation, popular culture, and other factors. Discourses should be understood... as systems of communication shaped through historical, social, cultural, and ideological practices, which can work to either confirm or deny the life histories and experiences of the people who use them... The proposition that language is neutral or non-ideological constitutes, in reality, an ideological position itself. (pp. 26–27)

The importance of these analyses and critiques cannot be over-stressed because it cannot be denied that our "innate design" develops in a social, historical, political context as argued by Vygotsky, and advanced by Freire, Macedo, Kincheloe, and many others, by giving special attention to the role that power plays in legitimizing certain knowledge and subjugating other knowledges (Kincheloe, 2005). Our individual ideas, collectively our worldviews, are therefore informed by particular philosophical paradigms (Malott, 2008).

Through philosophy our biological endowments, following this theoretical framework, can be put to work for or against others and ourselves. We might conclude that our biology is not political or controversial, as Chomsky contends, but its manifestation *is* both political and highly controversial because it always develops in a social-historical context, never in a vacuum, as noted by Macedo and his colleagues (2003). From this perspective, separating the biological from the social, or the internal from the external, represents the danger of what we might call over-reductoinism—which is, in a word, and at best, shortsighted. Simultaneously, however, while biological processes, in and of themselves, are not political, in practice, they are always political because they are always situated in a social context, and the social is never *not* highly political and contested. The biological, from a slightly different perspective, is thus fundamentally important to the pedagogical because it offers invaluable insights into how the mind works and constructs knowledge through practice and experience and *always* firmly situated in a social context.

Kinchloe (2005) reminds us that power is central to legitimizing types of knowledge particularly as it is expressed within the context of schooling. In the case of K-12 science teaching, school itself defines what counts as science knowledge for children. Science in school contexts goes through its own evolution as students' progress from early childhood through the secondary context. In early elementary classrooms, teaching often aligns pedagogy with children's innate ability to construct sophisticated arguments. For instance, the well-known early childhood science text *Science Experiences for the Early Childhood Years* (Harlan & Rivken, 2008) argue that when the "innate human desire for understanding the world is organized into careful ways of collecting, testing, and sharing information, it is called science" (p. 4). Chaille and Britain (2003) add support to this notion that children must use inquiry-based, constructivist practices as they wrestle with ways to better "understand the world" (p. 14). Constructivist approaches to science argue that learning is a result from observing the natural world, scaffolding that information with prior conceptions, and interacting with more capable peers to construct new understandings (Barba, 1998; Llewellyn, 2002).

Indigeneity and an LSDI Science Education

These approaches to classroom pedagogy are reflective of Native American approaches to teaching as a tool to understand the natural world. Traditionally, Indigenous students were taught using experiential learning that emphasized interaction, observation, and the involvement of traditional culture as opposed to the decontextualized formal instruction of the modern North American school system (Dyck, 2001). In his book, *Igniting the Sparkle: An Indigenous Science Education Model,* Cajete (1999) articulates a model for Indigenous science that must include: the space for students to approach science problems from differing pathways, extended learning experiences to include family and community members, a social context to connect to student lives and the cultural fabric of the community, authentic activities to facilitate experiential learning, emphasizes safe spaces for students to express their thoughts and findings, and lastly to provide students with opportunities to practice leadership skills. In this sense, utilizing students' cultural knowledge becomes an essential element to science education as opposed to a hindrance that must be overcome or abandoned.

Students in public schools in the U.S. are more likely to experience these types of pedagogical approaches, that mirror Native approaches to knowledge, during their early school years. However, as children progress through to higher grades, teachers are faced with increasing external pressures such as testing and more challenging abstract science content. In response to these challenges, teachers often fall back on traditional methods where constructivist science pedagogy is cast aside in favor of demonstrating control over students and preparing them to conform to traditional school hierarchies of domination and compliance (Gilbert, 2009). Wee et al. (2007) argued that, "inquiry presents an inconvenience, or even impediment, to traditional forms of teaching and learning in the science classroom" (p. 65). In a similar vein, Spector et al. (2007) demonstrated that upper elementary teachers often resist notions of inquiry, in their practice, claiming it gets in the way of the teaching what they *need* to do.

Jay Lemke's influential text (1990) *Talking science: Language, learning, and values* highlights how traditional teaching is often carried out in school contexts. This type of teaching and interaction is common at the secondary level. Lemke demonstrates how school language practices structure the authoritativeness of science, where students have no stake in creating their own scientific knowledge claims rather they must accept the word of the *experts*. Perkinson (1993) corroborates the idea of science as authoritative stating:

> Students must accept the statement as true because some authority (whatever it may be) says that it is true. Now, much can be said against authoritarianism in education; the most important criticism, however, is that authoritarianism prevents the growth of knowledge. Any knowledge justified by an infallible authority cannot be criticized, hence, cannot be improved (p. 50).

Consequently, making science authoritative is counter-productive to the creation of knowledge. This perspective highlights reasons that students, especially those without mastery of the dominant discourse ability, have difficulty mastering the thematic patterns that are associated with science education (Lemke, 1990). Given this move away from intellectual engagement pursuing questions that pertain to the interests and lives of students toward one of memorizing previously discovered "truths," it is not surprising that student interest in science wanes as they proceed through their elementary years (Matthews, 2004; Murphy & Beggs, 2003;Watters & Diezmann, 2007).

Drawing on critiques of Western science, we have argued that science education practices follow a capitalist science agenda without clear introspection for the consequences and exclusive nature of these approaches, which work to further the myth of objectivity and reason. To counteract this myth and develop more inclusive science pedagogy, educators must rethink several aspects of science education including: the nature of science and what counts as knowledge, connecting science to students lives, and reassessing the roles of students, teachers, parents, and the community (Cajete, 1999; Harding, 1993).

In addition, science educators must reject the notion of positivist science as objective, value-free, and neutral moving toward an idea of science as a human activity that is framed by experience, culture, language, and is a fluid and ever evolving process (Barton, 1998; Cajete, 1999; Cajete, 2000). To this end, Basu and Barton (2007) suggest that using students "Funds of knowledge" can achieve essential science education goals and long-term student interest in science itself. They define funds of knowledge as, "the historical and cultural knowledge of a community...That is, funds of knowledge are not stereotypes about cultural practices, but rather are the dynamic process of students' lived experiences within a particular family and community" (p. 468). The utilization of funds of knowledge can work to demystify the sanctity of science knowledge and represents science in a more realistic light, as opposed to a meticulous recipe for discovering "truth."

The research carried out through a funds of knowledge lens have repeatedly demonstrated powerful connections to science for students who exist outside of the traditional, Western, mainstream, science framework (Basu & Barton, 2007; Bouillion & Gomez, 2001; Hammond, 2001). Western science has demonstrated a consistent intolerance for multiple perspectives, which perpetuates a "culture of exclusion" where the voices of minorities, women, and other marginalized groups go unheard and unvalued (Hammond, 2001). This certainly limits democratic possibilities and determines the nature and quality of scientific understanding.

Conclusion

Building on this line of reasoning, we can view the biological as Chomsky does, that is, as highly complex and basically unalterable, but, drawing on Vygotsky, mediated by the social. What *is* subject to human intervention, therefore, from this combined approach, is the social context in which our *partial*-determinations develop. Intervening in the context of the political has traditionally been the task of philosophy. What this analysis demonstrates is that the hegemonic struggle to maintain a hierarchy of power and privilege in the material world, the concrete context, at its heart, is cultural, as argued by the likes of Vygotsky and Freire (again, among many others). Situating this struggle over the intellectual development of "the masses," and therefore the hearts and minds of men and women, and, as a result, the relationships that define our existence in the context of philosophy, Jonathan Israel (2006) notes

> Only philosophy can cause a true 'revolution'...A revolutionary shift is a shift in understanding, something which, though intimately driven by the long-term processes of social change, economic development, and institutional adaptation, is in itself a product of 'philosophy' since only philosophy can transform our mental picture of the world and its basic categories...Most modern readers [however] resist attempts to envisage 'philosophy' as what defines the human condition. (p. 13)

Philosophy, from this perspective, is the lens through which we view the world, and ultimately, informs our daily interventions and interactions in the world. Every conscious, functioning person has a malleable and particular way they think about and make sense of the world that is *not* biologically determined, which we can call our philosophy—everyone therefore has one.

CHAPTER EIGHT

Native American Democracy and Western Mathematics Curricula

What becomes obvious here is the recognition in Indigenous philosophy of the social and concrete nature of all forms of knowing, including, and perhaps primarily, mathematical forms. In this chapter we explore the ancient nature of human mathematical activity. Afforded significant attention in this role mathematics played in Enlightenment Europe as the model of reason and objectivity, and therefore the surest way to combat bias and create an enlightened society free from subjective inequality.

* * *

It can be stated with a fair amount of certainty that at least a limited range of mathematical operations, however rudimentary, were practiced by ancient man and woman very early, such as counting, that can reasonably be attributed to the genetically-determined repeating patterns of cell structures that are ubiquitous in nature, much of which are embedded with what appears to be an inherent dualism. That is, an overwhelming re-emergent theme of natural pairs exists within the organic world such as male and female; front and back; up and down; and one side (i.e. one hand) and the other side (i.e. the other hand), for example. From here it can be speculated that math originated in the concrete context of humans actively engaged in their world as the species' intellectual endowments naturally demand. Situating this analysis within our most recent ancient past we can look to the earliest evidence of recorded mathematics, found in Africa, and dated to 8000 B.C. (Sarton, 1952), that is, ten thousand years ago, suggesting a very long relationship with the development of mathematical habits of mind.

The ancient Egyptians, for example, thousands of years before the Greek mathematical philosophers of antiquity, conceived of the law of opposites or dialectics that conceptualizes the idea of naturally occurring positives and negatives with a constant zero at the center. This is the foundation of the notion of equilibrium and the balance between opposing forces or interests, such as good and evil or the oppressors and the oppressed, that, if equally distributed, theoretically, would cancel each other out, which can be represented numerically as positive one plus negative one equaling zero. In formulaic terms we can conclude that when we add the negative and positive representations of the same integer the result is always zero. This tension of opposites was understood to exist naturally within all entities from male and female to boss and worker. When we consider that math is organically contextualized, from this ancient model perspective, the decontextualized, reductionistic approach to contemporary Western mathematics instruction can be understood as highly controversial. In other words, when it is argued that mathematics should be kept separate from politics, the social context in which it has always been situated remains hidden. As a result, the economic ruling-class interests supported by this numerical approach to knowledge production are obscured and left behind what we might name the *ontological curtain*. As we will see below, this was the challenge of early scientists operating in a most intolerant Europe—that is, to enlighten the objective reality the church either obscured or thwarted the discovery of. This quest for certainty has been the driving force of modern science. However, in our search for a critical pedagogy that is not made to feel like a boss that demands absolute obedience, we will explore Critical constructivist insights that argue that there is *no objective reality* because all meaning is socially constructed.

In our exploration of the evidence that supports the claim that dominant approaches to knowledge production are not democratic, and therefore need immediate and fundamental reformation, we begin with an outline of traditional mathematics instruction. We then juxtapose these currents next to the revolutionary impulse of mathematics during Europe's Age of Enlightenment that found inspiration in both Native American democracy and the knowledge from antiquity preserved and substantially advanced by Islamic scholars during Europe's Dark Ages—an age of extreme pathology, barbarism and intellectual decline for many, if not most, of European's ruling elite. Finally, we explore the possibilities of critical pedagogical and critical constructivist approaches to mathematics instruction situated in an integrated paradigm of knowledge production.

Traditional Mathematics Instruction

The banking conceptualization of Western mathematics instruction, which tends to be based on the assumption that there is an objectively knowable reality out there awaiting discovery, and therefore external to the internal constructions of the mind, has been identified by critical educators as one of the primary culprits in perpetuating what has been coined as *number numbness* (Peterson, 2005). Bob Peterson (2005) alludes to what we can identify as pedagogical and curricular contributors to the widespread alienation engendered by mathematics. Looking at pedagogy Peterson (2005) identifies "rote calculations, drill and practice nauseum, endless reams of worksheets, and a fetish for 'the right answer'" as contributing to "number numbness" (p. 10). Curricularly, math is so thoroughly segregated from all other subject areas, it "is basically irrelevant except for achieving success in future math classes, becoming a scientist or mathematician, or making commercial transactions" and therefore "not connected to social reality" (Peterson, 2005, p. 10). The ubiquitous existence of number numbness is all but total because the process of abstracting numbers from real entities in the concrete world represents the dominant method of traditional mathematics instruction—it is everywhere all the time, especially pronounced in working class schools following the common assumption of a natural hierarchy of intelligence.

For example, when students are asked to calculate two plus two, it is understood that the answer, four, does not refer to any specific *thing* such as *four* abuses of power within objective reality, which would be from a Marxist perspective. However, critical constructivism challenges us to go beyond merely connecting abstract numbers to tangible *things* and consider the socially constructed nature of all signifiers—that is, every idea that represents a physical object, action, or emotion is a human creation, and every human unavoidably and subjectively creates knowledge based on who they are and the world they are dialectically related to as it shapes us while we simultaneously shape it (Kincheloe, 2005). The designification of numerical representations is therefore a hegemonized presupposition that can be overcome in many ways including the combined use of Marxist and critical constructivist approaches.

This work requires contextual awareness of not only the discipline of mathematics, but also an awareness of the relationship between the primary disciplines. For example, mathematics, like science more generally, tends to be treated by mainstream educationalists as a "pure subject" and therefore "taught in special, physically separated rooms, unsullied by common sense, aesthetics, economics, politics, or other characteristics of everyday life" and thus "a form of indoctrination to a particular worldview" (Roth & Barton, 2004, p. 3) informed by the mechanistic, decontextualized ontology of global capitalism. Mathematics has therefore been placed at the top, or near the top, of the *imaginary hierarchy of disciplines paradigm* because it has been socially constructed as the discipline that most closely approximates objective reality.

A consequence of this decontextualized approach to knowledge production is that corporate advertisers far too often construct images of themselves as part and parcel of the science that is understood to be benevolent and objectively *good*, thereby taking attention away from the destructive and deadly consequences of most industrial manufacturing. For example, in a recent *Bank of America* advertisement, aired throughout the United States during the Summer 2008 Olympics in Beijing China, it was proclaimed that "in America we do not let the sun *just* shine or the wind *just* blow, we put them to work." The primary message embedded within this public text could be interpreted as suggesting that the environmentally responsible and intellectually superior men, properly funded as they are in America, are benevolently putting their endowments to work providing consumers with a clean, renewable source of energy. Another interpretation of the message might be that the natural world exists for the purpose of being incorporated into the process of value production by the bosses, and therefore does not have an inherent right to exist outside the universe of market mechanisms, for such a place does not exist within the worldview of neoliberal capitalism. In both interpretations the labor capital relationship and industrialism are presuppositions.

In another 2008 Olympic commercial Exxon Mobile positions its math and science curriculum as a leading force responsible for producing the scientists that will "solve the problems" of these times, although such "problems" remain unmentioned in the advertisement. Rather than *solving problems*, however, the Exxon initiative is dedicated to producing more math and science teachers operating from the same industrial-capitalist, traditional, decontextualized, absolutist form of instruction responsible for the vast injustices of an irresponsible science. Such a paradigm, which dictates mainstream mathematics more generally, "does not account for the fundamental relationships between individual and society, knowledge and power, or science, economics, and politics" (Roth & Barton, 2004, p. 3). This particular approach has proven conducive to prepackaged curriculum materials and away from critical consciousness and an awareness of the central issues that threaten the viability of life on Earth itself, such as environmental devastation, nuclear weapons proliferation, and the privatization of the planet's genetic codes and fresh water supply (see Chapter Twelve and below).

Many students therefore become turned off to math (and science) because it is presented as an abstract higher order thinking skill with no real connection or relevance in the concrete context of both the larger society and the specificities of their micro-structural lives—simply stated as *number numbness*. The expected results have been substandard rates of mathematical literacy among the population.

Summarizing some of the recent quantitative evidence of these trends in a *New York Times* article Tamar Lewin (2008) writes that it has been widely reported that American students, internationally compared, can be described as "mediocre" when it comes to math achievement. Specifically, Lewin (2008) notes that "a 2007 assessment" found that "fifteen-year-olds in the United States ranked twenty fifth among their peers in thirty developed nations in math literacy and problem solving" (p. 2). For a nation with so many problems, from capitalist imperialism with its long history and foundation in genocidal colonialism to its white supremacist hegemonies and ecocidal consequences, it cannot be a positive indicator of fulfilling the democratic promises of the idea of a confederation of united states integrated around universal concepts of equality and freedom when its most current generation on the horizon of coming to age, has, at best, *mediocre* problem solving skills.

Given the exaggerated amount of attention and importance mathematics, conceptualized as a subject distinct from all others, is currently afforded in educational policy such as the No Child Left Behind Act, the preceding analysis, which suggests that there is something fundamentally wrong with how the content is taught, should cause such approaches to teaching the subject matter, as argued above, controversial. One might ask: would it not make better sense to seek out the best methods to teach the subjects considered to be the most important? We explore this question in the final section of this chapter in our engagement with critical pedagogy and critical constructivism. First, however, we explore a number of fundamental historical considerations that can serve as critical inspiration for contextualized approaches for the twenty-first century. Consequently, the following sub-section sets the stage for the final reflection of this chapter that takes as its driving force the transformative impulse of critical pedagogy *and* constructivism.

Mathematics and Revolution During Europe's Age of Enlightenment

Further underscoring the highly questionable nature of contemporary examples of Western mathematics instruction is the fact that it was only a few hundred years ago, during the seventeenth and eighteenth centuries, at the heart of Europe's Age of Enlightenment, that leading mathematicians of the day coined the term "Scientific Revolution." This should not be surprising given the perception of math which was considered "the greatest revolutionizing force" because it represents the most objective, clearest form of "rational thinking" and therefore the best suited to undermine the clerical bias and prejudice of the Inquisition (Hankins,

1985, p. 2)—the Church and Monarchies representing Europe's ruling classes of that time. Challenging divine-right dogmatism, scientists, armed with a Native American-inspired democratic universalism, took the concept of "reason" as the correct equalizing method, and, based on their judgment, argued that "the model of reason was mathematics" (Hankins, 1985, p. 2). The mathematical model of reason was particularly adept at providing a way to overcome the obscurity and "outlandish hypotheses" of the mechanical philosophy by studying "the vital phenomena themselves and attempt to reduce them to rule, without any suppositions about original causes or imagined mechanisms" (Hankins, 1985, p. 115). Before we continue it is worth mentioning that this scientific quest for certainty, even if democratically conceived, is challenged by a critical constructivist epistemology that sees within the vast diversity of human experience the instability of meaning (Kincheloe, 2005).

Through reason it was argued that *analysis* would serve as the "proper scientific method" (Hankins, 1985, p. 20) leading the disinterested scientist to the discovery of the hidden truths of *objective reality*. While modern scientists, such as Sir Isaac Newton, viewed analysis as representing the process through which "complex phenomena" could be reduced and synthesized into "simple components" (Hankins, 1985, p. 20), critical constructivists celebrate complexity and strive to "maximize" rather than "reduce" measurable "variables" (Kincheloe, 2005, p. 3). Summarizing this sentiment in his "Rules of Reasoning in Philosophy" Newton (1952/1987) comments that "Nature is pleased with simplicity" and therefore "the same natural effects we must, as far as possible, assign the same causes" (p. 270). Drawing on respiration as an example Newton (1952/1987) induces, in the name of simplicity and generalizability, that its internal design is essentially the same "in a man and in a beast" (p. 270). It was through observations and experiments that Newton drew such methodological conclusions. This method is known as *induction*. That is, the process was based on the assumption that if enough *singular* statements or evidence was gathered, then *universal* statements or theories could be postulated—the product of analysis being formulas and the unveiling of natural laws. In other words, the process consists of "inferring universal statements from singular ones," which has been critiqued for inevitably leading to "logical inconsistencies" (Popper, 1937/2007, pp. 4–5) due to the inherent fallacy of making quantitative conclusions from qualitative data.

Popper's work, first published in 1959, challenged the scientific community to rethink notions of certainty and theories of knowledge. Picking up on these critiques of Western epistemology during the 1970s and 1980s postmodern work began pointing to the highly political and prejudicial nature of indoctrinated human subjectivities, which are indicative of hierarchical societies, as one of the leading factors contributing to the uncertainty of human-created knowledge.

Considering these limitations of the scientific process of knowledge production to be valid has challenged me, as a Western-trained scientist-practitioner (sociology and education), dedicated to the pursuit of truth, to conduct research so informed.

As a Master's student in Sociology at New Mexico State University I attempted to construct a study that would produce the knowledge that would allow me to make both broad generalizations and paint fine detailed think descriptive pictures of concrete contexts and individual social actors. In other words, I sought to both reduce and maximize variables in an attempt to produce a richer and thicker construction than either approach alone. The result was a content analysis that produced both qualitative numbers through the use of statistics used to analyze large groups of data *and* think descriptive narratives of representative examples. The subject matter was the cultural spaces created by punk rockers and the quantifiable content was music lyrics. I was interested in how the messages and message presenters changed over time paying particular attention to hegemonic and counter-hegemonic sentiments. The presupposition behind this study was that the content of songs and the lead singes of signed bands reflected the composition and values and beliefs of the larger underground punk scene because of the communal and small-scale nature of the movement. To compensate for this leap of faith I triangulated the results with qualitative analyses of the larger punk scene (see Malott and Pena, 2004). Further attempting to contextualize this study I provided a detailed description of myself as a gendered, raced, and classed *being* whose capacity to produce knowledge is always and unavoidably mediated by this positionality.

Because the knowledge produced through science is inseparable from the subjectivity of the producers, and therefore vulnerable to biased and inconsistent logic, it's reductionistic tendencies, from the beginning, lent themselves to supporting the interests of power by reducing science so narrowly it becomes an easily manipulatable abstraction. For example, the Industrial Revolution was the product of the ruling class harnessing the power of science leading to great advances in chemistry as the boss's pursued their definitive occupation of plunder and in turn sought "improved methods of manufacture," leading to "new chemical techniques in metallurgy, ceramics, and textiles, especially in textile dying and bleaching" (Hankins, 1985, p. 84). Improving the methods of manufacture, from the bosses perspective, also included the scientific management of human labor power most notably through the behaviorist practices of Taylorism. The practice of war has always been part of the process of plunder and also benefited greatly from science during the Industrial Revolution with major developments in gunpowder and navigation. The subsequent irresponsible *abuses* of science, which are praised and celebrated in the schools and the wider societies of the West as evidence of progress and Euro-supremacy, represent the abstraction of the concrete context of human suffering and environmental degradation from the theoretical context of technical knowledge production and the accumulation of unpaid labor hours, that is, capital/profit/surplus value.

However, there remains something powerful and highly relevant within Newton's insistence that science must be taught not through rote memorization, but through *analysis* because "the proper way to learn was to duplicate the process of discovery" (Hankins, 1985, p. 21). Holding true to this ideal in the teaching of all subject matter might serve as a reliable safeguard and movement against the above mentioned dangers and injustices of disconnecting the processes of teaching and learning from the political context in which they are always intimately situated. During the early Enlightenment leading scholars of the time, such as Descarte and others, it was assumed that what we can call the *constructivist* method of learning had universal applicability throughout all the sciences including ethics or moral philosophy suggesting that *the road or pathway is most efficiently and logically constructed through the process of traveling or walking.* The primary difference between early forms of constructivism and the critical constructivism of today, of course, is that knowledge is no longer viewed as objective, but socially constructed through experience.

However, to the credit of early Western scientists it was posited that *reason* was not just applicable to the natural or *exact* sciences, but also to the social sciences and politics. In other words, Enlightenment thinkers tended not to be hindered by an interpretation of the *hard* and *soft* sciences as unrelated subject matters, which is a reductionistic distortion of what amounts to interrelated aspects of the same world, and therefore the same worldview. The idea was that the tight logic of science based on objective reasoning could serve as a safe-guard against the illogical characteristics of bias that stem from the motivations of profit and the accumulation of wealth. When the minds of men and women are corrupted by greed and power, they become incapable of objective and reasonable action—in short, unbiased science. This perspective was informed by the belief that a "science of society" should be guided by "human nature and the mutual needs of men and women" (Hankins, 1985, p. 159), which were considered to be minimal and conducive to the intellectual endowments of the species. Again, it is worth restating that these ideas were not understood to be social constructs produced by social actors situated in a particular historical time period, but as objective reality transcending time and place.

What these scientists struggled to better understand was the *endowments of the mind*, which have been the stuff of great philosophical and scientific contemplation throughout the recorded history of the species. The essence of humanness has long been understood to reside in our capacity for self-reflection, and therefore to be conscious of our own consciousness. It is within this capacity that renders humans necessarily creative beings—it has long been understood to be a genetically determined species characteristic. Karl Marx contributed to this field of study in his observation that because our natural vocation consists of remaking the world in our own image, when our creative capacities are hindered, we suffer. In other words, when our labor power is externally commanded and bought as a commodity as part of the capitalist process of value production, as it currently is, we become alienated from the external world and ourselves. Because these arrangements go against the grain of our natural inclinations, a certain amount of force, coercion, and manipulation is required to manufacture the necessary compliance and prevent or suppress the expected resistance it engenders.

This socially constructed hegemonic practice has served as the primary tool through which the population has been indoctrinated to fear freedom and internalize a negative conception of self that is based on the labor-capital relationship, and therefore consent to our own oppression by creating a religion out of work as wage earners. In such a scenario we seldom attribute our psychological maladies and material deprivation to the external ruling elite interests that benefit greatly from controlling our labor power. However, when we *do* read our world and pay particularly close attention to observing where power lies and how it is exercised, we begin to disconnect our identities from a deterministic conception of self-as-worker and replace it with an awareness of the ways we are limited by capital, but not determined by it. In so doing, we enter the process of liberation and counter-hegemonization conscious of assumptions informing the knowledge we produce.

In other words, democracy has not only been viewed as possible, but it represents the natural state of human sociability. Political decisions, according to the scientific perspective of early Enlightenment thinkers, should therefore not be informed by the hierarchies and illogical assumptions of the past but by the insights of a universal social science respectful of the democratic needs of humanity. While such notions of an objective social order have been co-opted to maintain the homogenizing injustices of antiquity, contemporary proponents of the democratic values of the early Enlightenment, such as Noam Chomsky, essentially argue that the minimalist logic of natural rights remains relevant for protecting the rich diversity found within human culture.

This *objective* study of humans led leading figures such as John Locke to conclude that the inherent free will and tendency toward independence found within human behavior renders the possibility of predicting it with absolute certainty impossible. The course of study was therefore taken in the direction of *probability theory*—that is, given certain experiences it can be predicted with various levels of probability that humans will respond in whatever observed ways. Here can be found one example of an intersection between the social and exact sciences. That is, we can understand mathematics as one of the common modes of knowledge production within all of the sciences, which continues to be dominant in not only chemistry and physics, but in sociology, anthropology, and other related fields. Such endeavourers led to further inquiries into the inherently subjective nature of *human judgment* rendering mathematical predictability highly tenuous as compared to inanimate objects. For example, while one can predict the *probability of events* in games of chance, such as coin tosses, with a high level of certainty, similar predictions cannot be made in regards to human behavior for randomness and instinct—the driving forces of the non-human world—have been superceded by free will and the highly variable tendency of our socially constructed schemas.

Again, what this analysis suggests is that the interpretive framework through which the results of inquiry were understood was thus transformed turning science into a revolutionary tool to attack the hierarchies and injustices of antiquity, and mathematics was to lead the charge. The boss's current model of mathematics instruction, as noted above, on the other hand, has been thoroughly hegemonized in the settler-states' institutions of education in Canada, the United States and the Western world more generally, and represents a gross distortion of seventeenth and eighteenth century Western conceptions of objectivity. However, this history is not widely discussed amongst the academic Left. As a result, there is a tendency among postmodern scholars, alluded to above, to take the boss's conception of objectivity as the true and only model. For example, it is argued that notions of scientific objectivity allow scientists to hide behind a false sense of neutrality and engage in their practice as if they were operating in a vacuum. While this postmodern analysis is verifiably accurate in modern times, critical scientists such as Noam Chomsky (2000b) suggest that a complete abandonment of objectivity would also be a mistake and that "we should work hard to embrace it in our pursuit of truth" (p. 20) assuming that "knowledge exists independently of our minds in a never-changing, fixed state" (Kincheloe, 2005, p. 13). Holding true to Galileo, Newton, and others Enlightenment values and ideals Chomsky (2000b) is not ambiguous in his position when he argues that "the pretense of objectivity as a means to distort and misinform in the service of the doctrinal system should be sharply condemned" (p. 20).

However, Chomsky (2002), among many others, reminds us, when considering the history of Western science and mathematics, that "as always, there are precedents" (p. 48), rendering our present discussion in need of an exploration into one of Europe's primary intellectual influences, that is, the Islamic civilization that flourished after the fall of ancient Egypt and during Europe's post-Roman Dark Ages. Providing an excellent summary of this historic era Wayne Chandler (1992/2008), in "The Moor: Light of Europe's Dark Age," notes that "the great empires of ancient Africa," due to internal "stresses and conflicts" and waves of "foreign invaders," faded into oblivion after "thousands of years of achievement in art, science, and philosophy" that "for so long inspired the world" (p. 151). After this foundational period of early human civilization that flourished in Africa, "a new culture began to develop" within the heart of the Black world, Islam, that "would generate a resurgence of activity in the arts and sciences" that subsequently played a central role leading Europe out of its age of darkness (Chandler, 1992/2008, p. 151), which the West has systematically *miseducated* itself about (Kincheloe & Steinberg, 2004).

For example, contrary to what the West's history books would have the world believe, it is not a coincidence that the areas of Europe that first began to emerge from the barbarism of the Dark Ages were those most southern regions, such as Spain, that were in the closest contact with the colonizing Black, Islamic Moors from the East. Situating this history within the framework of colonialism Jan Carew (1992/2008) describes the Moorish invasion of southern Europe as a "civilizing mission" that successfully brought stability to the "factional European tribes and kingdoms," and, as a result, they "were able to direct their energies from fighting amongst themselves to studying the very philosophies and sciences that would propel them out of their insular perspectives" (p. 254). However, after the successful *Reconquista* in 1492 and the expulsion of the Moors from Spain and elsewhere in Europe, the Catholic Church in particular went to great lengths to erase "any and all reference to the great influence the Moors had on their subsequent development" (Carew, 1992/2008, p. 254). These anti-intellectual efforts mark the beginning of the West's anti-Islamic impulses that have persisted and even intensified in the contemporary, modern era.

While the hegemonic ruling classes of Western societies, the United States most notably, portrays Islam as a primitive, backwards, dogmatic, authoritarian form of misogynistic religious extremism, the historical work that attempts to follow a more rigorous scientific objectivity, as alluded to thus far, provides a much different account. That is, the scholarship points specifically to 711 A.D. as marking the beginning of the Moorish invasion and subsequent nearly thousand year occupation of southern Europe, Spain in particular, which, again, led to the revitalization and expansion of the knowledge of antiquity within certain segments of the European elite. The center of the intellectual knowledge that the invading Moors brought with them to Europe can be traced to the Science Academy in Cairo Egypt, which was regarded as a world leader in science, mathematics, medicine, the arts, and literature. According to Beatrice Lumpkin and Siham Zitzler (1992/2008), the "African scientists," using Arabic as the "common language of learning," successfully developed the ability to:

> Communicate with their colleagues over the vast stretches of Muslim influence, from Spain and Italy on the West across Africa and Asia, to China on the East. This

was also a period of expanded trade. Muslim traders pushed energetically into every known corner of the world, expanding their wealth, and more importantly, spreading knowledge of the new Muslim mathematics and science. The convenient Arabic numerals and arithmetic, which we use today, were adapted from India and brought into Europe by the Moors of North Africa. (p. 383).

From Lumpkin and Zitzler's analysis here it becomes clear that today's modern capitalist global economy would not have developed when it did if it were not for the Moorish influence in the areas of commerce, mathematics, and scientific knowledge production more generally. Others have commented on the admiration an untold number Europeans had for the non-dogmatic and scientific aspects of Islamic intellectual culture (Van Sertima, 1992/2008). For example, all of the major European universities emerged around the same time in the twelve and thirteenth centuries and took as universal texts translations of Islamic works in Mathematics and science. In an attempt to downplay the significance of Moorish influence it is often argued that Islamic scholars merely preserved and passed on the knowledge of antiquity ignoring the vast bodies of doctrine created at such foundational institutions as the Cairo Science Academy mentioned above. Lumpkin and Zitzler (1992/2008) humbly speculate that maybe "it was the mathematical sciences" that the Academy's influence was the greatest noting that "the very word algebra is an Arabic word, adopted in Europe to describe some of the new mathematics that the Moors had brought into Europe" (p. 385).

CRITICAL PEDAGOGY AND MATHEMATICS

The critical modern challenge is therefore to re-inscribe the ideals and values of the European Enlightenment, which can be attributed to both Islamic science and the democratic gifts from Indigenous confederations such as the Haudenosaunee/the Six Nations Iroquois, who continue to occupy small reserves of their traditional lands in Western New York and South Eastern Canada, despite tremendous odds, into the notions of objectivity informing all subject matter such as mathematics instruction. The critical constructivist challenge, on the other hand, is to put the democratic ideals of social justice to the task of demonstrating that all knowledge is socially constructed and all knowers are also constructors.

Situated within this context of critical constructivism there is currently a very productive and enlightening movement amongst critical educators to reform and rewrite the traditional curriculum by connecting it with constructivism and critical pedagogy—that is, critical constructivism—and therefore to teach "mathematics for social justice" (Gutstein, 2006, p. 23). Because the vast majority of us have been uncritically reared with the ideology of the dominant society, preservice-teachers tend to undergo a shift in paradigm if they choose to embrace critical pedagogy/ constructivism. For example, critical pedagogy challenges its practitioners to view the natural hierarchy of human intelligence paradigm not as either a correct or incorrect interpretation of objective truth, but as a more or less "valid" "construction" of "reality" because ideas do not exist outside the context of human creativity and imagination (Kincheloe, 2005, p. 43), not even mathematical or biological ideas. Rather than viewing perceived intellectual difference hierarchically, critical constructivism views it as both socially constructed and the result of multiple, equally valid and useful intelligences.

Instead of pursuing truth and certainty, critical constructivism seeks "richer" and more "cohesive" "insights" and "portraits" of "phenomena" that reflect the many "cultural and historical contexts in which the phenomena is found," thereby paving the way for inclusiveness and social justice for "marginalized groups" (Kincheloe, 2005, p. 44). The constructed nature of social phenomena such as poverty are therefore understood to be the result of abuses and prejudices that stem from imbalances and inequalities in political power rather than the result of assumed deficiencies of the individuals who are poor.

Related to this paradigm shift is the need to view oneself as an active agent in the construction of knowledge and, in turn, the development of history rather than a passive bystander in the unfolding of events. We might take insights from the *history of science* literature and note that "transformations like these, though usually... gradual and almost always irreversible, are common concomitants of scientific training" (Kuhn, 1996, p. 111). Putting this tendency of the critically trained educator in a slightly different way Kuhn (1996) observes that as a result of these transformations of perception they "become an inhabitant of the scientist's world, seeing what the scientist sees and responding as the scientist does" (p. 111).

The revolutionary transformations of perception that are necessary for teaching subject matter, such as math, for social justice, from a critical pedagogical perspective, entails, as fundamental curricular objectives, not only the mastery of the content, socially and historically situated, and therefore "seeing what the scientist sees and responding as the scientist does" (Kuhn, 1996, p. 111), but expanding on those insights through self-reflection and becoming part of a more just world—this is the critical component of critical constructivism that is "concerned with the exaggerated role power plays in...construction and validation processes" (Kincheloe, 2005, p. 3). The manifestation of this critically conscious constructivism requires the empowerment that stems from students, and social actors in general, viewing themselves as "valued for their abilities to contribute to, critique, and partake in a just society" (Roth & Barton, 2004, p. 5). One way critical pedagogues have addressed this challenge is to privilege the subjugated knowledges of oppressed groups as a primary epistemological source for curricular development. For example, Luis Ortiz-Franco (2005) in "Chicanos Have Math in Their Blood," writing from an *ethnomathematical* perspective, argues that while "the process of counting" across the world has remained universal throughout history, "the symbols by which they represented specific quantities varied according to their own particular cultural conventions" (p. 70).

However, ethnomathematics is a little known approach to the subject matter within today's standards-driven educational landscape. Ortiz-Franco (2005) focuses specifically on the omission of Mesoamerican contributions in public schools and colleges and universities. These irresponsible deficiencies can be overcome at all levels by incorporating a wide array of epistemological approaches to mathematical operations, which, according to Ortiz-Franco (2005), "will expose students to the sophisticated mathematical traditions of other cultures and demonstrate that performing mathematics is a universal human activity" (p. 71). For Chicanos in particular, "studying pre-Columbian mathematics will allow them to learn more about their ancestors," and, as a result, contribute to the critical pedagogical goal of empowerment and movement-building against suffering and abuse. Highlighting the importance of such a program in the contemporary era Ortiz-Franco (2005) notes that, "despite a long and distinguished heritage in the sciences, arts, and letters in their own culture, Chicanos are one of the least educated groups in the country" largely due to the colonialist process of domination that has disregarded (or not given due credit) "the achievements of conquered indigenous civilizations" (p. 71).

The Native North American democratic impulse that provided the egalitarian spark that ignited the epistemological curiosity of Europe's intellectual community and working classes during the sixteenth and seventeenth centuries can provide Native Americans with a similarly empowering analysis as Ortiz-Franco's (2005) ethnomathematics. These insights are not only emancipatory for Native Americans, but they can provide people of European descent a conception of self not tied up in a false sense of superiority and the resulting debilitation of white guilt. The Indigenous aspects of Western science and mathematics also offers white people a respectful and democratic connection to indigeneity that can lead to socially just praxis largely absent within hegemonic schooling practices.

In action/practice a critical pedagogical approach to teaching and learning mathematics involves students and teachers "using mathematics...as an educational practice to analyze and affect society" (Gutstein, 2006, p. 23) while celebrating the rich history of the radical Enlightenment and the invaluable insights and gifts from Indigenous communities, cautious not to romanticize either. Gutstein (2006) draws on Freire's (2005) notion of reading the word and the world in his approach to mathematical literacy that draws on the analytical tools of the discipline to better understand "the sociopolitical, cultural-historical conditions of one's life, community, society, and world" (p. 24). Situating this challenge in a larger context we might begin by observing that virtually every major aspect of social life in the contemporary era—from warfare, to the human genome project, to economics—involves increasingly complex manifestations of numeric epistemology. Within this framework, mathematical literacy can be understood as fundamental to acquiring the competence necessary for reading the world and actively participating in the unfolding of history.

One of the most celebrated mathematical tools that social justice educators make use of in their attempts to assist their students in learning to read their world and combat number numbness is the concept of *percent*. Percent is a powerful tool because of its simplicity, which can provide clear, comparative images of large and highly complex contexts marked by vastly unequal distributions of power and wealth. Presenting a similar argument Bob Peterson (2005) comments that "an understanding of math and how numbers and statistics can be interpreted is essential to effectively enter most debates on public issues such as welfare, unemployment, and the federal budget" (p. 10). Another aspect of the concrete context mentioned above, the global water crisis, would be almost unintelligible without the use of percent, a seemingly rudimentary analytical devise. For example, the rate of water consumption is doubling every twenty years with the two leading consumers of water, globally, being agribusiness with their vast and highly inefficient irrigation systems and the telecommunications industry in the production of computer chips. As a result, it has been estimated by the United Nations that by 2025, less than twenty years, two-thirds of the world's population will be living in a context of serious *water shortage* and one-third living in *absolute water scarcity* (Juhasz, 2006).

Given these material conditions, it is not surprising that even the mouthpieces and regulating agencies of capital, such as *The New York Times* and the World Bank, have warned that water will soon take the place of oil as the primary driving force of international markets and the next major wars will be over this infinitely more valuable substance (Juhasz, 2006). Situating this crisis in an even larger global context Antonia Juhasz (2006) notes that "given the increased scarcity of water, a global race to privatize and commodify the planet's remaining water is already well under way, with billions of dollars at stake" (p. 109). That is, the water business, as it were, is already a four hundred billion dollar industry (Juhasz, 2006). Juhasz (2006) notes that as the world's fresh water reserves dry up, corporate plunderers put increasing pressure on "places where Indigenous peoples have maintained their resources and traditional uses" (p. 109). Indeed, from the beginning of Europe's colonization of the Americas colonialists were always set on taking over the most water-rich and inherently wealthy regions, rendering current trends part of that much older legacy. However, these attempts to privatize the planet have not been met without opposition as the global movement against neoliberal privatization has reminded us as they have made real gains in what we might call the communalization of water. Summarizing the potential of this movement Juhasz (2006) comments that "the good news is that during the last few years, a tremendous wave of resistance to the privatization of water has emerged on every continent, with some very notable early successes" (p. 109)—in a word, hope.

Central to critical pedagogy is this notion that hope, however tenuous it may seem at times, can never be completely lost because it is an ontological need (Freire, 2005) of the species. We can explain this *need* arising out of the genetically determined creative use of language, which is infinite in both its newness and the possibility for increasingly complex sentences that remain comprehensible. This character trait of the species requires that the individual language user be in control of her own creative capacities/labor power and therefore interacting with other humans and the world as an intuitively-engaged, independent, democratic agent. When fully matured adult humans spend the majority of their days with their labor power externally controlled as wageworkers, as the vast majority currently, and in the foreseeable future, do, their creative use of language in the making and re-making of the world is suppressed, and, consequently, they tend to feel oppressed, stifled, alienated, stressed, and so on. While these impulses, and the critical insights they engender, can be suppressed or misguided through the process of hegemony, they cannot be completely wiped clean because that would require a genetic alteration, which, thankfully, is not possible. Again, critical constructivism challenges this Western scientific approach to knowledge production to rethink the certainty and epistemological exclusiveness its conclusions suggest. While these Western scientific interpretations of phenomena undeniably do contain some valid constructions, they represent only one perspective.

In other words, the usefulness of this Western philosophy resides in the conclusion that our *most special gift*, commonly known as *free will*, is part of our biological endowment guaranteeing, with a fair amount of certainty, that the presence of a hegemony will *always* manifest a counter-hegemony, as Gramsci (1971) theorized. Simply stated: when humans are oppressed, they have a natural propensity to resist, which is as widespread as it is varied in its manifestation ranging from private thoughts of grievance to full-blown, organized and integrated revolutionary movements. Encouraging and advancing this tendency toward movement for social justice is the work of critical pedagogy. The task of critical pedagogues is therefore to connect the learning of concepts, such as *percent*, to the concrete context of the world and the lives of the students, which are all interconnected by many systems, both human-made, such as global capitalism, and those that are naturally occurring like ecosystems, but all dependent for survival on the Earth's finite stream of what amounts to be an increasingly polluted and squandered supply of fresh water.

Gutstein and Peterson's (2005) *Rethinking Mathematics: Teaching Social Justice by the Numbers* offers teachers many such practical teaching examples and ideas about "how to weave social justice issues throughout the mathematics curriculum and how to integrate mathematics into other curricular areas" (p. 1). For example, in "Poverty and World Wealth" Susan Hersh and Bob Peterson (2005) provide an introductory example of how to engage students in critical understandings of the relationship between poverty and wealth placed in a global context. This lesson combines math, geography, writing and the social studies. The first part of the activity engages students in thinking about the regions where the world's population of approximately six billion people is concentrated. The next component challenges learners to compare where the world's wealth is located and how that differs from where people are concentrated. The goal is to push student thinking about the nature of the labor/capital relationship. Some possible discussion questions that might facilitate the development of student thinking are presented here as a call to action:

- How did the accumulation of wealth come to be the dominant economic goal of the world?
- How did the distribution of wealth get to be so unequal?
- Who do you think decides how wealth is distributed?
- Should wealth be distributed equally?
- Is the accumulation of wealth the best goal for a population to pursue?
- Who creates wealth, workers or the stock market?
- What is the relationship between rich and poor?
- Within our community is wealth distributed equally?
- What can be done about the unequal distribution?
- Who could we contact to find out more?

A final and on-going component of these types of engagements should always include writing and reflection. In other words, writing is a central aspect of critical learning because it provides an opportunity for students to logically think through how they see their new insights informing their practice in the world. Students can do follow-up research on related topics such as: the role colonialism and neo-colonialism have played and are playing in global poverty, for example. However, these issues and studies should be part of larger curricular reformations. In the short term, on the other hand, critical engagements with teaching and learning can be aligned with, and substantiated by, current learning standards, which is not a difficult task given their vague nature.

CHAPTER NINE

Native American Literacies and the Language Arts Curriculum

The rich traditions of Native American literature are explored in terms of how they have and *can* enhance mainstream conceptions of what is ontologically and epistemologically possible in both the written and oral traditions. What is underscored is the powerful use of narrative and story in fostering critical consciousness in the critical pedagogical sense. The data informing much of this chapter was collected and analyzed by Candy on the Menominee Indian Reservation in the classroom of a veteran traditional Menominee teacher, Mrs. Teller (see *Appendix A* for an example of her unpublished work critically analyzing the Poem of Hiawatha).

* * *

An appropriate place of departure for our present discussion centered on the *language arts* curriculum, which, in Western-based societies such as the United States and Canada, has been dominated by Euro-centric conceptions of literacy, might be the oral traditions Indigenous to many Native American Nations. Contextualizing this writing-centric justification for the civil-savage scale, and therefore the paternalistic practice of colonization and subjugation, Linda Tuhimai Smith (2005) notes that, "writing has been viewed as the mark of a superior civilization and other societies have been judged, by this view, to be incapable of thinking critically and objectively, or having distance from ideas and emotions" (pp. 28–29).

Similarly, James Paul Gee (2008) challenges the view that writing, on one hand, and oral traditions, on the other, are two separate stages on the same universal, hierarchal scale of development, and instead, argues that they represent the social and cultural variability of human difference. That is, the difference between oral-based and writing-based cultures is not biological or predetermined but rather socially constructed. Clarifying his position Gee (2008) notes that what *is* the result of the species' genetic code, and therefore universal, is the use of "lines and stanzas," which he goes on to conclude are "the products of mental mechanisms by which humans produce speech" (p. 130). The difference between how distinct cultural groups use this propensity for organized language, from this perspective, should not be understood as evidence of less advanced and more advanced civilizations, but the result of naturally occurring epistemological diversity worthy of great celebration and encouragement. However, because the historical record clearly shows that globally-oppressive European colonizers have and continue to demonstrate a strong bias to subjugate that which is considered to be non-Western ways of knowing, students who have "retained substantive ties with an oral culture" (Gee, 2008, p. 130) tend to possess discourse styles not valued by schools and their overwhelmingly Eurocentric learning standards and goals, pedagogy, and curriculum.

The Native Oral Tradition: A Brief Introduction

The folktales and fairytales, the myths and legends, and the tall tales and fables that children love today came from the oral tradition (Savage, 2000). All cultures and societies had or have an oral tradition where culture, traditions, and history were passed down from generation to generation by word of mouth. Today there are approximately 500 different tribes who speak 200 different languages in the United States. All of these tribes passed their history, culture, and customs on to their children through the oral tradition because very few had a written alphabet. Many Native Americans still have a strong oral tradition today that impacts their lives.

For example, the Inupiat people of Point Hope Alaska are living proof of the power of the oral tradition. Sakakibara (2008) studied the use of storytelling by the Inupiat as a coping mechanism for climate changes their environment is encountering with global warming. Inupiat storytelling helps them make important connections to places and people in their changing world. McCeough, et al. (2008) advocate the use of oral storytelling by teachers and students because they see it as a precursor to reading and writing for Aboriginal children in Canada. They argue that oral narrative "fits with Aboriginal epistemology—the nature of their knowledge, its foundation, scope and validity" (p. 148). They hope to develop a program incorporating culturally appropriate oral storytelling to support early literacy development.

The Menominee Indian Tribe of Wisconsin provides another rich example of a Native American Tribe who has a strong oral tradition. The Tribe has had and continues to have many great orators. The best speakers were able to tell the people stories as they spoke. In the old days certain tribal members by virtue of their clan affiliation were designated as speakers for the Tribe. Al Dodge, Gordon Dickie, Mani Boyd, and Earl Wescott were some of the great contemporary Menominee leaders who spoke at various tribal functions. Their voices and their verbalization and their prose were truly spellbinding.

In fact, Al Dodge was called the senator by his fellow Menominee because of his gifted oratory and the ability to distill issues to their simplest form. During some of the most difficult times for Menominee people, he was significant part of negotiations. Dolores Boyd called him the smartest Menominee to ever live.

THE POWER OF MENOMINEE STORYTELLING AND ORAL TRADITION

It is implicit in the Menominee oral tradition that the power is in the spoken word (Teller, 1985). This does not mean the stories themselves are sacred, but in telling them the people are recalling the collective memory of deceased relatives. Storytelling in Menominee tradition is a valued skill and naturally pedantic. It is the domain of the elders and both males and females may participate. No summation is given to the stories as they are told, for it is believed that every person must determine the meaning of the story for himself or herself. The stories shared in the following pages demonstrate the beauty and value of the oral tradition. Because these stories were not originally designed to be written texts, thanks must therefore be extended to the Menominee Elders who told these stories over the years knowing they would be reproduced in books.

The first example we highlight below is a creation story because all cultures and societies have their own unique versions of creation stories (Campbell, 1988). Many Menominee children are familiar with the following story that tells us the genesis of the Menominee Nation:

> We begin at the beginning. This is the story of the origin of the Menominee and our organization of the cosmos. It is said that the Menominee people descend from a Great Bear who sprang from the earth, and became a fair skinned man. He was alone until he called the Eagle to join him, and the Eagle became human. Soon all of the other animals saw them and they took human form. Yet, all was not well with this world; the evil Underground Spirits did not like to see what was happening, and set out to destroy the human beings. The Creator felt sorry for the human beings, and did not want them to fall prey to the murderous Underground Spirits, so he sent Thunderbird to protect them. Everything was good for awhile until the

Underground Spirits grew too powerful, and Thunderbird could no longer beat them back. So the Menominee sent their best young men out to fast and pray for help. The young men went without food and offered their pain as a gift to the Creator. They rubbed dirt on their faces, believing that they were deriving strength from the earth. The young men then set out alone, separate from one another, and began to observe all the while praying for their safety. After some time past the men began to return to the camp. As they returned, one by one, they began to recount the same vision: Each man saw a Grandfather in the four directions. He spoke to them and told them to go back and tell the people what they had seen. He instructed them not to worry, but to know that the Spirits of the four directions were sent to help the people. Thereafter the Menominee have paid homage to the Guardian Sprits of the four directions. (Teller 1985)

The story tells us that the Creator is everywhere, just like the Grandfathers that dwell in the four directions. Additionally, this story represents the roots of the Pipe Ceremony we see in Menominee culture today. It is said that to turn the pipe skyward with the stem offered to the Spirits of the four directions is like smoking with God. Promises and prayers made within this ceremony are therefore sacred. Within the religious dances the special drum that is used is treated like it is our Grandfather; it has a spirit. It is carefully cared for and never touches the earth without a blanket covering.

Another story that is commonly known by Menominee people today relates to a monument on Wisconsin State Highway 55, called Spirit Rock. Many people do not know this, but there are many Spirit Rocks. Here are the stories that tell us how the rocks gained a spirit, and how Maeqnapus, the son of the sun, came to live with the Menominee:

> According to legend there were six young people who, in defiance of tradition, decided they were going to play lacrosse at night. They painted a ball white and stealthily left the camp after sundown. They played a rambunctious game; causing the ball to be tossed further and further away from the camp, until, they suddenly realized that they had been victims of magic. The ball they had been chasing all night had become a white rabbit: it led them to the water's edge and no one remembered the way back home. The evil spirits rose up, ready to devour them, when suddenly Saba, a good giant, came to their rescue. Saba took them on his shoulders and carried them away from the evil spirits, over to an island in the middle of the lake. The young people were frightened and knew that they were in the throes of a great wonder. They sat down together and decided they must be very careful about what they would do next. A voice spoke to them and asked them what they desired. They agreed they must ask for something to help their people. Each of them stepped forward and spoke to the voice: I ask to be a great hunter so I can feed my people, I ask to know medicine so I can heal the people, I wish to be a great speaker so I can lead the people, and so on. The last young man to speak thought to himself, "My brothers have all asked for

gifts for our people so it shouldn't matter if I ask for something I want." He stepped forward and said to the voice, "The thing I desire most is not to have to suffer and die. I want to live forever." The voice answered, "Granted."

The young people fell into a deep sleep. When they awoke they saw a blinding light coming from the east (the sun), and from the light a man came toward them. He told them he was the child of the sun. He was sent to take them home and to teach them all the things they needed to know. The young person that had the temerity to ask for everlasting life was turned to stone; a rock lasting longer that a lifetime.

There came a time when the Menominee were dying from a smallpox epidemic. They had no resistance to illnesses of the respiratory system, but this one was especially deadly. Those that lived were unwilling to go on when they saw their scarred faces; many committed suicide. The Menominee knew that this plague was brought to them by the United States Army. The Army had given them blankets in Peshtigo and soon after the epidemic swept through the Tribe. The people were desperate, they asked the Creator for help. He sent a dream to the people that they would find a rock, it would be in the shape of a human, and they were to make offerings to the rock. The Manito would hold the destiny of the people within it; from now on they would be like the rock, when the rock crumbles, and is no more, the Menominee would be extinct.

The old people remember when the rock was large and in the shape of a man, but now it is small and its mass is indistinguishable. There was a time when the Menominee would ride by, in horse and buggy, and place their offering without leaving their mount. Many believe it was the tourist that came and hacked off pieces of the rock for souvenir. No one knows for certain what has happened, but for sure the rock has nearly disappeared. (Teller 1985)

Through the Spirit Rock story, the strength Menominee derived from the mother earth can be appreciated. The story also delineates the respect and connection between the people and the earth. In the 1920s the anthropologists, George and Louise Spindler, came to study and write about the Menominee people. Mrs. Teller's father remembered them talking with his grandmother, Sally Corn, about Menominee culture and traditions. They wrote a book that they called *Dreamers Without Power,* which was clearly a play on the idea the Menominee had about themselves as important dreamers. Later the title was changed to *Dreamers With Power* when the book was reissued. Here is a common story that is told about Menominee dreamers:

> The old people say that the Menominee were noted for the ability to dream dreams that foretold the future. It came to pass that Tecumseh sought the predictions of the Menominee Dreamers. Tecumseh was a great Shawnee leader of the 17th century. It was his vision that all nations must join together to push the English, French, and Spaniards out of this country. He believed that we could reclaim our lost lands if the Indian people all banded together. He traveled the waterways speaking to the bands he found there. He needed to win the Great Lakes coalition if he was to succeed. He sought council with the Menominee Dreamers because he knew that their

vision would sway all the other tribes in the area. The Dreamers told the council that there was no way that Tecumseh could win; they had seen that the invader was like the leaves in the trees, in the autumn they die, but in the spring they always come back, more in number. It would be useless to fight them because they could not be destroyed. (Teller 1985)

Joseph Campbell (1988), one of the foremost experts on mythology, said that dreams are a part of our mythic imagination. He believed that dreams are a part of our spirit. Myths are public dreams we all share. There was a time in Menominee history when the bands had not yet organized themselves into a tribal group and clans. There is a story of how this came about:

> Long ago the people were divided by a river. The Bear on one side and the Eagle on the other. There was plenty of fish for everyone until the Awassa people damned the river, and the sturgeon no longer came to the Kinew waters. The Eagle leader sent his son to ask his Awassa uncle to remove the dam and let them share the fish. The Awassa said yes he would remove the dam and let them share the fish; Awassa then grabbed the young Kinew and branded him in the forehead with a copper marking iron. He laughed and sent the boy back to his people. The young Kinew was humiliated and covered his face with his robe. He told his father that the Bear agreed to remove the dam; but when his father saw how Awassa had cruelly marked his son he became enraged. Kinew sent a war party to the Awassa camp. When the Eagle caught up with the elder Awassa he tied him up and stuffed his mouth with fish. The Kinew said, "From now on your name will Akwinemay because you are always chewing!" A long time later a council was called. The Awassa was traveling to it, took the wrong route, and began going up the Wisconsin peninsula. He realized his mistake too late, and he knew he would not have time to double back and still make it to the council. The Eagle flew overhead and understood Awassa's difficulty. He came down from the sky and offered to share his wing with the Bear. Awassa wondered if this could be done. They both agreed it would not be easy but they were willing to try it. It is said, that with great difficulty, the Eagle flew the Bear over the escanabe, at the mouth of the Menominee river, to the place of the minikani. From then on the Menominee people did not make war on one another and became a tribe. (Teller 1985)

The Eagle and the Bear story is about the importance of sharing within tribal society. This story is a wonderful example of the value of sharing that is so commonly attributed to Native American culture. Another part of Menominee culture that contains examples of the relevance and importance of the oral tradition can be found in a study of ceremonial names. Metaphor used in naming ceremonies worked to reinforce desirable behavior; it was sometimes used for healing purposes and was an integral part of an individual's social identity. Metaphor in naming was non-generic, and designed for the individual's clan, deed, or disposition. Children were not given names at birth for it was believed that they belonged to the women until they had shown they were ready for a name (usually around eight years old). The occasion of name giving was a feast and family gathering. It was proper for the elder to name the child through dreams, which he or she sought months before the time of naming. At the naming ceremony the elder would lay hands on the child and pronounce their new name in unison, usually following the naming there was a great deal of discussion as to the origins and meaning of the name. (Before a child given a name he or she is called by fondness given to them by the women.) Yet, there were occasions when it became necessary to attempt a cure for colic.

There is the story of an infant that cried constantly, and his parents could not soothe him. His family became distraught and sought the help of a man that was known for his gift of prophecy, and his ability to speak to babies. The "Dreamer" concluded that the child wanted a Menominee name right away. A feast was called and the child was named Saba. Saba was a good giant that had carried six young men away from the cannibalistic Moyaki. The boy baby became like Saba; a good strong man who would help his people.

Sometimes, one name was not enough for an individual. It was believed that a good name could alter or strengthen a person's karma. Mani Boyd, a respected Menominee elder and native speaker, told the following story about himself. When he was a small boy his mother and sisters called him Mamahkatehkamek, which means, wonderful. Later he was named Kuhkiw. Kuhkiw is the Menominee word for the lumberjack bird. Kuhkiw is noted for being a bird that steals, often swooping into camp unannounced. It became apparent, as Mani grew into adolescence, that the name Kuhkiw was having a detrimental effect on his behavior. It was decided that he needed a new name. Kuhkiw, a bird that steals, became Napus. Napus literally means lead rabbit, but we must refer to it's mythological origins to fully understand the metaphor involved. The lead rabbit refers to the wapus spirit that posed as a white ball to fool lively young people. In the story the adolescents were led to meet Maeqnapus, the teacher of all good things, and they learn to accept the responsibilities of adulthood. Napus is the spirit that leads young people to wisdom.

This underscores the fact that the Menominee felt some energy derived from language. It is also clear that great care went into the creation and tailoring of each person's name metaphor. This indicates two important concepts in Menominee culture, which many people believe today. They placed great importance in the individual and believed their names could help them. Naming incorporates four major themes: description of natural phenomena, historical and mythological events is characters, extraordinary accomplishment, and a view of the cosmos.

> The old people have said that it is believed that when we die we no longer need our name. When we leave this world our name becomes the property of our relatives, who

are free to give it away to someone else. It is our duty to keep our name unblemished, so that the next one receiving it will be getting a good name (Teller, 1985).

In Menominee culture a person is judged by what he gives away and by how well he gets along. Spiritual power is very important and it is a complex entity. It is important to achieve old age and wisdom, which not all Menominee people are able to do. In European culture, material wealth is the measure of success and the means of acquiring it become uppermost in their society. Spiritual power, its acquisition and maintenance is what dominates Menominee culture and story.

Other Examples of the Oral Tradition

The Iroquois Confederacy represents another extraordinary example of the oral tradition. Gifted speakers recite every year in the Longhouse The Great Law of the Iroquois Confederacy from memory. They have learned the law from attending ceremonies and by being mentored by older speakers. This process has been in existence for at least 1000 years. This recitation takes approximately eight days and utilizes only wampum beads to mark the order and progress of the recitation. It should be kept in mind that older speakers will correct the younger speakers in a discreet way during the recitation.

In addition, since 1799 the Code of Handsome Lake is recited every other year. This recitation takes about four days. The Great Law tells Iroquois people how to treat each other. It outlines the roles of mothers, fathers, children, clans, and the Nation. The Code of Handsome Lake deals with how Iroquois people are to interact with non-Indians and their influence on the Iroquois. Anthropologist William Fenton adds validity to the Iroquois oral tradition. He first heard the Great Law in the 1930s at the Cold Springs Longhouse and did not hear it again until the 1960s. He recorded little or no change in the recitation.

Through the last 200 years, Native American leaders have spoken eloquently about Native American issues and history. Red Jacket from the Seneca, Chief Seattle from the Duwamish and Chief Joseph of the Nez Perce were all considered great orators in their time and have left a legacy of wisdom in their words that have been saved for posterity. We wish to share some snippets of their well-known speeches to show the beauty of their language and their inherent wisdom.

Red Jacket in 1805 spoke to missionaries who wanted to convert the Seneca to Christianity. Red Jacket was chosen by the Seneca women to speak for them at Council and this is where his power came. In the 1800s, Red Jacket's words were recorded and printed in the *New York Times*. The following is his "You have got our country, but are not satisfied; you want to force your religion upon us" speech from Bliasdell's *Great Speeches By Native American:*

> There was a time when our forefathers owned this great island. Their seats extended from the rising to the setting sun. The Great Spirit had made it for the use of Indians. He had created the buffalo, the deer and other animals for food. He had made the bear and the beaver. Their skins served us for clothing. He had scattered them over the country and taught us how to take them. He had caused the earth to produce corn for bread. All this he had done for his red children because he loved them. If we had some disputes about our hunting ground, they were generally settled without the shedding of much blood. But an evil day came upon us. Your forefathers crossed the great water and landed upon this island. Their numbers were small. They found us friends and not enemies. They told us they had fled from their own country on account of wicked men, and had come here to enjoy their religion. They asked for a small seat. We took pity on them and granted their request, and they sat down amongst us. We gave them corn and meat; they gave us poison [rum] in return.
>
> The white people, brother, had now found our country. Tidings were carried back, and more came amongst us. Yet we did not fear them. We took them to be friends. They called us brothers; we believed them, and gave them a larger seat. At length their numbers had greatly increased. They wanted more land; they wanted our country. Our eyes were opened, and our minds became uneasy. Wars took place. Indians were hired to fight against Indians, and many of our people were destroyed. They also brought strong liquor amongst us. It was strong and powerful and has slain thousands.
>
> Brother, our seats were once large, and yours were small. You have now become a great people, and we have scarcely a place left to spread our blankets. You have got our country, but are not satisfied; you want to force your religion upon us.
>
> Brother, continue to listen. You say that you are sent to instruct us how to worship the Great Spirit agreeable to his mind; and if we do not take hold of the religion which you white people teach, we shall be unhappy hereafter. You say that you are right, and we are lost. How do we know this to be true? We understand that your religion is written in a book. If it was intended for us as well as you, why has not the Great Spirit given to us—and not only to us, but to our forefathers—the knowledge of that book, with the means of understanding it rightly? We only know what you tell us about it. How shall we know when to believe, being so often deceived by the white people?
>
> Brother, you say there is but one way to worship and serve the Great Spirit. If there is but one religion, why do you white people differ so much about it? Why not all agree, as you can all read the book?
>
> Brother, we do not understand these things. We are told that your religion was given to your forefathers, and has been handed down from father to son. We, also, have a religion which was given to our forefathers, and has been handed down to us, their children. We worship in that way. It teaches us to be thankful for all the favors we receive; to love each other, and be united. We never quarrel about religion, because it is a matter which concerns each man and the Great Spirit.
>
> Brother, we do not wish to destroy your religion or take it from you; we only want to enjoy our own.

Red Jacket's perspective is important because it disrupts the colonizers' mythology that Europeans came to the Americas and paternalistically *gave* the primitive savages, that is, *Indians*, the comforts of civilization in return for land. This mythology that permeates settler-state schools cannot be attributed solely to innocent social amnesia, as the apologists would have us believe, because counter-evidence is so abundant. The historical misinformation that red Jacket's analysis subverts serves a larger more purposeful function, which is to provide a national story that legitimizes the basic structures of power. The American public possesses a national identity that is just and democratic. *The truth*, as it were, can thus engender a crisis in legitimacy for the ruling class/elite. Searching for a truly democratic education consequently brings us to the view from below and a genuine engagement with subjugated knowledges. Let us therefore continue hearing such marginalized and ignored voices from Indigenous master orators.

Chief Seattle has been written about a great deal and there are numerous websites dedicated to his life and legacy. Unfortunately, there is considerable debate about what the true text of his speech was (Nodelman, 1999; Stott, 1995). Translations of speeches were always an issue for Native Americans and often caused problems in regard to treaty agreements because the accuracy depended on the skill and honesty of the interpreter. Here is one of his recorded speeches from 1854:

> Your God seems to us to be partial. He came to the white man. We never saw Him; never heard His voice; He gave the white man laws but He had no word for His red children whose teeming millions filled this vast continent as the stars fill the firmament. No, we are two distinct races and must ever remain so. There is little in common between us. The ashes of our ancestors are sacred and their final resting place is hallowed ground, while you wander away from the tombs of your fathers seemingly without regret.
>
> Your religion was written on tables of stone by the iron finger of an angry God, lest you might forget it. The red man could never remember nor comprehend it.
>
> Our religion is the traditions of our ancestors, the dreams of our old men, given to them by the Great Spirit, and the visions of our sachems, and is written in the hearts of our people. (Blaisdell, 2000)

Like red Jacket, Chief Seattle clearly highlights the contradiction of a religion that claims to represent all of humanity, but was supposedly only given to an elite few by God. The value of pointing out such glaring contradictions serves a counter-hegemonic function in the critical thinking of democratic praxis, and therefore embodies an incalculable usefulness. One of the most famous and documented Native American speeches is Chief Joseph's speech "I will fight no more forever" represents one of the more interesting examples. Chief Joseph supposedly spoke these words when he surrendered to General Oliver Howard at Eagle Creek Montana on October 5, 1877. Chief Joseph was a Nez Perce Indian from Washington, who valiantly fought the onslaught of the white man:

> Tell General Howard I know his heart. What he told me before I have in my heart. I am tired of fighting. Our chiefs are killed. Looking Glass is dead. Too-hul-hul-sote is dead. The old men are all dead. It is the young men who say yes or no. He who led on the young men is dead. It is cold and we have no blankets. The little children are freezing to death. My people, some of them, have run away to the hills, and have no blankets, no food; no one knows where they are-perhaps freezing to death. I want to have time to look for my children and see how many of them I can find. Maybe I shall find them among the dead. Hear me, my chiefs. I am tired; my heart is sick and sad. From where the sun now stands I will fight no more forever. (Blaisdell, 2000)

These speeches are noteworthy because of the importance of the oral tradition to Native people. Guthrie (2007) observed that Euro-Americans "relished being able to penetrate Indian speakers and believed oratory rendered the otherwise obscured native accessible" (p. 522). Furthermore, he argues that Euro-Americans, in an attempt to discredit their potentially counter-hegemonic insights, portrayed Native people as *children of nature* who were in a more primitive developmental stage than their European counterparts. Many European writers of the nineteenth century therefore led their audiences to believe that Native orators had to rely on metaphor due to the poverty of the languages. Again, it is the hierarchy of civilizations paradigm that those working to ensure the continued occupation of Indigenous lands draw on in the manufacture of legitimacy.

Traditional Storytelling in the Menominee Classroom Today

Leslie Teller teaches remedial reading and junior English at Menominee Indian High School in Keshena, Wisconsin. She has been a teacher for over 20 years and regularly uses storytelling as a part of her teaching—stories she learned from various Menominee elders throughout the years. Many of the stories noted above are the very stories Mrs. Teller tells her students.

As a child Mrs. Teller, who was born and raised on the Menominee Indian Reservation, always loved stories. Her earliest memory is when she was very young and thought she saw "little people" walking on her windowsill. Her grandmother was taking care of her at the time and she was not at all afraid. A good storyteller, her stepfather, Mani Boyd, taught her storytelling. She pursued her interest in storyteller and has collected many stories over the years.

As an educator, she had to look at what works with children in teaching them to control impulsivity and to try to socialize them in a good way. She believes that these are things storytelling does. For example, all storytelling asks the listener to be quiet and put him or herself in a state where they are receptive to language and imagery. This is not always an easy task for children to do.

In the Menominee way, it is important to realize that stories mean something different to each person at different ages. In other words, there is not just one correct way to interpret a story. Age of the listener, for example, effects how one sees the world, and therefore how they understand and interpret stories. Students will often say they have heard a story before. But it should be noted that a story might mean one thing at age four and another at age fourteen. This is not like television. Students are told that this is a story you need to remember so you can tell this story again to someone else. Mrs. Teller lets her students know that these stories were told to her several times so she could learn them and could thus tell them again.

As mentioned previously, stories are considered sacred because they are from the collective memory of ancestors. Consequently, Teller begins to tell stories in the early winter during the traditional time for storytelling. *When the snow comes* is the traditional time for storytelling for the Menominee and other Native Americans.

Mrs. Teller has come to the conclusion, after decades of practice, that storytelling represents an important component of a successful pedagogue. Students seem to appreciate and enjoy the storytelling days. Many times they ask for storytelling, but she sets asides a special storytelling time on Fridays. Her storytelling is ritualized. Students are told that they cannot make fun of the language and the Indian words used in the stories. They are expected to respect the story and the words within the stories because they come from the ancestors. It is expected that all students respect these predetermined rules, regardless of what difficulties they may be faced with in their lives. This sends the message that all students are capable of learning, even if they are poor and have many problems. This is a democratic choice Mrs. Teller consistently makes. Even though classroom management can be difficult with Menominee children, Mrs. Teller does not have a problem getting students to follow her rules.

Mrs. Teller has occasionally taught mixed classes of Natives and non-Natives Native mythology. In such contexts Teller reported differences she observed between non-Menominee children and Menominee children. Native American children have a special place in their culture for the oral tradition. She believes that this is not something Native people have lost. Natives, unlike non-Natives, have retained this respect for storytelling. It has given Menominee children a reverence for language because it is a ritualized form of oration. Students become very involved in the storytelling process and are almost transported to another place.

Teller observed that when she is telling a story and there is a disturbance (if the phone rings or if someone comes to the door or knocks on the door) the students are awakened like someone startled them from sleep. It seems like a hypnotic state and there is a relaxation and receptiveness to this experience on the part of her students.

The process engenders language development observed by the rich student discussions after the storytelling is over. This is another aspect of successful pedagogy, that is, ensuring there is sufficient time for students to speak and create knowledge collectively. Teller believes that this is important because students have their own stories to tell. The difficulty with Native American storytelling is that each story is connected to the other, and Native Americans, because of life experiences, sometimes have low attendance rates. That is, the stories are interconnected and in order to go to the next week they have to be there for the first installment. These are stories that are sequential and so students have to understand foundational knowledge such as why Maeqnapus is a trickster and a demigod.

Part of the reason that Teller surmises that she is successful with the storytelling in the classroom is that the students are hungry for knowledge about themselves. There is no better place to find it, but in the traditional stories. Stories teach traditional values such as the importance of the Menominee language, reverence for silence, and to respect and foster a silence within their own minds. It validates Menominee students and their human experience. Teller sees a need for more teachers to become storytellers and she thinks it should be a part of the curriculum. She maintains that storytelling can be "powerfully healing, powerfully soothing" and it can help children to learn. Storytelling could be considered a part of Native American mental traditions. As educators, it is important to build on the strengths of the student. The oral tradition is a positive attribute of many Native American children and should not be disregarded when exploring every avenue to increase their success.

In addition to using storytelling in her classroom, Teller uses Longfellow's *The Song of Hiawatha* in her junior English classes to teach pre civil war literature. The students are enthralled with Longfellow's work. In fact, she had a group of University of Wisconsin student teachers observing her classroom and they were amazed at how engaged they were. In analyzing the poem, Teller has become convinced that Longfellow patterned the story after Maeqnapus, in Menominee mythology. She has identified Menominee words interspersed throughout the poem that she shares with her students. Always searching for new experiences, Teller has plans to do Storytelling Theater with her students based on Longfellow's Hiawatha. She is firmly convinced that this poem and Longfellow's "noble savage" saved what was left of the Native American in the 1850s. It seems Longfellow preserved many Menominee legends and stories.

In other words, while the *noble savage* myth essentializes Indigeneity by placing it at the bottom of a false hierarchy of civilizations, it *has* produced sympathetic attitudes among the settler population reducing *some* hostility toward Native Nations. However, these myths and stereotypes are unfortunately not a thing of the past, but continue to be reproduced within the settler society. What follows is a critical examination of contemporary children's literature that deals with Native Americans. What is highlighted is that stereotypical attitudes are perpetuated by non-Natives and Native alike demonstrating that the power of cultural hegemony.

Bias, Stereotyping, and Inaccuracies in Native American Literature

In 2002, there were approximately 5,000 children's books published and approximately 10% of these books fell into the category of multicultural literature (MCL) (CCBC, 2002). MCL is so important in today's changing society. Children must learn about other cultures so that they can appreciate the diversity of the world. It goes without saying that many of the goals of multicultural education can be achieved through sharing multicultural literature with children. This section of the chapter will examine how MCL should be evaluated and examples of literature that do not meet these important criteria will be provided.

Data collected by the School of Education's Cooperative Children's Book Center at the University of Wisconsin indicate that there are not a great number of Native American books written for children. That is, only sixty-four books out of a populations of five thousand were coded as possessing Native American content. Nodelman (1999) argues that the publishing industry underwent dramatic changes when large corporations absorbed small independent companies in the late 1980s and early 1990s. This transition subverted the professional values of quality and historical integrity with the corporate value of profit, that is, money. As a result, children's literature became commercialized and historical figures such as Pocahontas were reduced to "Disneyfied" caricatures. Summarizing Disney's historically inaccurate and stereotypical portrayal of Pocahontas Conel Pewewardy (1998) notes:

> Disney's Pocahontas has an...instant attraction to...John Smith. Yet historians agree that Pocahontas and John Smith had no romantic contact. In short, Disney has abandoned historical accuracy in favor of creating a marketable New Age Pocahontas...Pocahontas is rooted in the "Indian princess" stereotype, which is typically expressed through characters who are maidenly, demure, and deeply committed to some white man. (p. 61)

Given the corporate tendency to sacrifice historical accuracy for feel good stories, our first criteria for evaluating MCL is accuracy. That is, do the author and illustrator accurately and respectfully portray their subject matter (Norton, 2003)? This criteria cannot be stressed enough in light of *False Face* by Welwyn Wilton Katz (1987). Katz has won many writing awards for her children's books. From a strictly mechanical perspective *False Face* is a well-written book. According to the book cover:

> One day Laney and Tom discover two terrifying, old Indian masks in a nearby bog. But even more horrible is what lies beneath them.
>
> As the mystery surrounding the masks, Laney, an ordinary thirteen-year old caught between her divorced parents, and her friend Tom must come to grips with the power of the masks, and the danger they pose to those who try to control them.

The story is set in London, Ontario. Both young people are troubled. Laney is having a hard time dealing with her conniving mother. Tom is unhappy since his Mohawk father died and he had to leave the Grand River Reserve with his white mother. Laney and Tom accidentally find Iroquois artifacts. One is a pipe and the other is an actual false face, which is sacred to the Iroquois. The story leads to the false face taking possession of Laney's mother who wants to sell it and make money. The boy and the girl have to work together to save the mother and return the false face to the bog where they had found it and where it would be safe.

Katz (1987) observes that her resources for the book came from W.N. Fenton's *Masked Medicine Societies*, Gertrude Prokosch Kurath's *Dance and Song Rituals of Six Nations Reserve*, and the Museum of Indian Archaeology in London, Ontario. She is proud of the fact that she has attempted to be accurate about Iroquois songs and false face rituals. The Canada Council for the Arts even sponsored her work.

However, the title and plot of the book are disturbing because the False Face Society of the Iroquois is sacred and not shared with the general public. The Grand Council has decreed that false faces should not be used for commercial gains and exploitation. It is obvious this decree relates to fictional stories depicting elements of the False Face Society.

The Iroquois, or more accurately the Haudenosaunee, would certainly not appreciate their sacred False Face Society being used as a Stephen King plot device in a children's book. When we look at evaluating multicultural literature, we believe authors and illustrators must be culturally accurate. Writers like Jane Yolen endorse this idea and she has written some excellent MCL (*Encounter*). However, we need to add one more criteria to the evaluation tool. Writers must be culturally accurate and also culturally sensitive. Because we have accurate cultural knowledge does not mean that we should use it to write a story.

Along this same line and an excellent example of the use of stereotypes, the reader can read *Indian in the Cupboard* by Lynne Reid, which was published in the 1980s when people should have been more enlightened about MCL. This book is actually a five book series because it was so popular. The story, in a nutshell, is about an English boy named Omri, who receives small plastic figures of an Iroquois Indian named Little Bear and a cowboy for his birthday. He also has a magic heirloom key to a magic cupboard where the plastic figures come to life when locked inside. The plot revolves around the problems that arrive as result of yanking these characters from their time period. Omri has great fun controlling the life of Little Bear.

Taylor (2000) sees the book as troubling because it represents the "contrast between Indian and non-Indian perspectives about it" (p. 371). Some people believe this book is a classic to be included in any children's library while others view the book as the epitome of what is wrong with children's multicultural literature (Taylor, 2000). In 1981, the Times Educational Supplement, *The Junior Bookshelf, Publishers Weekly*, the *Horn Book Magazine*, the *Bulletin of the Center for Children's Books* and the *New Yorker* all published reviews of the book that were positive (Taylor, 2000). This is somewhat disturbing because librarians and teachers use these magazines to measure the quality of children's books.

Taylor (2000) notes that "Native Americans almost from the first moment of encounter with non-Indians, have faced and lived with, and died from, the paternalism of societal attitudes incarnated as governmental policy and law intended to take care of the misguided s*avage* by remaking Natives into Euro-Americans and coincidentally divesting them of resources" (p. 375). *Indian in the Cupboard*, according to Taylor (2000), is an example of Euro-centric paternalism. Even the icons of children's literature have been challenged for their stereotyping of Native people in their books.

For example, Slapin and Seale (1998) take both Dr. Seuss (Theodore Geisel) and Maurice Sendak to task for their portrayals of Native Americans in their alphabet books. Dr. Seuss as P.D. Eastman repeatedly portrays Native Americans as caricatures in his alphabet book. The pictures resemble his drawings of the Japanese during WWII, which some people have deemed highly racist. Maurice Sendak, a Caldecott award winner for *Where the Wild Things Are*, dresses an alligator up in a full Western headdress as an Indian to represent the letter "I" in his book *Alligators All Around* (1961, 1991*)*, which is still on the market.

When we review MCL, the setting must be genuine and accurate (Norton, 2003). This is a major concern for all cultures. One of the best examples of this in Native American children's literature is the Cinderella story called *Rough Face Girl* by Rafe Martin and illustrated by David Shannon. This Algonquin story begins on the shores of Lake Ontario and tells the tale of an Invisible Being who lives with his sister in a wigwam near the forest. However, the initial illustration shows a huge teepee common to the Lakota Indians from South Dakota. A Native American folktale is ruined by inaccurate illustrations and the Westernization of the story (Stott, 1995). Each tribe is unique and different, which many authors and illustrators fail to take into account when they are producing Native American stories.

Finally, the author of any MCL must be "qualified" to write about the culture and minority characters (Norton, 2003). The person or author who writes the stories is a major issue for many minority groups and cultures (Stewart, 2002). For instance, it is important to many Native American people who write Native American stories. Native American people are concerned about the authenticity of illustrations in Native American literature. Through the years many non-Native people have written stories based on traditional legends, myths, and history. This has disturbed many Native American people because the interpretations have not always been accurate.

Perry Nodelman in his book the *Pleasures of Children's Literature* discusses the idea of cultural appropriation in multicultural literature. Nodelman (1999) defines cultural appropriation as "the act of claiming or appropriating the right to give voice to what it means or feels like to belong to a particular group" (p134). Nodelman (1999) and Stott (1995) use the book *Brother Eagle, Sister Sky* by Susan Jeffers as the best example of this problem. This book is beautifully illustrated and the text is poetic. Environmentalists use the text as their credo. The book is supposed to be the speech Chief Seattle of the Suquamish Nation made in 1854 at the signing of the last treaty his people made with the United States government.

The reality, however, is that the words in the book were actually penned by Ted Perry, who was a Hollywood scriptwriter and a professor at a small college in Connecticut. This book has created a firestorm of controversy in Indian country. If readers even just search the Internet, they will discover a great deal of information about Chief Seattle and this book. Jeffers has also received a great deal of criticism because she portrays tepees, horses, and canoes in her illustrations, which are not representative of the culture of the Suquamish people. In summary Stott (1995) observes that:

> ...No matter how well-intentioned Susan Jeffers is, no matter how great her respect for traditional and contemporary Native Americans, her book is another example of the creation of a "white man's Indian," a construct which reflects not realities but a view of what a white author, painter, motion picture director, actor, politician, missionary, activist, or conservationist believes Natives peoples to be, wants them to become or wishes they already were. (p. 20)

Another book that has created similar controversy is *Turkey Girl* by Penny Pollock, who is from the Wyandotte Tribe. The story is a pourquoi story, which is a story that explains how things came to be and is a common type of story in Native American literature and oral tradition (Stewart, 2002). It has also been used as an example of a Zuni Cinderella story (Reese, 2007). Pollock's story is about a "poor orphan girl" who tends the tribe's turkeys and who longs to attend the Dance of the Sacred Bird. The turkeys dress her in beautiful clothes for the dance and warn her to return home before dawn. She fails to do so and the turkeys leave forever. Stewart (2002), who is non-Native, sees the book as encompassing Native American structures and values instead of European structures and values. She believes a Native American may understand what it means to be Native American in ways that an outsider cannot.

On the other hand, Reese, who is a Nambe Pueblo Indian woman, has a very different opinion of the story. Reese (2007) compares Pollock's version to Zuni Tribal member Alvina Quam's translated stories from *The Zunis: Self Portrayals*. Pollock used Frank Hamilton Cushings translations of Zuni stories. Reese argues that Quam's version is not only more straightforward, but it is truer to Zuni values. She does an interesting job of comparing and contrasting the two versions in regard to Zuni values and beliefs. Reese believes that Pollock actually makes her story fit what a mainstream audience expects, that is, a *Disneyfied* interpretation.

NATIVE LITERATURE AND WRITERS

Some of the best literature written about Native Americans is based on myths and legends. These stories fit the picture storybook category perfectly because of the beautiful illustrations that can be produced from this material. Through the years Caldecott awards have been given to such books telling Native American stories like *Arrow to the Sun*, and *The Girl Who Loved Wild Horses*. The chapter book *Walks Two Moons* is a Newbery award-winning book. However, Native Americans wrote none of these books. There is an increasing amount of Native American literature available today, but there are still few published Native American authors.

Again, who writes the stories is an issue in the Native world because of authenticity (Stewart, 2002). Many Native people feel only Natives should write the stories. Some people will even question what Natives write *what* stories. This takes the insider versus outsider conflict to a new level. For example, some reservation people may feel urban Indians have different values and beliefs from themselves because of their acculturation and assimilation.

Stewart (2002), on the other hand, sees certain characteristics as being important in defining authentic Native stories no matter who writes the story.

For instance, Native American literature may utilize multiple narrators or perspectives as in the oral tradition. The story is also not written in a linear fashion as Western children's literature is but takes on the Native view of time as being cyclical (Stott, 1995). The essence of storytelling is incorporated into the story through different stylistic devices (Stewart, 2002). Native stories do not focus on conflict resolution, but on the integration into community and the larger community group. Native American myths are often a part of the story as well as other cultural beliefs. The connections Native people have with Mother Earth and nature may also be incorporated into the story. Finally, the recovering or rearticulation of an identity is the center of Native American fiction or as Stewart says "homing in" (p. 191). We will briefly examine a number of authors of Native American literature and their writings in the following paragraphs taking into account some of our discussions above.

Joseph Bruchac

Bruchac lives in Greenfield Center, New York with his family in the same house where he was raised by his grandparents. Bruchac is well-known for his Native American stories. He is proud of his Abenaki culture and heritage, which he has attempted to revive and preserve. Bruchac holds a Bachelor of Arts degree from Cornell University, Master of Arts from Syracuse in literature and creative writing and his PhD in comparative literature from Union Institute of Ohio. He worked as an educator for a number of years before his writing took center stage. Bruchac is a traditional storyteller and a flute player. For 25 years, he has visited schools doing presentations for educators (Stott, 1995). He believes that this is an important endeavor so that non-Native people can hear about Native culture and traditions.

Bruchac is a prolific writer and has written over 70 books for adults and children using his Native, Slovak and English background. He believes that anyone who writes Native American stories must have a "deep knowledge" of the culture learned from the elders. Too many authors only do library research or use biased and inaccurate texts, which leads to the "best of intentions but deeply flawed" books (Stott, p. xii). Bruchac is an award winning author. He has received such awards as the Cherokee Nation Prose Award, the Knickerbocker Award, and the Hope S. Dean Award for Notable Achievement in Children's Literature. The following are some of his well-known picture books and chapter books: *A Boy Called Slow*, *Crazy Horse's Vision*, *The Heart of a Chief*, *Jim Thorpe's Bright Path*, and *Geronimo*.

Bruchac's book, *Eagle Song*, published in 1999, is about a fourth grade boy named Danny Bigtree. Danny is a Mohawk, who moves from the reservation to

Brooklyn, New York. He finds it a difficult transfer because he is ridiculed and made fun of by his classmates for being Indian. *Publishers Weekly* gives the book a positive review while *School Library Journal* was negative about the story dialogue and character development. Leslie Teller read the book for an adolescent literature course a number of years ago. She loved the book. In the 1960s when she was in junior high her parents moved to Chicago from the Reservation. She was forced to attend a girls' Catholic school. She identified with the experiences of Danny and believes Brushac got the story *right*.

Sherman Alexie

Alexie is interesting because he was born and raised on the Spokane Indian Reservation. It might be said that he has lived the stories some authors write about regarding Native people. He was born in 1966 and is therefore a relatively young writer. In personal accounts he has admitted to having had alcohol problems in his early 20s. He started school on the reservation and opted to transfer to an all white high school off the Reservation when he was older. In 1985 he graduated from Reardon High School. He went on to college at Gonzanga University for two years and then transferred to Washington State University. He graduated with a BA in American Studies and an interest in poetry and writing. Alexie received a Washington State Arts Commission Poetry award in 1991 and the National Endowment for the Arts Poetry Fellowship in 1992.

His foray into children's literature is *The Absolutely True Diary of a Part-Time Indian*. This book was published in 2009 and it is classified as a book for young adults. It would be considered contemporary realistic fiction, which Norton (2003) says is severely lacking in Native American Literature. The book is autobiographical and parallels Alexie's high school experiences. The story is about Arnold Spirit, who is 14 years old from the Spokane Indian Reservation. Arnold was born with water on the brain and was targeted by bullies all the time. He is a good basketball player, which he uses to buy his way into being accepted at the white high school. His Reservation friends can't understand why he has chosen to transfer to the high school off the Reservation and he suffers for it. Part of the story is told though the cartoons he draws relating to his experiences. The book is quite graphic.

Lynn Skenadore, a school librarian, has uncertainties about the book because of the message it sends about life on the Reservation. She admits life can be difficult but there is beauty also. In addition, it would be difficult for her to use the book in the library because of the language used. Her daughter, an English teacher at the Menominee Indian Reservation high school, thinks the book is hilarious and enjoyed it thoroughly.

Paul Goble

Goble was born on September 27, 1933 in England where he grew up. He studied at the Central School of Art in London. In his early career, Goble worked as a furniture designer, industrial consultant, and art instructor. Goble has lived in the United States since 1977 and he became a citizen in 1984. He currently lives in Rapid City, South Dakota. He initially visited the United States in 1959 where he toured the Sioux and Crow Reservations and returned there many times. At this time, he published his first children's book (*Red Hawk's Account of Custer's Last Battle*) while still living in England. Goble writes and illustrates his own books.

Goble has had a fascination with Plains Indians since he was a child. He was intrigued by Native American spirituality and their culture. He takes great pride in the fact that his first books were historical fiction told from a Native American perspective. He has commented, "I feel that I have seen and learned many wonderful things from Indian people, which most people would never have the opportunity to experience. I simply wanted to express and share these things which I love so much."

An issue for many Native Americans, as discussed above, is the cultural appropriation of Native stories and who tells their stories. Goble has made a practice of only telling the stories of the Plains Indians as culturally accurate as possible. Chief Edgar Red Cloud and other Native Americans served as mentors in helping him learn about the culture, history, and mythology. History says he was adopted by the Yakima and Sioux Tribes and given the spirit name of Wakinyan Chikala (Little Thunder) by Chief Edgar Red Cloud.

Stott (1995) notes that Goble's writing and illustrations are the result of a "long and arduous process" (p 27). Goble's texts are brief, which is similar to the actual oral tradition, while he "uses his illustrations to expands and deepen the written texts" (Stott 1995, p 27). Gobles illustrations involve "extensive research into the art and culture of the traditional peoples of the northern plains, and accurate observations of the land and *skyscapes* in the midst of which these people lived" (Stott 1995, p 29).

In the summer of 2008, Lynn Skenadore was in Rapid City and had lunch with Goble and his wife. She found him to be a humble and private person, who leads a simple life. He does not use the Internet, but will answer any letter he receives, particularly from children. Skenadore has taught his books to her students for years and the students would share their thoughts and observations about his books with him. He always wrote back to the students. Although Goble is not Native American, Skenadore believes he has the heart of a Native American demonstrating sensitivity to cultural and historical accuracy.

Underscoring this point Goble reflects on an invitation he received from the Zunis to come to their Pueblo noting that, "I was once with the Zunis at the invitation of their schools; they wanted me to write stories of their mythology. But can I? I know almost nothing about them, and would make minor mistakes all the time."

READ ALOUDS & THE ORAL TRADITION

Because the Menominee and other Native Americans have a rich oral tradition, the use of *Read Alouds* is an intriguing tactic to use with Indian children. Many of the benefits of storytelling are the same benefits children receive from *Read Alouds*. Storytelling and *Read Alouds* can be magical, enchanting, and fun. Storytelling and *Read Alouds* reinforce the concept that language learning in story form is a valued activity. Both activities enhance listening skills and enrich vocabulary. A wonderful strategy to incorporate in teaching Native American children to read is therefore the *Read Aloud*. Native American people have a rich oral tradition. History, culture, and traditions are all passed down by word of mouth. The *Read Aloud* follows this same line and capitalizes on this practice.

Jim Trelease, the guru of *Read Alouds*, advocates the idea of advertising reading. He believes that it is important to entice our children to read and to instill in them the desire to read. He has an annotated bibliography of books to use as *Read Alouds* at all grade levels. He also sees parents as an important part of the process. This would certainly be true in Native American communities. We need to have parents, along with the classroom teachers, actively involved. Mem Fox (2001) also expresses her support of *Read Alouds* in her book, *Reading Magic*. Note the following statement:

> If every parent understood the huge educational benefits and intense happiness brought about by reading aloud to their children, and if every parent—and every adult caring for a child—read aloud a minimum of three stories a day to the children in their lives, we could probably wipe out illiteracy within one generation. (p. 12)

As a literacy expert, she shares with us her personal observations relating to the power of *Read Alouds*. Fox (2001) writes extraordinary children's books, which certainly adds to her credibility. Her book is a good source to read in learning how to do great *Read Alouds*. In addition, the *Read Aloud* helps Native American children learn literary elements, story structure, intonation and fluency, and vocabulary that they need to become successful readers. It will also give Native American children language patterns to use in reading and in everyday language. The read aloud is a fun, culturally sensitive way to teach Native American children a love of reading and books. In addition, many Native American children speak non-standard English. They speak what is known as American Indian English (AIE), a term coined by William Leap (1993). As a consequence, they need to hear the Standard English that *Read Alouds* provide.

Teaching Menominee Students a Love of Reading

Lynn Skenadore is an enrolled Menominee woman, who has lived on the Menominee Indian Reservation all her life. She is a strong believer in the importance of Menominee culture and she treasures her Native heritage. As a young girl and woman, she participated in the historic pageants at the Woodland Bowl, which we will discuss in the section on the Oral Tradition. Her spirit name is Kaeqsiw wapan, which means "cold morning." She proudly carries her mother's name.

Skenadore worked in numerous jobs on the Reservation, including the county librarian for many years. She even served as the chairwoman of the Tribe when she was on the Menominee Indian Tribal Legislature. After her children were grown, she returned to school and earned her teaching degree from St. Norbert College in Green Bay. Because her mother always promoted education, it was important for her to complete her formal schooling.

Lynn Skenadore has been the school librarian for the past eight years and former third grade teacher at Menominee Tribal School (MTS) for seven years. The MTS is situated in the small village of Neopit, Wisconsin along the historic Wolf River. MTE and the tribal lumber mill are also located there. MTS is positioned in the old St. Anthony Catholic School building. Since 1990, it has been funded by the Bureau of Indian Affairs and designated a contract/grant school. Approximately 40% of the teaching staff are Menominee or Native American.

Parents who want their children to be exposed to Menominee Language and culture send their children to MTS. Students in grades K-5 learn Menominee Language and Culture once a week and Middle school students have classes five days a week. The students have the opportunity to participate in such things as wild rice gathering and learning traditional beadwork. Menominee test scores in reading at the elementary level are the best in the BIA system, placing them in the top three percent. The school uses the Accelerated Reading Program and there are two reading specialists who work closely with the students and teachers in improving reading skills.

Mrs. Skenadore has always done *Read Alouds* with her students. She has a love for literature and has tried to pass this love onto her students no matter what their grade level. She has an incredible amount of knowledge about children's books and authors. She works very hard to promote the importance of reading to parents and to her students. When she first started doing *Read Alouds* in her third grade classroom, it was to sell the enjoyment of reading to her students. As a librarian, she uses *Read Alouds* to advertise different books to her students. Mrs. Skenadore says she initially was just trying to get children to read. MTS has an enrollment of 241 students, but during the last five years students checked out an average of over 12,000 books a year. This was much higher than the checkout rates in the other schools on the Reservation. She credits this rate to her hard work, the fact that students are required to read 20 minutes a day, and the new Accelerated Reading Program in the school.

According to Skenadore, it has been her experience that students at all grades and reading levels enjoy *Read Alouds*. She thinks that they should by read to by their teachers and parents. Sometimes we think because students are gifted or older that they do not need to be read to, but this is not true. Menominee children love rhythm, repetition, and word plays included in many of the books. This corresponds with the singing and drumming, which is an integral part of the native culture. Menominee children have a great sense of humor and they love the ridiculous and exaggeration that can be showcased in *Read Alouds*.

Recently, Skenadore was using multicultural literature picture storybooks to teach comprehension skills to her middle school students. Some books they studied included Deloris and Roslyn Jordan's *Salt in His Shoes*, Jane Yolen's *Encounter*, Robert Coles' *The Ruby Bridges Story*, and Holly Keller's *Grandfather's Dream*. The story, *Grandfather's Dream*, caused an interesting reaction in the students. The name of the main character in the book is "Nam" and as a result the students thought that the story was Native American. A common traditional name on the reservation today is "Namakesa" (Little Thunderbird), which is often shortened to "Nam." They were more than a little surprised to find out the story was about a Vietnamese boy and his grandfather living in the Mekong Delta after the Vietnam War. The Sarus cranes disappeared during the war and the boy's grandfather believed that the cranes would return when the rain came and flooded the land. Cranes are the Vietnamese symbol for family and life. The students were sure that "Nam" was a Menominee boy and they argued with Mrs. Skenadore about it. Actually, they were especially convinced of this fact after the mention of cranes in the story because the Menominee have a Crane Clan and the children see cranes on the Reservation all the time. She was amused by her students' confusion and their realization of how closely connected dissimilar parts of the world can be.

Mrs. Skenadore notes that she usually does books in themes and her book selections can change from year to year depending on the students and the new books available. She has a very limited budget to work with at $4000 a year, which is not a generous amount of money when you look at the cost of books today. As a result, she sticks with award winning books and authors who have demonstrated excellence in the past. She can't afford to purchase books that she calls "duds." She has a collection of over 13,000 books and each year she adds 500 more. Among her stacks, she has consciously built a large collection of Native American books.

The library has a special table where books are advertised. Before the end of library skills class, Mrs. Skenadore will discuss some of the books on the table and try to entice the children to read them. One of the things she has found that works wonders in getting children to read a particular book is to read it aloud. Invariably, after a book is read aloud children will find the book and check it out.

Sometimes students will choose a particular book that has been advertised or read aloud and take it to their teachers to read in class. Teachers are strongly encouraged by Mrs. Skenadore to do *Read Alouds* in their classrooms. In fact, a *Read Aloud* workshop was presented to the teachers and staff on the importance of read alouds. Many of the teachers are keeping track of the number of minutes a day they spend on their read alouds.

Mrs. Skenadore knows a book is liked if students read it over and over again. It is important to note that when children have not been read to from time they were babies, it will take time to teach them to enjoy the read aloud the older they get. Patience is the key.

Every year Mrs. Skenadore has a fall Scholastic book sale. She promotes this activity for two reasons. Most importantly, she gives parents an opportunity to purchase books for their children. Each year parents and students purchase hundreds of dollars worth of books to take home and read. In addition, she receives special credits she can use to purchase more books and materials for her library.

JOHN SATTERLEE: EARLY MENOMINEE EDUCATOR

John Satterlee, who was an early educator on the Menominee Reservation, taught in what was known as Crow Settlement. Interestingly, he taught school in both English and Menominee, which was long before the bilingual approach to education was implemented. Another strategy used by Satterlee was that he had his students memorize poetry and recite it because it had a rhythmic quality to it. He knew that the first sound we hear is the heartbeat from our mothers, which is why we like the rhythm of poetry.

Satterlee, as a teacher in the late 1800s, developed a strategy that is still useful with our children today. In our *Read Aloud* research on the Reservation, we discovered that Menominee children particularly loved rhythm, repetition, and word plays included in many of the read aloud books. We think that this corresponds with the singing and drumming, which is an integral part of Menominee culture and other Native cultures. Unfortunately, *Read Alouds* are not the magic wand educators have all been looking for to cure the educational problems that plague Native American children. However, it can be a simple, inexpensive way to help Native American children begin to acquire the literacy skills they will need to be successful in school based on their connection to the oral tradition in their culture.

Conclusion: Readers' Theater & the Oral Tradition

Readers' Theater (RT) is simply the act of reading aloud from a script in a dramatic style usually based on a picture storybook or a chapter book by two or more readers. No sets, costumes, or props are necessary for the production. Emphasis is on interpretive oral reading. Tyler and Chard (2000) say that Readers' Theater is effective with both older students and elementary students. This strategy or technique builds on the oral tradition of Native American children. Any children's book can be used in Readers' Theater, whether it is a picture storybook or a chapter book. Young and Vardell (1993) advocate using reader's theater with nonfiction trade books to increase active involvement with the material and to make it more interesting to the students. Furthermore, Readers' Theater would work well in teaching social studies and world events.

Where did RT come from and how did it begin? This is an excellent question and it has several answers. S. Jay Samuels in the 1970s began research on the use of repeated readings with children who were problem readers. He and other researchers found success in having students reread short reading passages until they reached a successful fluency level (Samuels, 1979). Problem readers were motivated and enthusiastic about the gains they made in fluency. The repeated reading technique is based on Samuels' automaticity theory. Samuels believed that a fluent reader decoded text automatically while a problem or beginning reader had to pay attention to their decoding. Beginning readers or problem readers struggle with their comprehension as a result.

The guru of readers' theater by many accounts is Aaron Shepard, who began his work around 1975 with Chamber Readers (Shepard, 1994). Shepard has published many books on RT available today for use by teachers. Between 1986 and 1991, Shepard was a professional actor with the Chamber troupe where he scripted and directed many of its performances. He led workshops for teachers and students for many years before he began a career as a children's author. In addition, he has a popular web site called Aaron Shepard's RT Page, which is a popular resource.

Research shows that reader's theater in special education classrooms helps to improve fluency because of the repeated oral readings (Corcoran & Davis,

2005). Fluency is described "as the appropriate grouping or chunking of words into phrases that are characterized by correct intonation, stress, and pauses" (Tyler & Chard, 2000, p. 163). Good reading fluency is important because it frees student attention to work on comprehension. In addition, it can positively reinforce children in their reading skills and they will develop a more positive attitude toward reading. The best part of readers' theater is that children at all reading levels enjoy it because it is fun. This is notable because children's attitudes impact the process of their becoming literate (McKenna & Kear, 1990).

Rinehart (1999) believes readers' theater improves sight word knowledge by the repeated repetition of the scripts. Sight word knowledge helps with their automatic processing, which is essential in children learning to read (Chard, Vaughn, & Tyler, 2002). Martinez, Roser, and Streaker (1999) see RT as a way "to offer teachers a way to incorporate repeated readings within a meaningful and purposeful context" (p. 333). In their study of inner city second graders, they introduced an instructional model of thirty-minute daily sessions in RT. The children were ethnically mixed of low socioeconomic status. From their pre and post assessments of students, it was evident that nearly all the children posted gains in their rate of reading; some even had dramatic gains.

Worthy and Prater (2002) indicate that readers' theater leads to increased engagement with literacy for very resistant readers. They believe that increased fluency helps students comprehend what they are reading. RT should be a regular part of the curriculum and instructional activities. The more opportunities reluctant readers have to practice with the teacher, tutor, or friend in a safe atmosphere the more confident they will become. After using RT in the classroom, many teachers report finding that it is a motivating, effective reading activity.

Worthy and Broaddus (2002) note that in their research fluency instruction has not played a major role in classrooms or intervention programs, even though oral reading fluency is an important part of mature reading. Students with inadequate fluency are likely to avoid reading for fear of failure and negative attitudes. Often times in the upper grades, struggling readers are not given the opportunity to practice and to successfully perform. This is unfortunate for struggling readers as it continues to reinforce their low self-confidence. The researchers advocate teacher read alouds, choral reading, and shared readings, in addition to RT in helping students improve their fluency. Students can use poetry, speeches, as well as other literature of interest for RT. They have compiled an interesting list of literature that is suited for RT.

As schools move into the twenty-first century, the school population will become more diverse. The school curriculum must reflect the contributions of many cultural groups and integrate their perspectives throughout. A simple way to infuse cultural and ethnic diversity into the classroom is to use multicultural literature as a part of reader's theater stories. These reading strategies, to meet the demands of an increasingly unjust world, must also focus on the imbalance of power and why some cultural groups possess more cultural capital than others. In other words, relevant literacy programs must not only challenge the mechanical approach to reading and writing by infusing them with cultural knowledge, but they must always be critical, which demands that pedagogy and curriculum always problematize basic structures of power, such as colonization and capitalism, and how they effect the goals and outcomes of education. While it is easy to lose sight of these larger structural issues of where power lies and how it operates in the context of extreme poverty and countering years of outsider-induced educational neglect, as is the case in many working-class urban areas and on Indian reservations, it is only a critical pedagogical approach that will move education beyond the important work of assisting our students in surviving within the world that exists, and engage them in transforming that world by challenging unjust hierarchies of power.

Conclusion

CHAPTER TEN

Knowledge Production in an Age of Economic Meltdown

Within this chapter we examine the history and continuity of Western knowledge production within a more contemporary context. We examine the dialectics of Western thought from Durkeim, Marx, Lippmann, Keynes and Friedman. We also consider the ways Indigeneity can inform knowledge production for a democratic society in the twenty-first century.

* * *

Epistemology, or the study of knowledge, is at the heart of all teaching, learning and *knowing* in general. When setting out to examine and understand the knowledge produced by any system, it is imperative that one focus on the most central and underlying assumptions informing the knowledge production process. Because we are interested in the knowledge produced by both capitalism and neoliberal capitalism, we will begin our investigation looking at its ideological structure, historically contextualized. We pay particular attention to what knowledge is deemed valid and which knowledges are deemed invalid (Kincheloe, 2005) within the social universe of capital as a central aspect of understanding the role power plays in the validation process.

COMPETING CONCEPTIONS OF SOCIAL CLASS

What defines capitalism more than any other characteristic is that it is a class-based system. At its most basic level social class can be understood as the hierarchical grouping of people based on similar economic and occupational characteristics giving way to the collective experience of social rank and caste, such as lower/working class and upper/ruling class, and the manifest relationships between and within such stratum. Associated with the notion of class, and especially with caste, is the idea that it is predetermined by government power or noble authority, who loosely determines, by birthright, what occupations are available to what groups.

Because occupation is not judicially determined by birthright in North America—the United States, Mexico, and Canada, among much of the world—the ontological perspective that differences in wealth and power exist *not* because of social class, but rather, are indicative of the division of labor that roughly represent the natural distribution of intelligence and drive, represents the dominant, hegemonized perspective, which tends to not be overtly stated in the knowledge production process, but rather, is implied. From this perspective *socioeconomic difference* becomes no more or less important to human diversity than eye color or body type, that is, one of many *neutral* differences that are entitled to universal respect and dignity. Class *difference* is therefore not something to be resisted, but rather, *tolerated*. Within this interpretative framework, through which praxical knowledge about *being* in the world is produced, the concept of social class, to reiterate, is rarely discussed or included. In other words, within the knowledge production process of the bosses/the ruling class social class is constructed as nonexistent.

As the vast majority of humanity, with varying levels of severity, are oppressed as wage workers by this hierarchal system of neoliberal capitalism, it should be no surprise that there exists an ancient tradition of knowledge production from working-class/subjugated perspectives, which, in different ways, have argued that the unequal relationship between what we might call bosses and workers is not the natural outcome of genetically-determined endowments and deficiencies but is the result of a long legacy of abuse. We might begin naming this *legacy* as coercive, brutal, and manipulative manifesting itself in highly concentrated accumulations of wealth and power that are as nearly deterministic as birthright in reproducing class structure and social relations more generally affirming the central role class plays in capitalist society. Within this paradigm the concept of social class is most fundamentally represented in the relationship between the vast majority, divested from the means of production, therefore possessing only their labor to sell as a commodity, and the few who hold in their hands the productive apparatus, land, and resources, and the vast fortunes accumulated from purchasing the labor power of the landless multitudes at a price far below the value it generates. In short, this antagonistic relationship between social classes represents the heart of what capitalism *is*.

Drawing on the insights of Adam Smith, Noam Chomsky (2007), summarizing what we can understand to be the ontological perspective of the profiteer or capitalist, notes that, "the 'principle architects' of state policy, 'merchants and manufacturers,' make sure that their own interests are 'most particularly attended to,' however 'grivious' the consequences for others" (pp. 41–42). Similarly, outlining the primary self-serving invention of the capitalist, *the corporation*, Joel Bakan (2004) observes that, "corporations have no capacity to value political systems, fascist or democratic, for reasons of principle or ideology. The only legitimate question for a corporation is whether a political system serves or impedes its self-interested purposes" (p. 88). Because safety and environmental regulations are a cost to production and thus encroach on margins, they are frequently violated as corporations sacrifice the public to satisfy their own self-interests.

Since The Great Depression of 1929 it has been increasingly difficult in North America to externalize these costs to those who rely on a wage to survive. For example, to appease an increasingly rebellious underclass the Bretton Woods system was established in 1944, which, among other things, limited the mobility of capital, and, as a result, weakened the deadly grip of capital. However, with the assistance of an intensified emphasis on the propaganda machine, including schools and the corporate media, that have been designed to manufacture the consent of the working and middle classes to support their own class-based oppression as normal and natural, Bretton Woods was dismantled in 1971, which gave way to an era of unrestricted capital movement, and, consequently, the massive redistribution of wealth upwards (Chomsky, 2008). This focus on the use of consent/the control of ideas/hegemony has resulted in the production of knowledge taking on a renewed importance within American and Canadian settler societies. The struggle over the purpose and goals of the education system has consequently become one of the primary battlegrounds where the working classes and ruling class vie for political power to determine the course of history.

From this epistemological perspective, as long as social class exists, that is, as long as there are two antagonistically related groups, workers and bosses, rich and poor, or oppressed and oppressors, there will not be consensus on what explains the basic structures of society because what tends to be good for one group tends not to be beneficial for the other. For example, the idea that social class does not explain the inequality rampant in capitalist societies, but is the result of natural selection, is good for the beneficiaries of market mechanisms. At the same time, the notion that the violent class relation that can only ever offer cyclical crisis and perpetual war is at the core of capitalist society has provided much fuel against capitalism. In short, the class struggle that is indicative of capitalism itself is represented in the "fact" that higher wages are good for workers because they increase their standard of living, but hurt the bosses by encroaching on margins/profits.

From here a smart place of departure might be to observe the current post-Bretton Woods economic structure of North America. A look at the data indicates that in the last ten years in the United States the wealth of the ruling class has exploded while the middle class has simultaneously experienced a steady period of decline as the off shoring trends of the 1980s and 1990s have dramatically effected not just blue collar manufacturing jobs, but white collar service sector employment as well. As a result, <u>the ranks of the poor and the pissed off have continued to swell.</u> No longer able to finance a middle class lifestyle, consumer debt also skyrocketed during this period. Setting off a system-wide pandemic of foreclosures, the bosses ensured the public that the economy was fine largely ignoring the high cost the public was paying. According to Greider and Baker (2008):

> In the long run, the destruction of concentrated wealth and power is always good for democracy, liberating people from the heavy hand of the status quo. Unfortunately, many innocents are slaughtered in the process. As the US manufacturing economy was dismantled by downsizing and globalization, the learned ones (Alan Greenspan comes to mind) told everyone to breathe easy—ultimately this would be good for the workers and communities who lost the foundations of their prosperity. Now that "creative destruction" is visiting the bankers, we now observe they are not so accepting of their own fate." http://www.alternet.org/story/988

Reflecting on this quote in a personal communiqué Joe Kincheloe observed that, "now that 'creative destruction' is reaching the corporate elite, they are not so sanguine about the situation," which is to be expected because, from the boss' perspective, "the pain of structural adjustment for the privileged is more distressing than it is for the poor." It was only a matter of time before the mega-banks collapsed into their own self-made house of cards constructed of worthless defunct mortgages. The current crisis and the government's attempts to "bail out" the capitalists with an unprecedented 700 billion dollar "bill," which increased to nearly a trillion dollars before it passed both the Senate and the US House, has exposed the self-destructiveness embedded within the logic of capital.

The knowledge being produced about the bailout aired through the corporate media focuses on the ways the bailout will benefit "mainstreet," that is, the workers of capital, which, in a way, has some element of truth to it because the financial capitalists cannot operate on their own. That is, they depend on other capitalists involved in industry, commercialization, real estate, etc. to borrow money and invest in human labor as a commodity who actually do the work and produce the wealth that is then appropriated, reinvested, gained, lost, etc. It should therefore not be surprising that the majority of representatives of the House and US Senators, in making their case for the bill, stressed, over and over, the benefits that the "small people" will incrue as justification for their "yea" rather than "nay" votes. But using that indirect "benefit" to obscure the basic antagonistic relationship between labor and capital, which, as long as it remains in tact, the majority of humanity will suffer, can be viewed as nothing short than an aplogoy for the inevitable injustices of capitalism.

We might therefore say that the mere existence of capitalism, its ruling classes in particular, represents the constant risk of an uprising, and the more powerful the bosses, the greater the inequality between the oppressors and the oppressed, and therefore the greater the probability of an uprising or frontal assault designed to seize control of state and private power. The bosses tend to have this awareness, and it is for this *ruling-class class-consciousness* that the hammer is always in the background. However, the elite are more interested in avoiding *disruption* because that kind of *instability* is not good for business. The ruling class perceive those who rely on a wage to survive as a constant pontential threat because their existence as labor is structually, by definition, set against their own creative human impulse.

From this perspective, labor is always instinctively operating at some level of uprising in their struggle to relieve themselves from the chains that bind them. The objective of the capitalist is therefore to keep working class resistance at the lowest possible level through the combined use of force and consent, placing special emphasis, for obvious reasons, on consent, that is, the control of ideas. It has been argued by mainstream-progressive sources that the slight hesitation to pass the recent trillion dollar bailout "bill" represents a victory for democracy because of the public's overwhelming disapproval and the swelling "crisis in confidence."

This crisis in confidence does not merely refer to the reluctance to spend money, as the corporate media would have us believe, but runs to the very core of capitalism as a viable economic system. United States President George W. Bush alluded to this reading of the world in a special television appearance where he reassured his audience, the "small people," that "democratic capitalism is the best system that ever existed." Similarly, White House Press Secretary, Dana Perino, offered similar reassurance arguing that the United States is "the greatest capitalist country in the world" and that the public only needs to be willing to suffer for a short time so "we" can, once again, "enjoy prosperity." Of course the bosses would never offer workers a choice in the matter, so we will suffer unless we fight back and challenge policies that treat the well-being of the public as incidental. That is, as long as the basic structures of power remain in tact and wealth is flowing to the elite, the well being of the public is not a concern.

Let us now situate in an historical context the ways in which knowledge is and has been constructed to explain and account for these trends and inequalities. The remainder of this chapter examines different approaches to these class-based issues. We end our discussion with critical pedagogy, which has recently begun to emerge as a leading force in emancipatory educational practice.

* * *

It is worth restating, risking unnecessary repetition, that social class and related concepts, within Western political discourse, have traditionally been articulated along an antagonistically related continuum. On one end, there is the idea that the existence of social class is evidence of the natural evolution of human society increasingly necessary as civilization becomes more complex and advanced. On the other end of the spectrum, it tends to be argued that the existence of social class is the result of the appropriation of the naturally occurring division of labor, and therefore conceived as an unequal relationship that has been continuously and rather violently forced upon humanity. These two positions do not merely represent *both sides*, as it were, each possessing equal weight, and therefore embodying independent existences, unaware or unaffected by the other. What is demonstrated below is the intimate relationship between these competing perspectives on social class, one hegemonic, and therefore endowed with the power of the capitalist-state, (supporting the interests of the rich and the powerful), the other, counter-hegemonic, and as a result, historically marginalized by the dominant society, (representing the interests and concerns of the vast majority).

However, there has emerged within the critical conception of social class—and the social more generally—a tradition of thought that challenges the assumption of an external objective reality that the mind can neutrally comprehend with as much accuracy as a mirror reflects objects. As a result, such approaches refocus the debate from questions of *accuracy* to questions of *certainty*. While this shift may seem qualitatively insignificant, its ontological implications have immense pedagogical and curricular consequences. That is, if knowledge exists outside the realm of human intervention, then *truth* can be absolutely known and externally imposed. However, critical pedagogy argues that knowledge, democratically conceived, cannot be pre-scripted because it is constructed through active participation. Democracy is a way of *being* in the world informed by common values such as social justice, equality, freedom, responsibility, and so on (Freire, 2005). While the practice of democracy undoubtedly requires complicated theoretical knowledge, it also requires that those insights be actively engaged with the concrete context, making it much more than a way of knowing—again, it is a way of *being*. These pedagogical issues are discussed in greater detail in the final sections of this chapter.

In the process of outlining this dialectical discourse, we have demonstrated the complex and contradictory nature of the concrete context thereby underscoring both the conceptual limitations and benefits of the hegemonic/counter-hegemonic dichotomy outlined above. We begin investigating the assumptions underlying the production of knowledge under capitalism in Europe because it was the European model of class society that was reproduced around the world through the process of colonization, which, in most regions, such as North America, continues to serve as the dominant paradigm.

Discourse Wars: Knowledge Production within Capitalism

Among the many scholars who have engaged an in-depth study of the innermost workings of Europe's model of class society, that is, capitalism, Karl Marx's has proven to be the most influential, resilient, relevant, and responded to (both positively and negatively). One of the most widely read constructions of knowledge of all time, the *Manifesto of the Communist Party* (1848/1978), by Karl Marx and Frederick Engels, has touched, in one way or another, every major revolution around the world rendering its conceptualization of social class particularly important for the study at hand.

By the end of the *Manifesto's* first sentence—a relatively short sentence—Marx and Engels have clearly broken with the idealist romanticism of bourgeois scholarship by firmly situating their analysis of class within an historical dialectics of antagonistically competing interests noting that "the history of all hitherto existing society is the history of class struggles" (p. 473), and taken to its logical conclusion underscores the tenuousness of the present moment. The duo continue, linearly and temporally, from a European-centered perspective, naming what they understand to be the stages of conflicting interests that define human social development situating its beginning in ancient Rome and Greece, which would eventually give way to the modern, capitalist, bourgeois era.

Euro-centric, as suggested by the late Senegalese scholar and scientist, Cheikh Anta Diop, because there is evidence that suggests that capitalism is not, as Marx suggested, a relatively recent human construction because it existed in ancient Egypt. For example, Diop (1955/1974) argues that in rural and urban centers during Egypt's Middle Kingdom (2160–1788 B.C.) there existed "marginal capitalism" as evidenced by the labor force being "free" and "contractual" and the existence of "a business class who rented land in the countryside and hired hands to cultivate it" motivated by the sole purpose of generating "huge profits" (p. 210). In the cities Egyptian capitalists engaged in what seems to be very modern business practices such as "interest-bearing loans, [and] renting or subletting personal property or real estate for the purpose of financial speculation" (Diop, 1955/1974, p. 210). While Diop (1955/1974) argues that it was the "inalienable liberty of the Egyptian citizen" (p. 210) that prevented the development of "strong capitalism" with more power over the populous than the state or nobility, the contradictions within Egypt's hierarchical arrangements did lead to a series of unsuccessful internal revolutions.

Again, Diop's analysis, examined next to Marx and Engels' (1848/1978) history of human social development, underscores the latter's European-centered perspective. That is, naming what they understand to be the stages of conflicting interests, beginning with ancient Rome, which transitioned into the Middle Ages, and finally giving way to the modern bourgeois era, Marx and Engels (1848/1978) comment: "freeman and slave, patrician and plebeian, lord and serf, guild-master and journeyman, in a word, oppressor and oppressed" (p. 473). However, while Marx and Engel's timeline and family tree of humanity might be inaccurate, the conclusion that is drawn from the developmental concept remains highly relevant and instructive: the oppressors and the oppressed "stood in constant opposition to one another, carried on an uninterrupted, now hidden, now open fight, a fight that each time ended, either in a revolutionary reconstitution of society at large, or in the common ruin of the contending classes" (p. 474).

This observation is particularly relevant, as capital's current crisis, discussed above, has exposed, in stark relieve, that the very existence of capitalism is an elite class war continuously waged in a never ending quest to increase the bottom line, which can only come from more and more unpaid labor hours put to work grinding up more and more of the Earth's vital ecosystems. As part of the process of abstracting and distorting these class relations, the stock market is incorrectly presented as the producer of value. Challenging the assumption that the "profits and losses that result from fluctuations in the price of" stocks represent "an index of genuine capital accumulation," that is, "reproduction on an expanded scale," Marx (1894/1991), in *Volume Three* of *Capital*, rather, argues that they are "by the nature of the case more and more the result of gambling, which now appears in place of labour as the original source of capital ownership, as well as taking the place of brute force" (pp. 607–609) or the exertion of labor power.

With the development of global capitalism Marx (1894/1991) saw financial capitalists or bankers taking on a more central role as "imaginary money wealth" created on the stock market "makes up a very considerable part" of the money economy. As a result, bankers have become "intermediaries between the private money capitalists on the one hand, and the state, local authorities and borrows engaged in the process of reproduction on the other" (p. 609). Providing an analysis of how this system, with its built-in upward pulling gravity, without strict regulations, inevitably leads to an imbalance of commodities to consumer ratio, and therefore to a disruption in the actualization of value, Marx (1894/1991) observes that "if there is a disturbance in this expansion, or even in the normal exertion of the reproduction process, there is also a lack of credit" creating a crisis in the confidence of the actual value of credit, which is indicative of "the phase in the industrial cycle that follows the crash" (p. 614).

Marx (and with Engles), despite his shortcomings, therefore seems to offer what has proven to be a valid observation, that is, human society tends not to stand still—it is always in a stage of development—and as long as the old oppressed class become the new oppressors, society will remain pregnant with a new social order. Returning to the *Manifesto*, in making their case that the relations of production under capitalism will eventually be *burst asunder*, Marx and Engels (1848/1978) document the process by which Europe's (concentrating on France, England, and Germany) bourgeois capitalist class emerged "from the ruins of feudal society" (p. 474) playing "a most revolutionary part" (pp. 474–475) in that transformation.

The massive amounts of wealth extracted from the Americas by European powers led Marx and Engels (1848/1978) to the conclusion that "the discovery of America," as they called it, was one of the primary driving forces behind "the increase in the means of exchange and in commodities generally" and therefore to the "revolutionary element in the tottering feudal society, a rapid development" (p. 474). The argument is that the small-scale feudal arrangements were not equipped to organize the large armies of labor necessary for transforming the massive amounts of raw materials imported from the Americas needed to meet the exploding European demand for commodities, which was fueled by the influx of unprecedented resources. What is more, unlike Europe's nobility whose power stemmed from their possession of land, the emerging bourgeoisie, without land, gained their advantage through the accumulation of capital due to the mercantile role they played in the extraction of American and African wealth. Summarizing the bourgeoisie's transformation from the oppressed to the oppressors Marx and Engels unveil their most feared and celebrated prediction—that the bourgeoisie, who are still in power, like all of the oppressors before them, too will fall. A Marxist analysis might therefore view each new crisis of capital, such as the most recent one, part of capitalism's march toward its own inevitable demise. Consider Marx and Engels' (1848/1978) description of the capitalist class:

> The bourgeoisie, wherever it has got the upper hand, has put an end to all feudal...relations. It has pitilessly torn asunder the motley feudal ties that bound man to his "natural superiors," and has left remaining no other nexus between man and man than naked self-interest, than callous "cash payment"...It has resolved personal worth into exchange value, and in place of the numberless indefeasible chartered freedoms, has set up that single, unconscionable freedom—Free Trade...The weapons with which the bourgeoisie felled feudalism to the ground are now turned against the bourgeoisie itself...The bourgeoisie forged the weapons that [will] bring death to itself; it has also called into existence the men who are to wield those weapons—the modern working class...(pp. 475–478)

While the broad strokes painted in the *Manifesto of the Communist Party* are useful for beginning to understand why knowledge produced by subjugated populations through the lens of Marx's work continues to be both feared and exalted, we must focus more centrally on his more elaborated work on the division of labor as a transition into the perspectives of his *pro-boss, non-solidarity* critics, which continue to hold political sway in the contemporary context of global capitalism. In one of his major classic works, *Capital: Volume 1*, Marx's (1867/1967) discussion of primitive accumulation as part of the historical development of the capitalization of humanity, which, as alluded to above, began in its "strong" form in England roughly a decade before Columbus set foot in present-day Haiti, is useful here in understanding Europes' engagement in the Americas in particular and global affairs in general. Because of the light it sheds on the discussion that follows, a sizable excerpt taken from *Volume One* of *Capital* (Marx, 1867/1967) is presented here:

> The so-called primitive accumulation...is nothing else than the historical process of divorcing the producer from the means of production. It appears as primitive, because it forms the pre-historic stage of capital and of the mode of production corresponding with it.
>
> The economic structure of capitalistic society has grown out of the economic structure of feudal society. The dissolution of the latter set free the elements of the former.
>
> The immediate producer, the labourer, could only dispose of his own person after he had ceased to be attached to the soil and ceased to be the slave, serf, or bondman of another. To become a free seller of labour-power, who carries his commodity wherever he finds a market, he must further have escaped from the regime of the guilds, their rules for apprentices and journeymen, and the impediments of their labour regulations. Hence, the historical movement which changes the producers into wage-workers, appears, on the one hand, as their emancipation from serfdom and from the fetters of the guilds, and this side alone exists for the bourgeois historians. But, on the other hand, these new freedmen became sellers of themselves only after they had been robbed of all their own means of production, and of all the guarantees of existence afforded by the old feudal arrangements. And the history of this, their expropriation, is written in the annals of mankind in letters of blood and fire....
>
> The starting point of the development that gave rise to the wage labourer as well as to the capitalist was the servitude of the labourer. The advance consisted in a change of form of this servitude, in the transformation of feudal exploitation into capitalist exploitation....
>
> The expropriation of the agricultural producer, of the peasant, from the soil, is the basis of the whole process. The history of this expropriation, in different countries, assumes different aspects, and runs through its various phases in different orders of succession, and at different periods. (pp. 714–716)

From Marx's work we can begin to *read* or *construct* the entire modern world as mediated and dictated by the Westernized process of value production through the capital-labor class relation. In other words, we can understand the entire process, from the on-going need to primitively accumulate and expand, to the establishment of petrol-chemical industrialism, as a form of class struggle that began as a counter-hegemony, but has since developed into perhaps the most oppressive, destructive, and irresponsible hegemony in recorded history. Put another way, capitalism was initiated by Western Europe's bourgeoisie against their feudal lords, some of the last remnants of Europe's "Dark Ages," but now rule with more barbaric force than ever before imagined. Ultimately, it has been the vast majority of humanity, disconnected from the soil and therefore from their Indigenous culture, who have suffered from centuries of bourgeoisie pathology. In his examination of the historical development of class relations Marx points to the division of labor as offering a place of origin.

That is, Marx argues that during the early stages of human development the division of labor was a naturally occurring by-product of age and sex-based physical difference, but also, and we would add, it is the result of the non-hierarchical creative diversity/multiple intelligences unique to human consciousness, as well as to the unpredictable nature of complex events, such as the establishment of purposeful economic systems. Within the division of labor, from this perspective, reside the most basic structural roots of organized society. Commenting on the *division of labor* Marx (1867/1987) notes:

> Within a family, and after further development within a tribe, there springs up naturally a division of labor, caused by differences of sex and age, a division that is consequently based on a purely physiological foundation, which division enlarges its materials by the expansion of the community, by the increase of population, and more especially, by the conflicts of different tribes, and the subjugation of one tribe by another. (p. 351)

The issue of one tribe subjugating another will be taken up later. For now I would like to focus on the context Marx situates this naturally occurring division of labor in. Marx (1867/1967) hones in on the place-specific nature of tribal communities commenting that "different communities find different means of production, and different means of subsistence in their natural environment" (p. 351). In other words, the development of technology is informed by the specific characteristics of physical place or geography such as climate, terrain, arable land, game, waterways, distance and accessibility to other human communities, and so on. As a result, human societies have developed vastly different technologies based on geography, which constitute the original source of commodities, that is, products produced in one context and consumed in another. For example, civilizations that emerged close to large bodies of water have tended to create ship-building technology, whereas those communities whose traditional lands are covered with ice, such as in the Arctic, have developed technology conducive to more efficiently navigating the snow such as sleds and snow shoes.

In the following analysis Marx begins to break, however slightly, from his Euro-centric, linear analysis, acknowledging the persistence of ancient communities in the "modern" era. As an example, Marx (1867/1967) points to "those small and extremely ancient Indian communities, some of which have continued down to this day, are based on possession in common of the land…and on an unalterable division of labor" (p. 357). However, "each individual artificer" operates independently "without recognizing any authority over him" (Marx, 1867/1967, p. 358). Marx attributes this independence, in part, to the fact that within these arrangements products are produced for direct use by the community and therefore do not take the form of a commodity and therefore avoiding the value-generating process associated with it. As a result, the alienating division of labor engendered by the exchange of commodities is also avoided. Marx defines commodities as products consumed by others rather than those who produced them, and those who produce, under capital, are not independent craftsmen, but externally commanded.

Marx (1867/1967) quickly returns to Europe and goes on to argue that the guilds, who more or less labored independently, resisted the bourgeoisie's commodification of production and therefore "…repelled every encroachment by the capital of merchants, the only form of free capital with which they came into contact" (p. 358). Marx notes that the guild organization, by institutionalizing stages of production as specialized trades separate from one another such as the cattle-breeder, the tanner, and the shoemaker, for example, created the material conditions for manufacture, but "excluded division of labor in the workshop," and as a result, "there was wanting the principal basis of manufacture, the separation of the labourer from his means of production, and the conversion of these means into capital" (p. 359). Marx stresses that the process of value production is unique to capitalism and is therefore a "special creation of the capitalist mode of production alone" (p. 359), and therefore not an original or natural aspect of the division of labor. Driving this point home Marx critiques the "peculiar division" of manufacture, which "attacks the individual at the very roots of his life" giving way to "industrial pathology" (p. 363). Because of the forcefulness and accuracy of much of Marx's work, many proponents of capitalism have been forced to attempt to refute the idea that capitalism is a form of pathology, and that the capitalist relations of production, the relationship between what we might crudely call bosses and workers, is negative or harmful for those who rely on a wage to survive, the vast majority of humanity. What follows is therefore a brief summary of some of Emile Durkheim's pro-capitalist constructions that continue to dominate official knowledge production in the Western world, which, with slight variations, are all capitalist.

* * *

Widely influential French sociologist, Emile Durkheim, is considered to be one of the "fathers" and founders of sociology and anthropology. Through the late 1800s Durkheim challenged much of Marx's analysis, setting out to demonstrate that the deep inequality between social classes that drew much attention from critics such as Marx—a central aspect of the Industrial Revolution that began in England—was a natural product of the development of human societies, and should therefore not be resisted, but encouraged through such sorting mechanisms as schools. Essentially, what Durkheim (1893/2000) argues is that humanity (those relegated to the status of worker) would be wise to divest itself of any illusions of maintaining an independent existence and rather "equip yourself to fulfill usefully a specific function" (p. 39) because society requires it, that is, to bend ourselves to fit within the system that exists, to submit ourselves to the labor it requires. What Durkheim suggests is that the bourgeoisie, rather than a ruling class that embodies its own negation, represents the end of history and therefore the manifestation of the final and most advanced stage of human social evolution.

However, Durkheim could not ignore the class antagonism highlighted above by Marx, due, in part, to the intensity of the class struggle of his time and the recent memory of the worker's Paris Commune of 1871. Acknowledging the human need of not being made a slave or being externally controlled, while maintaining his belief that inequality serves a necessary function in advanced societies, Durkheim notes that "moral life, like that of body and mind, responds to different needs which may even be contradictory. Thus it is natural for it to be made up in part of opposing elements..." (p. 39). In effect, Durkheim tells us that "progress" has a price—a price that tends to cause distress within the individual—but that is the nature of the universe, and it is not wise to challenge laws of nature. Building the foundation for this "functionalist" approach to sociology in his dissertation Durkheim (1893/2000) theorizes:

> We can no longer be under any illusion about the trends in modern industry. It involves increasingly powerful mechanisms, large-scale groupings of power and capital, and consequently an extreme division of labor...This evolution occurs spontaneously and unthinkingly. Those economists who study its causes and evaluate its results, far from condemning such diversification or attacking it, proclaim its necessity. They perceive in it the higher law of human societies and the condition for progress. (pp. 37–38)

Again, Durkheim does not stop here in his analysis of *objective reality* as he reaches ever deeper into the grandiose, going on to argue that the division of labor does not just occur within the realm of economics, but can be identified within every aspect of life, and within all forms of life, rendering it a "biological phenomenon," and therefore a law of nature. By claiming that capitalism happened "spontaneously" and "unthinkingly" Durkheim effectively rewrites history erasing the long struggle against the commodification of humanity that was anything but spontaneous or without thought. Essentially, Durkheim takes Marx's idea of the naturalness of the division of labor and divests it of its independent and communal nature, and replaces it with the notion that inequality and subservience to power are necessary manifestations of the advanced development of the division of labor.

This basic formula, with roots in Platonic epistemology that views intelligence as naturally and unevenly distributed, continues to exist in contemporary hegemonic discourses of the ruling elite—it is the presupposition informing the entire foundation of ruling class policy and practice. As a side note, the current crisis in confidence, discussed above, can, in part, be understood as stemming from the seeming incompetence and confusion coming from the political bosses in Washington and elsewhere. Not only does Durkheim support this idea of a naturally-occurring hierarchical conception of class within societies that undergoes intensified scrutiny during times of crisis, but he ranks civilizations/nations on a similar scale. Essentially, Durkheim argues that there is a tendency among societies that demonstrates that as they grow larger, the division of labor grows more specialized and entrenched, and as a result, they become more advanced. However, confronted with the existence of larger non-white nations, Durkheim argues that there are exceptions to this rule, which seems to stem from his belief in racial hierarchy. Consider:

> The Jewish nation, before the conquest, was probably more voluminous than the Roman city of the fourth century; yet it was of a lower species. China and Russia are much more populous than the most civilized nations of Europe. Consequently among these same peoples the division of labor did not develop in proportion to the social volume. This is because the growth in volume is not necessarily a mark of superiority if the density does not grow at the same time and in the same proportion...If therefore the largest of them only reproduces societies of a very inferior type, the segmentary structure will remain very pronounced, and in consequence the social organization will be little advanced. An aggregate of clans, even if immense, ranks below the smallest society that is organized, since the latter has already gone through those stages of evolution below which the aggregate has remained. (p. 49)

Durkheim's implied white supremacy was not his own invention, nor was the idea of a natural hierarchy among Europeans represented within the division of labor new to him either. However, it is beyond the scope of this essay to trace the origins of those ideas. What follows, rather, is an analysis of how hegemonic conceptions of the division of labor have influenced policy in the United States situated in a more contemporary context from Lippmann to Friedman. Beginning with Lippmann we investigate how the idea of a natural hierarchy represented in the existence of rank-able social classes informed his ideas and practice concerning both domestic and foreign affairs.

However, as we will observe, Lippmann represents the progressive end of the elite political continuum of hierarchy—progressive, primarily because he was a proponent of British economist John Maynard Keynes (1936/1997) who advocated for a series of restrictions and taxations placed on accumulated wealth in order to "get rid" of the "objectionable characteristics of capital," such as "instability" (p. 221). Lippmann (1937/2005) argued that taxing the rich was necessary in "relatively rich societies," such as the United States, because "there is a strong tendency for the supply of capital to become so large that the rate of interest falls to a level where there is little inducement to invest it in new enterprise" (p. 229). In other words, when the profit gained from investing x amount of capital becomes so minimal that taking the economic risks that accompany speculative enterprise leads to dramatic reductions in investment and the resulting economic instability, government intervention becomes a necessity for the perpetuation of capitalism. When capitalists hoard capital, Lippmann (1937/2005) reasons, substantial sums of "wealth" are "withheld from use," which slows down production, increases unemployment, and leads to "the extreme poverty of the marginal workers" (p. 229). Lippmann (1937/2005) concludes that "under these circumstances" it is necessary to use "taxing power" to "pump the surplus funds of the rich out of the ordinary capital market and into public investments" (p. 229).

Keynes (1936/1997) points to the "separation between ownership and management" and "the development of organized investment markets," that is, the *Stock Exchange* system, as contributing to both increased investment, which, from a capitalist perspective, is positive, but also to "greatly" enhancing "the instability of the system" (pp. 150–151). For example, Keynes (1936/1997) observes that because the Stock Exchange is primarily designed to "facilitate transfers of old investments between one individual and another," there is a propensity to "spend on a new project what may seem an extravagant sum, if it can be floated off on the Stock Exchange at an immediate profit" (p. 151). As a solution Keynes (1936/1997) suggests that capital should be made "less scarce" to "diminish" the "excess yield" or profit, which can be done "without its having become less productive—at least in the physical sense" (p. 213). This ability to stabilize markets through regulating "the competition of the rate of interest on money" led Keynes (1936/1997) to "sympathize" with the observation that all value "is produced by labor" (p. 213).

Propaganda and Capitalism in the United States

While John Maynard Keynes is responsible for developing the economic theory known as *social democratic liberalism*, which was harshly condemned during the 1950s and beyond by Friedman and other neoliberals as *socialist* or *collectivist* and therefore *misguided* (Hill & Kumar, 2009; Hursh, 2008; Porfilio & Malott, 2008), Lippmann can be said to have situated the theory within a propagandist framework. Walter Lippmann, to be sure, was a highly influential architect of this discursive model contributing significantly to the implementation of its practice, a point world-renowned scholar/activist Noam Chomsky (1999) has consistently given much attention to. For more than fifty years Lippmann was perhaps the most respected political journalist in the United States "winning the attention of national political leaders from the era of Woodrow Wilson through that of Lyndon B. Johnson" (Wilentz, 2008, p. vii). Again, within the Western tradition of hegemonic philosophy and practice, Lippmann's ideas tended to fall on the liberal end of the spectrum. That is, while he believed it was the paternalistic responsibility of democratic government, comprised of those endowed with a naturally superior intelligence, to mold "the will of the people," it must be for *the common good* and carried out without the conscious manipulation of propaganda. Set against what he believed to be the crude tactics of McCarthyism and the Red Scare, Lippmann was concerned with purifying "the rivers of opinion that fed public opinion" (Steel, 2008, p. xv).

Like Durkheim before him, Lippmann too, discounted the ideals of democracy (such as the notion that the will of the people does not need to be externally commanded) as an "illusion" referring to it in *Public Opinion* (1922) as "the original dogma of democracy." As we will see, Lippmann constructed a theory of humanity, assumed to represent *objective reality*, as being too ignorant and steeped in prejudice and bias to be able to achieve the necessary competence to know what is best for themselves rendering the theoretical idea of democracy a fantastic vision, but not conducive to the imperfect reality of human depravity. Lippmann biographer Ronald Steel (2008), in his forward to the recently re-issued *Liberty and the News* (1920/2008), reasons that:

> The horrors of World War I had shattered his optimism about human nature. His propaganda work, reinforced by the repressive activities of the government's propaganda bureau, the Committee on Public Information, had made him realize how easily public opinion could be molded. He had always believed that a free press was the cornerstone of democracy. He still believed that, but with a new qualification. (pp. xii-xiii)

That "qualification" was his assertion that democracy itself is an unachievable ideal. Contributing to his belief in the inferior intelligence of the general public was his engagement with the emerging field of psychology that reinforced his beliefs about the nature of human perception rendering most people unfit to participate in the democratic process. For example, in *The Phantom Public* (1927) Lippmann argues that, "man's reflexes are, as the psychologists say, conditioned. And, therefore, he responds quite readily to a glass egg, a decoy duck, a stuffed shirt, or a political platform" (p. 30). Lippmann was clearly informed by the idea that the public is limited to perceiving the world only as it has been trained to. As a result, there tends to be a great gap between what is believed about the world and the actual world, or, *objective reality*.

Highlighting the persistence of this paternalistic attitude the U.S. House of Representatives recently discounted the people of the United States' overwhelming objection of the trillion dollar bailout bill, arguing that the public is unable to comprehend the severity of the problem, and thus only see clear skies blind to the approaching storm. According to Lippmann (1927), not only is the public inherently limited in its sense of perception, but in its desire to know commenting that "the citizen gives but a little of his time to public affairs, has but a casual interest in facts and but a poor appetite for theory" (pp. 24–25).

Summarizing his position Lippmann (1927) concludes that it is false to "…assume that either the voters are inherently competent to direct the course of affairs or that they are making progress toward such an ideal. I think it is a false ideal. I do not mean an undesirable ideal. I mean an unattainable ideal…" (pp. 38–39). Lippmann therefore viewed education no more suitable to achieve democratic ideals than any other false sense of hope. As it turns of then, the United States, who has long presented itself as *the* world's leading proponent of democracy, has a history of being influenced by thinkers who believe in hierarchy and supremacy and therefore view the theoretical context of democracy as not representative of the concrete context of human nature, and therefore an unwise goal to pursue. However, not only was democracy portrayed as unwise, but dangerous. Summarizing this point in classic prose Lippmann (1927) notes:

> A false ideal of democracy can lead only to disillusionment and to meddlesome tyranny. If democracy cannot direct affairs, then a philosophy which expects it to direct them will encourage the people to attempt the impossible; they will fail, but that will interfere outrageously with the productive liberties of the individual. The public must be put in its place, so that it may exercise its own powers, but no less and perhaps even more, so that each of us may live free of the trampling and the roar of a bewildered herd. (p. 145)

Of course men like Lippmann, armed with their superior capacities, do not suffer from the afflictions of inadequacy or the illusion that the public man is of the same mind as the public. From this perspective the division of labor is largely based on the naturally occurring unequal capacities of *men* rendering some more fit to lead and design the social structure, while the most useful function for the vast majority reside in their physical ability to follow direction and labor—as passive spectators rather than active participants. The responsibility of those most fit to lead, the responsible or capable men, is therefore to regiment the public mind as an army regiments its troops. This is the boss's moral and paternalistic "commitment," as Lippmann (1943) referred to it. Because Lippmann's conception of class was based on the assumption of a natural hierarchy, he was logically able to claim a moral relativism as well, which stands in stark contrast to Marx's privileging of democratic relations over the unjust relationship between labor and capital, that is, between the oppressed and their oppressors. In making this case—a case ultimately against democracy—Lippmann (1927) proclaims, "it requires intense partisanship and much self-deception to argue that some sort of peculiar righteousness adheres to...the employers' against the wage-earners', the creditors' against the debtors', or the other way around" (p. 34).

The peculiar nature of Lippmann's political relativism is further brought to the fore in his discourse on U.S. foreign policy where he draws on the notion of "justice" as it pertains to the use of force. Lippmann's analysis in *U.S. Foreign Policy* (1943), seems, in many ways, to be a direct response to the arguments presented in the highly publicized *War is a Racket* (1935/2003) by anti-war activist, World War I veteran, and Brigadier General Smedley D. Butler. Summarizing his position on war Butler (1935/2003) comments:

> War is a racket. It always has been. It is possibly the oldest, easily the most profitable, surely the most vicious. It is the only one international in scope. It is the only one in which the profits are reckoned in dollars and the losses in lives. (p. 23)

Reflecting on the United States' involvement in the First World War Butler (1935/2003) notes that, "we forgot, or shunted aside, the advice of the Father of our country. We forgot Washington's warning about 'entangling alliances'" (p. 26). In *U.S. Foreign Policy: Shield of the Republic*, published eight years after *War is a Racket*, Lippmann (1943) invests a significant amount of time making an argument against the pacifism alluded to in *War is a Racket*, without, however, referring directly to Butler or his work. Like Butler, Lippmann too draws on the legacy of General George Washington, but draws almost opposite conclusions. Consistent with his usual style, Lippmann (1943) paints a picture of the benevolent leader whose responsibility it is to protect the national interest—the interests of the rich—which *he* must have the military capacity to do. Otherwise, through his vulnerability, he is inviting his enemy's provocation, and therefore irresponsibly putting those who rely on his paternalistic protection at unnecessary risk.

> Washington did not say that the nation should or could renounce war, and seek only peace. For he knew that the national "interest, guided by justice" might bring the Republic into conflict with other nations. Since he knew that the conflict might be irreconcilable by negotiation and compromise, his primary concern was to make sure that the national interest was wisely and adequately supported with armaments, suitable frontiers, and the appropriate alliances. (Lippmann, 1943, p. 51)

Lippmann's reasoning here is simple enough: an empire, such as the United States, will not survive without room to grow and the muscle needed to protect its "interests," that is, the interests of the rich or responsible men which include the subjugation of their own population during crises of confidence and the extraction and concentration of wealth. The essence of his argumentation lies in the same age-old paternalistic guardianship and moral relativism that allows questions of justice to be freed from issues of domination and subjugation. In making his argument Lippmann cites the Monroe Doctrine of 1823 as evidence of the United States' "commitment" to extend its "protection…to the whole of the Western hemisphere" and that "at the risk of war, the United States would thereafter resist the creation of new European empires in this hemisphere" (Lippmann, 1943, p. 16). Monroe's doctrine has come to be interpreted as "professing a unilateral US 'right' to circumscribe the sovereignty of all other nations in the hemisphere" (Churchill, 2002, p. 335) influencing its aggressive dealings with Indigenous sovereigns within its boundaries and those within its hemisphere such as Cuba and Jamaica and all other Latin American and Caribbean nations (Malott, 2008, 2007; Malott & Malott, 2008).

The context Lippmann situates U.S. foreign policy in provides a useful lends for understanding the nation's current policies, such as those concerning not only Cuba, but globally. After all, it is the responsibility of the more capable men to make decisions for less capable men, and any illusions concerning democratic principles only restricts the natural development of the division of labor worldwide. As we will see below, Milton Friedman (1962/2002) picks up on this line of reasoning arguing that restrictions on the extraction and accumulation of wealth and the further entrenchment of class antagonisms only threatens the freedom of "progress," that is, capitalism, and of men and women pursuing it.

* * *

Milton Friedman, pro-capital, economist extraordinaire, received worldwide recognition in 1976 winning the Nobel Memorial Prize in Economic Sciences and has been touted as the world's most influential economist of the twentieth century. Friedman has drawn the attention of the likes of internationally-renowned political analyst and activist Noam Chomsky (1999) who referred to him as a "neoliberal guru" while vociferously critiquing his (1962/2002) *Capitalism and Freedom* for hegemonically equating "profit-making" with being "the essence of democracy" and that "any government that pursues antimarket policies is being anti-democratic, no matter how much informed popular support they might enjoy" (p. 9).

Friedman's supposition that the surest way to freedom is through capitalism is informed by the ancient hierarchy of intelligence paradigm that views economic competition the playing field most conducive to fostering the environment that will encourage and enable the superior individuals to rise to the top and assume their place as leaders and decision makers, that is, capitalists. Attempts to legislate against exploitation and abuse to ensure a functioning democracy, from this approach to knowledge production, is viewed as an attack on freedom because it prevents the naturally endowed masters from assuming their biologically determined place within the hierarchy. This construction is an unquestionable aspect of *objective reality*. Informed by this logic, the primary responsibility of government is therefore to "preserve the rules of the game by enforcing contracts, preventing coercion, and keeping markets free" (Friedman, 1955, p. 1). Connecting Friedman's philosophy to practice Chomsky (1999) observes:

> Equipped with this perverse understanding of democracy, neoliberals like Friedman had no qualms over the military overthrow of Chile's democratically elected Allende government in 1973, because Allende was interfering with business control of Chilean society. (p. 9)

In order for government, and society more generally, to fulfill their scripted functions, reasons Friedman (1955), they require social stability, which is not possible without "widespread acceptance of some common set of values" and "a minimum degree of literacy and knowledge" (p. 2). Friedman (1955) reasons that the government should subsidize these *basic* levels of education because it "adds to the economic value of the student" (p. 4) and capitalists should invest in their labor just as they invest in machinery. The public is therefore viewed as a resource to be manipulated by the natural leaders for the *common good*. Making this point Friedman (1955) argues that education "is a form of investment in human capital precisely analogous to investment in machinery, buildings, or other forms of non human capital" and can be justified as a necessary expenditure because "its function is to raise the economic productivity of the human being" (p. 13). For Friedman (1955) then, knowledge production as an actively engaged endeavor is reserved for the elite, rendering the vast majority subject to the necessary "indoctrination" needed to ensure the widespread acceptance of "common social values required for a stable society" even if it means "inhibiting freedom of thought and belief" (p. 7).

As one of the world's leading theoreticians of free market capitalism, it should not be surprising that Friedman (1955) was a strong supporter of the privatization of, and thus the corporate control over, public education, masking it with a discourse of *choice*. In more recent times Milton Friedman acknowledged that the testing-based No Child Left Behind Act (NCLB) touted as the surest path to increasing achievement was really designed to lend weight to the *choice* and voucher movement by setting schools up to fail and then handing them over to private managing firms such as Edison Schools (Kohn, 2004). Critical educator Alfie Kohn (2004) has commented that "you don't have to be a conspiracy nut to understand the real purpose of NCLB" (p. 84). That is, NCLB is nothing more than a "backdoor maneuver" (Kohn, 2004, p. 84) constructed around conceptions of *choice* allowing private for-profit capitalists to take over public education. Friedman's theory paved the theoretical pathway for these *neoliberal* tendencies of the public realm being handed over to corporations to be realized.

Friedman's theory is based on the assumption that the competition for education dollars would push, out of the necessity to survive, education investors to offer superior products to attract customers. Schools that offered a sub-standard product would not be profitable, and would therefore be forced to either improve or close. Again, the NCLB of George W. Bush has served as a standards-based approach to usher in Friedman's desire to privatize public education, which has had disastrous results on the knowledge production process. As a result, a major blow was leveled against the practice of education as an active engagement designed to understand the world and to transform it, taking aim specifically at the labor/capital relationship and its manifest hegemonies such as white supremacy and patriarchy.

These developments, however, are well documented. For the purposes of this discussion we will turn our attention to the larger Euro-centric vision of Friedman's discourse, which is equally relevant as we approach a potentially new era in knowledge production in North America. That is, the Democratic presidency of Barack Obama, while pro-neoliberal capitalist in principle, claims to "believe" that "teachers should not be forced to spend the academic year preparing students to fill in bubbles on standardized tests" (Obama Biden). The manifestation of this desire would provide critical pedagogues much needed breathing room to engage in counter-hegemonic knowledge production and critical praxis after this long period of Friedman inspired privatization.

Friedman leaves little room for misinterpretation regarding his conceptualization of democracy and social class, which, we will see, is, in many ways, almost the exact opposite of Marxism, underscoring, in a sense, a testament to Marx's continued relevance in terms of directly and indirectly informing popular democratic movements challenging basic structures of power and therefore demanding a response by the architects of contemporary U.S. public hegemonic discourse and policy. Within his paradigm Friedman (1962/2002) situates capitalism as the central driving force behind human evolution and therefore responsible for the "great advances of civilization" such as Columbus "seeking a new route to China" (p. 3), which consequently led to the emergence of vast fortunes generated by Europe's colonialist empire building, slavery, genocide/depopulation and repopulation, and on a scale so massive, so horrendous and so utterly barbaric as to render comprehending its manifestation as a criminal act carried out by real living, breathing, feeling people almost unimaginable (Malott, 2008). Friedman, therefore, does not seem too different from his predecessors. That is, describing Columbus coming to the America's as one of the great advances in civilization can only be understood as callous and thoroughly Euro-centric.

But again, Friedman draws on the example of Columbus for the "advances" that have resulted from the "freedom" to pursue private "economic interests," and therefore as evidence to support capitalism. Friedman (1962/2002) goes so far as to argue that free market "capitalism is a necessary condition for political freedom" (p. 10). Friedman's thesis can be understood as a direct response to the popular support for nationalized economies designed to promote an equal distribution of the wealth generated by the productive apparatus arguing that "collectivist economic planning has...interfered with individual freedom" (p. 11). Individual freedom, for Friedman, stems from unregulated market mechanisms "stabilized" by a limited government whose function is to "protect our freedom both from the enemies outside our gates and from our fellow citizens: to preserve law and order, to enforce private contracts, and to foster competitive markets" (p. 2). Friedman points to the Soviet Union as an example of what he argues is the coercive tendency of government intervention in economic affairs. It is not surprising that Friedman does not mention the infinitely more democratic and egalitarian nature of Cuba's centrally-planned economy compared to the US-supported free-market systems in the Caribbean and Latin America (Malott, 2007, 2009; Malott & Malott, 2008).

The "law and order" referred to by Friedman can best be understood as the way in which "the descendents of European colonizers shaped...rules to seize title to indigenous lands" (Robertson, 2005, p. ix) and to "enforce" these "private contracts." Similarly, the Monroe Doctrine, touted by Lippmann (1927) as bounded by "law" and "custom," can be understood as extending the United States' "sphere of influence" to the entire Western hemisphere. That is, to ensure that the resources and productive capacities of not only this region, but much of the world, would be controlled by U.S. interests. These self-endorsed "commitments" of the United States have been upheld with deadly force explaining the U.S.'s simultaneously open and hidden war against the Cuban Revolution and Castro's trouble-making in the hemisphere (Chomsky, 1999; Malott, 2007). While the hegemony of US power has seemed all but total, it has not been without critique and resistance from not only Cuba and Latin America, but within the US as well. At the heart of this counter-hegemony has been the on-going development of critical pedagogies, one of the primary philosophical influences of which can be traced to both Southern and Northern Native America.

CRITICAL PEDAGOGY AND INDIGENEITY: DEMOCRATIC PRAXIS AGAINST SOCIAL CLASS

Although he is certainly not the first critical pedagogue, the late Brazilian radical educator, Paulo Freire, is, however, the practitioner credited with the founding of what we have come to know in North America as *critical pedagogy* with his first book being published in Brazil in 1967. Freire's *Pedagogy of the Oppressed*, initially published in the United States in 1970, is arguably the seed from which critical pedagogy in education in North America has sprouted. Freire and other critical theory-trained, Latin American, critical pedagogues were highly influenced by liberation theologists such as Leonardo Boff (1971/1978) and Leodardo Boff and Clodovis Boff (1987) of Brazil, Peruvian Gustavo Gutiérrez (1973/1988), and world-renowned Archbishop Oscar Romero (1988/2005) of El Salvador who was assassinated in 1987 after becoming "known across the world as a fearless defender of the poor and suffering" earning him "the hatred and calumny of powerful persons in his own country" (Brockman, 1988/2005, p. xv). What is common among these leaders is that they all practiced (practice) and developed their theologies with the poorest and most oppressed sectors of their societies, who, wherever Indigenous peoples are found, tend to be Indigenous peoples. Within these theologies of liberation we can therefore find the democratic impulse that can be treated, risking romanticization, as a common characteristic among a diverse range of traditional Indigenous communities.

Critical pedagogy has always been concerned with challenging the discourse of hierarchy that legitimizes oppression and human suffering as indicative of the natural order of the universe. Rather than viewing intelligence as unequally distributed and therefore the practice of democracy extremely limited, critical pedagogy is based on an armed love and radical faith in people's ability to tend to their own economic and political interests in the spirit of peace and mutuality. In a recent series of interviews with David Barsamian, international activist, Noam Chomsky (2007), describes the characteristics of what he understands to be the praxis of democracy, that is, widespread political participation

> There can't be widespread structural change unless a very substantial part of the population is deeply committed to it…If you are a serious revolutionary, you

don't want a coup. You want changes to come from below, from the organized population. (p. 121)

This unyielding democratic impulse of Western-trained, North American critical pedagogy can be largely attributed to the generous philosophical gifts of not only Native South Americans but Native North Americans such as the Haudenosaunee. According to Donald A. Grinde (1992) in "Iroquois Political Theory and the Roots of American Democracy" many of the "founding fathers" of the U.S., Benjamin Franklin most notably, rejected the anti-democratic European model drawing instead on the brilliance of the Iroquois system of shared governance designed to ensure democracy and peace by putting power and decision making in the intelligent hands of the people united in a confederation of nations and not in the divine right or assumed superiority of a ruler. Grinde and others in *Exiled in the Land of the Free* (Lyons & Mohawk, 1992) document, in great detail, the generosity of the Iroquois leaders in assisting Euro-Americans, before, during and after the American Revolution, in creating a unified Nation composed of the original thirteen colonies as the foundation for long-term peace, freedom, liberty and democracy in North America. Putting the American Revolutionary war in a context foreign to traditional social studies instruction, Grinde (1992) notes that "the first democratic revolution sprang from American unrest because the colonists had partially assimilated the concepts of unity, federalism, and natural rights that existed in American Indian governments" (p. 231). It is abundantly clear that the gift of democracy received by the United States government by the Haudenosaunee has all been but subverted. For examples of the democratic tradition in contemporary times, outside of Native communities themselves, we have to turn our attention to the highly marginalized critical tradition.

However, we might say that this democratic tradition, commonly associated with European critical theory (i.e. Marxism), is an appropriation because the Native American source of these generous gifts, in the contemporary context, tends not to be cited. For those already engaged in the life-long pursuit of knowledge, this is an easily amendable flaw—requiring of such Western-trained critical theorists/educators an active epistemological and material engagement with Native Studies and Indigenous communities the world over (Ewen, 1994; Kincheloe, 2008). We might say that the critical theoretical tradition, rooted in Indigenous conceptions of freedom and liberty, represents a rich history of opposition to anti-democratic, authoritarian forms of institutionalized power—private (corporate), federal (state), and religious (Clergy/Church)—for it is this unjust power that poses the greatest barrier to peace. The example of the Haudenosaunee is relatively indicative of this tradition, which stands in stark contrast to the anti-democratic model perpetuated by Durkhiem, Lippmann, Friedman, and the like.

QUESTIONS OF CERTAINTY, ISSUES OF PEDAGOGY

Questions of absolutism and certainty also become epistemologically central in the realm of pedagogy and the theory of our educational practice. Postmodern analyses challenge us to question the deterministic absolutism characteristic of enlightenment science. However, it would be foolish to take these critiques as an excuse not to consider what seem to be the more useful conclusions of modernist social science in regards to the role power plays in the legitimation process. For example, Marxists and other Enlightenment science radicals have gone to great lengths to quantify and reduce social trends concluding that the doctrinal system of the elite consistently portrays a distorted imagine of reality as neutral and therefore *just how it is*. This has been accomplished in the contemporary era through the establishment of a ruling class controlled propaganda machine, employing schools, the government, and the mass media, which serves the function of maintaining social control. Some scientists argue that this control must be established, by either force or consent, whenever people are oppressed, because the species has a predetermined propensity for freedom and democracy, which is therefore built into the genetic design as an endowment.

Skeptical of any absolutisms regarding the highly complex and little known phenomena of consciousness and free will, that is, the human condition, we might argue that it only appears that humans are naturally democratic because the values of democracy have long been accepted and internalized by the vast majority of humanity rendering it easy to confuse that which has been socially constructed for a biologically determined characteristic. Rather than attempting to make a deterministic case for the human condition, as either democratic or competitive, we might argue that behaviorism has demonstrated that humans' socially constructed schema are vulnerable to external manipulation suggesting more of a *blank slate* or *environmental* theory. Instead of putting this knowledge to work in the service of domination as the behaviorist tradition has done, we evoke it here to raise caution against anti-democratic practice.

However, we take issue with the radical or progressive scientific tendency to treat either of these analyses as *more or less* accurate representations of *objective reality* even when they are grounded in the *facts* and not based on a desire to oppress and dominate. Following the postmodern insights of critical constructivism we therefore challenge the assertion that there *is* an objective reality that exists independent of the senses because it is the schemas of the mind that constructs ideas, explanations, and guides the practice of choice. Pedagogy based on the presupposition of an external objective reality can too easily lead to a form of anti-democratic critical banking and therefore not inclusive of the multitude of subjugated knowledges based on the multiple positionalities of oppression. We argue, on the other hand, that students should be actively engaged in the process of discovery or knowledge production based on a dialectical relationship between their own experiences and the theory of the social that suggests that there exists a macro-structural hegemonic power base that represents the common class enemy of the vast majority, despite the vast epistemological diversity found within human culture and individuality.

Again, it is not our aim to challenge critical descriptions of capitalism, especially those coming from the Marxist tradition, but to reframe them not as *objective reality* but as social constructions that, for now, do seem to best represent the phenomena in question (Kincheloe, 2005), that is, neoliberal capitalism. In so doing, we invite learners to become actively engaged in the discovery process, or the process of naming and renaming the concrete context through the production of knowledge. Ultimately, the epistemological goal of critical pedagogy is not only to construct *accurate* and useful knowledge about the concrete context and the self, but to construct knowledge about how to transform the self as part of the process of transforming the world. For Marxists this means challenging and dismantling the labor/capital relationship and creating new relationships between people based on an inherently different set of values and ideals that challenge the hierarchies of antiquity that continue to dominate. We might understand this critical approach to knowledge production as part of the democratic process of becoming.

Conclusion

Reflecting on the current crisis of capitalism, working people, as always, will bare the burden because the bosses will not pay the costs if they can defer it to "the simple people," as US Congressmen and women so often paternaliistically refer to the *American people* as. So they pay. But sometimes it takes a trillion dollar reward for systemic irresponsible deception—the loving touch capitalism has always afforded "the bewildered herd"—to waken the sleeping giant of those who rely on a wage to survive. The crisis in confidence *is* the sleeping giant waking up, which goes much deeper than the reluctance to spend/consume. That is, the questoining goes to the heart of the modern world—the process of value production and its dehumanized underlying driving force, which is the quest for profit, whatever the consequence. While the *sleeping giant* metaphor can be useful and powerful, however, the risk is that it is a form of reductionism. That is, reducing the infinitely vast diversity of consciousness to a single entity flattens out the richness of all the contributing parts. We therefore must be careful not to confuse the individual parts for the whole (Kincheloe, 2005). To illustrate this point we might say that while the left pinky toe seems to effectively stimulate the epistemological curiosity of many people, it alone cannot account for the complexity of the entire giant.

As critical pedagogues it is within these instances of overt crisis that is our time to shine and do what we do: teach and engage with democratic principles, that is, help that big old giant stand up, become self-actualized, reach its full non-deterministic potential, and mature gracefully. Pedagogy is always critical at this juncture because the dominant paradigm does not recognize that we are all unique *free wills* and not things to be directed because it can't. If the system did, it would not be what it is. It would be something different, and that is what we want. What will life after capital be like? Who knows? Maybe we'll decide to call it Fun Style. Who is against fun? To be successful we must continue to rigorously strive to name the world, as it currently exists. We might call this the struggle over *the meaning of our language*, and thus, the meaning of the world and ourselves.

For example, despite the central role social class plays in determining the conditions of human life in capitalist society, it is a concept that receives very little attention in corporate media outlets. On rare occasion when it is introduced, it tends to be treated as the objective state of falling within a particular income bracket and is therefore just one of the many ways people are diverse, no more or less special than being male or female, or short or tall, for example. What is implied is that inequality is the natural state of humanity, and that any centrally-planned attempts to democratize the distribution of wealth is therefore *un*natural because it limits the individual's freedom to create his or her own economic destiny, allowing the cream to rise to the top, as it were. The entire history of coercion, propaganda, genocide, and conquest that paved, and continues to pave, the way for class society to exist, and the on-going resistance against it, tends to be left out of these discussions, almost without exception. Making a similar observation Chomsky (1993) plainly states that "in the United States you're not allowed to talk about class differences" unless you belong to one of two groups, "the business community, which is rabidly class-conscious" and "high planning sectors of the government" (p. 67).

It is therefore not saying too much that the class-perspective found in the work of Durkheim, Keynes, Lippmann, and Friedman has greatly influenced the business press, which tends to be "full of the danger of the masses and their rising power and how we have to defeat them. It's kind of vulgar, inverted Marxism" (Chomsky, 1993, p. 67). What we find is that this self-serving perspective of those who benefit from class-based inequalities, in mainstream, dominant society, is presented as objective reality—as normalized and naturalized. However, because our humanity can be limited, but never completely destroyed, hegemony cannot be complete, and the less so, the more serious we take the wisdom of those who counter-hegemonically came before, and those who continue to generously contribute to the critical tradition.

Appendix A

This analysis of Longfellow's Hiawatha is part of a lesson that Mrs. Teller shared in part with one of 11th grade English classes in their study of American literature a number of years ago. It was an eye opening experience for the students because they had only been familiar with the poem from the mockery and disdain in cartoons.

THE SONG OF MAEQNAPUS BY LESLIE TELLER

The Song of Hiawatha by Henry Wadsworth Longfellow is based upon the sacred Medicine Dance stories of my blood, the Menominee and Ojibwa people of the Great Lakes region. In 1855 Longfellow, with the help of an Ojibwa man named Kah-ge-gah'bowh (p. x), takes the Medicine Dance stories, the oral traditions of the Great Lakes people, and crafts them into an epic poem. There are twenty-two cantos in *The Song of Hiawatha*. I have chosen to interpret the third canto titled "Hiawatha's Childhood." *The Song of Hiawatha* is not a strict translation of the Medicine Dance stories, but it maintains much of the thematic structure of the original work. I will discuss differences between Longfellow's *Song of Hiawatha* and the Medicine Dance stories, which may reveal some of the ways the mythology of the Indian people were distilled for American consumption. I will discuss the theme of the Indian people's belief system within the canto "Hiawatha's Childhood," specifically the earth as a living organism. I will explore the theme of maturation within "Hiawatha's Childhood"—or the hero's journey as he travels from child to man; a transition that demands a connectedness to Mother Earth. I will also examine Longfellow's word choices as an imitation of the structure of the Algonquin language family.

* * *

The Hiawatha character in Longfellow's epic poem was a real Onondaga chief (p. vii) who had helped to build the Six Nations Confederacy of the Oneida, Seneca, Onondaga, and Mohawk, Cayuga, and Iroquois Tribes. The authentic name of the culture hero God in the sacred Medicine Dance stories of the Great Lakes people is Namebozho (p. vii) in the Ojibwa language or Maeqnapus in the Menominee dialect. In the introductory notes (p. x) Longfellow changed the name to Hiawatha because the sound was more euphonic to the American ear. Longfellow shows us the Hiawatha character is of his creation:

> Thus was born *my* Hiawatha... (p. 27 line 9)

For purposes of our discussion, I will refer to Longfellow's Hiawatha in his authentic Menominee name of Maeqnapus (pronounced MAH'-NA-PUS). What makes Maeqnapus a hero God? He is not like you and me. His grandmother is the daughter of the moon and his father is the West-Wind. In "Hiawatha's Childhood" we see how Nokomis, the grandmother of Maeqnapus, came to live on earth, "From the moon fell Nokomis..." (p. 25 line 13). Nokomis is seen as a star that falls to earth, later she bears a daughter. Wenonah, Nokomis warns her beautiful daughter often:

> Oh, beware of Mudjekeewis.
> Of the West-Wind, Mudjekeewis... (p. 26 lines 14, 15)

Wenonah fails to heed the warnings of her mother, and succumbs to the advances of the West-Wind, Mudjekeewis. In the original story Wenonah was not seduced by Mjdjekeewis, instead she was raped. Longfellow cloaks the rape of Wenonah because sexual impropriety was not polite to write about in Longfellow's time and he omits it in *The Song of Hiawatha*. The Menominee Ojibwa original legend, on the other hand, tells of how Wenonah was raped by Judjekeewis. Longfellow leaves evidence of this:

> Till she bore a son in sorrow
> Bore a son of love and sorrow. (p. 27 lines 7, 8)

This son, Maeqnapus, becomes the central character of the story and we are shown his transition from young boy to manhood. The role of Maeqnapus, throughout

"Hiawatha's Childhood," is to travel from a child to man. In the beginning, Longfellow's Hiawatha is shown as a child quieted by his grandmother:

> Hush! The Naked Bear will hear thee! (p. 28 line 11)

Maeqnapus later becomes a brave who slays his first deer:

> As he bore the red deer homeward… (p. 33 line 23)

Maeqnapus is raised by his grandmother Nokomis because his mother, Wenonah, has died. Wenonah fails to listen to Nokomis and as a result is impregnated and dies, according to Longfellow, of a broken heart:

> Hiawatha's gentle mother,
> In her anguish died deserted
> By the West-Wind, false and faithless
> By the heartless Mudjekeewis. (p. 27 lines 12–15)

It is not Wenonah's anguish, as we are led to believe, that is the cause of her death. According to the original Menominee/Ojibwa legend, a second baby is born after Meaqnapus, his twin brother the Rock Monster. It is this baby made of rock which is the cause of Wenonah's death. The second child tears the mother and she bleeds to death. This detail is most likely excluded in Longfellow's work for 1850 American Sensibility. However, the consequence of not listening to the warnings of wise grandmothers is maintained. Wenonah dies because she did not heed the warning of her mother, the daughter of the moon.

Maeqnapus slays the deer because one of the rights of passage in traditional Indian culture is the first kill. Maeqnapus matures from a child to a young, brave, hunter who has brought his first kill to the people of the village. In "Hiawatha's Childhood" we are told Maeqnapus is given a special bow and arrows and embarks on a task of killing a red roebuck. After a successful hunt, Maeqnapus returns to the village with deer and is honored with a special feast and is given new names of manhood:

> Called him Strong-Heart, Soan-ga-taha!
> Called him loon-Heart, Mahn-go-taysee! (p. 34 lines 5, 6)

These are traditional rights of passage for Maeqnapus and exemplify the transitional theme of "Hiawatha's Childhood."

Another theme of this story is the connection with the earth—the earth as Mother. Maeqnapus knows the language of each and is able to speak to all the consciousness within it: the wind, the water, the animals, and the plants. An example of the linguistic gifts of Maeqnapus is found in the following lines:

> "Minne-wawa!" said the pine trees,
> "Mudway-aushka!" said the water. (p. 29 lines 8, 9)

They all speak to him and he understands them:

> Then the little Hiawatha
> Learned of every bird its language
> Learned their names and all their secrets...(p. 30 lines 23–25)

Maeqnapus speaks with the insects, the birds, the rabbits, and all creatures of the earth because they are his relatives. The deer he slays is glad to give his life to him and is shown in the line:

> Leaped as if to meet the arrow...(p. 33 line 15)

The purpose of the arrow making its mark is because Maeqnapus is a hero God whose arrow sings the song of the earth. His arrows are straight because his heart is pure, he is the orphan son of the West-Wind and his grandmother is the daughter of the moon. We are more powerful, our arrows are straight, when we connect to earth as our mother, when what we take from her is life affirming. The idea that the earth is a living organism requires us to speak to her in a common language.

The syntax Longfellow chooses to use in *The Song of Hiawatha* follows the form of the spoken Algonquin language. This form choice assists in our understanding of the Indian from the perspective of the Indian people. It is interesting to note that despite the immense popularity of this work from 1855 on, the text has gone largely unnoticed as an accurate depiction of the syntax of the Algonquin language. The English language, when translated from the Algonquin equivalent, results in word order that sounds much like what we might call *Yoda-speak* from Star Wars. For example, Longfellow writes:

> 'From the sky a star is falling.' (p. 26 line 3)

However, if you examine the Menominee/Ojibwa language source from which Longfellow derived his Hiawatha, you must hear the syntax of the original Indian language. In the Menominee language you would say:

> *Eneh mihekaehsaehseh kes-painohnaew enoh enaeniw.*

In English this phrase literally translates to:

> *That path on he did walk that man.*

Longfellow imitates the word order of Menominee/Ojibwa language to create the sound of a Native American story. This choice is further enhanced through the use of actual Algonquin names of characters such as Nokomis (grandmother), Opeechee (robin, and Ajiidamoo (squirrel). Longfellow's use of authentic language and syntax makes the work imitate the Menominee and Ojibwa language.

In conclusion, Longfellow changed the name of Maeqnapus to Hiawatha; he expunged the rape of Wenonah and her death in childbirth, but he maintained the basic themes of the sacred Medicine Dance stories. Maeqnapus, a child of the sacred Mother Earth, makes the journey from an infant to a man who feeds his people showing a transitional theme. Longfellow used the syntactic structure of the Algonquin language and incorporated many Algonquin language names and words. The original Medicine Dance stories were told in the ceremonies of my ancient people of the Great Lakes region, Longfellow borrows them for his song of Hiawatha. Aho!

References

Acuña, R. (1988). *Occupied America: A History of Chicanos.* New York: HarperCollins.
Adams, D. (1995). *Education for Extinction: American Indians and the Boarding School Experience 1875–1928.* Lawrence, KS: University Press of Kansas.
Aguilar-Moreno, M. (2007). *Handbook to Life in the Aztec World.* Oxford: Oxford University Press.
Bakan, J. (2004). *The Corporation: The Pathological Pursuit of Profit and Power.* New York: Free Press.
Banks, L.R. (1980). *Indian in the Cupboard.* New York: Doubleday.
Banyacya, T. (1994). Thomas Banyacya: Hopi Elder (North America). In Alexander Ewen (Ed.), *Voice of Indigenous Peoples: A Plea to the World.* Santa Fe, NM: Clear Light Publishers.
Barba, R. (1998). *Science in the Multicultural Classroom.* Needham Heights, MA: Allyn and Bacon.
Barton, A.C. (1998). *Feminist Science Education.* New York: Teachers College Press.
Barton, A.C. (2003). *Teaching Science for Social Justice* with Jason L Ermer, Tanahía A. Burkett and Margery D. Osborne. New York: Teachers College Press.
Basu, S. & Barton, A. (2007). Developing a sustained interest in science among urban minority youth. *Journal of Research in Science Teaching,* 44, 466–489.
Bernal, M. (1987). *Black Athena: The Afroasiatic Roots of Classical Civilization.* New Brunswick, NJ: Rutgers University Press.
Bernal, M. (2001). *Black Athena Writes Back: Martin Bernal Responds to His Critics.* London: Duke University Press.

Bigelow, B. (1998). "Discovering Columbus: Re-reading the past." In Bill Bigelow and Bob Peterson (Eds.), *Rethinking Columbus: The Next 500 Years*. Milwaukee, WI: Rethinking Schools.

Bigelow, B. (2003). Standards and Multiculturalism. In Linda Christiansen and Stan Karp (Eds.), *Rethinking School Reform: Views from the Classroom*. Milwaukee, WI: Rethinking Schools.

Blaisdell, B. (2000). *Great speeches by Native Americans*. Mineola, New York: Dover Publications, Inc.

Blumm, M. & Bodi, L. (1999). "What the Treaties Promised the Indians." In Joseph Cone and Sandy Ridlington (Eds.), *The Northwest Salmon Crisis: A Documentary History*. Corvallis, Oregon: Oregon State University Press.

Borneman, W. (2007). *The French and Indian War: Deciding the Fate of North America*. New York: Harper Perennial.

Bouillion, L.M. & Gomez, L.M. (2001). Connecting school and community with science learning: Real world problems and school-community partnerships as contextual scaffolds. *Journal of Research in Science Teaching*, 38, 878–889.

Brayboy, B.M.J. & Castagno. (2008). How might Native science inform "informal science learning"? *Cultural Studies of Science Education*, 3, 731–750.

Brosio, R. (2000). *Philosophical Scaffolding for the Construction of Critical Democratic Education*. New York: Peter Lang.

Bruchac, J. (2000). *Crazy Horse's Vision*. New York, NY: Lee and Low books Inc.

Bruchac, J. (1994). *A Boy called Slow*. New York, NY: Philomel Books.

Bruner, J. (1990). *Acts of Meaning*. London: Harvard University Press.

Bruner, J. (1996). *The Culture of Education*. London: Harvard University Press.

Butler, S. (1935/2003). *War Is a Racket*. Los Angeles: Feral House.

Byrd, M. (2002). *An American Health Dilemma: Race, Medicine, and Health Care in the United States*. New York: Routledge.

Cajete, G. (1999). *Igniting the Sparkle: An Indigenous Science Education Model*. Skyand, NC: Kivaki Press.

Cajete, G. (2000). *Native Science: Natural Laws of Interdependence*. Santa Fe, NM: Clear Light.

Campbell, J. (1988). *The Power of Myth*. New York: Anchor Books.

Carew, J. (1992/2008). Moorish culture bringers: Bearers of Enlightenment. In Ivan Van Sertima (Ed.). *Golden Age of the Moor*. London: Transaction Publishers.

Castile, G.P. (1998). *To Show Heart: Native American Self-Determination and Federal Indian Policy, 1960–1975*. Tucson: The University of Arizona Press.

Chaillé, C. (2008). *Constructivism Across the Curriculum in Early Childhood Classrooms: Big Ideas as Inspiration*. Boston: MA. Pearson.

Chandler, W. (1992/2002). Trait-influences in Meso-America: The Africa-Asian connection. In Ivan Van Sertima (Ed.). *African Presence in Early America*. London: Transaction Publishers.

Chandler, W. (1992/2008). The Moor: Light of Europe's Dark Age. In Ivan Van Sertima (Ed.). *Golden Age of the Moor*. London: Transaction Publishers.

Chard, D., Vaughn, S., & Tyler, B. (2002). A synthesis of research on effective interventions for building reading fluency with elementary students with learning disabilities. *Journal of Learning Disabilities*, 35(5), 386–406.

Chomsky, N. (1988). *Language and Problems of Knowledge: The Managua Lectures*. London: The MIT Press.

Chomsky, N. (1993). *The Prosperous Few and the Restless Many*. Interviewed by David Barsamian. Berkeley, CA: Odonian Press.

Chomsky, N. (1999). *Profit Over People: Neoliberalism and Global Order*. New York: Seven Stories.

Chomsky, N. (2000a). *New Horizons in the Study of Language and Mind*. Cambridge: Cambridge University Press.

Chomsky, N. (2000b). *Chomsky on MisEducation*. New York: Rowman & Littlefield.

Chomsky, N. (2002). *On Nature and Language*. Cambridge: Cambridge University Press.

Chomsky, N. (2007). *What We Say Goes: Conversations On U.S. Power in a Changing World*. Interviews with David Barsamian. New York: Metropolitan Books.

Chomsky, N. (2008). Anti-democratic nature of US capitalism is being exposed. Irish Times. http://www.irishtimes.com/newspaper/opinion/2008/1010/1223560345968.html

Churchill, W. (1995). *Since Predator Came: Notes from the Struggle for American Indian Liberation*. Littleton, CO: Aigis Publications.

Churchill, W. (1997). *A Little Matter of Genocide: Holocaust and Denial in the Americas 1492 to the Present*. San Francisco, CA: City Lights.

Churchill, W. (2002). *Struggle for the Land: Native North American Resistance to Genocide, Ecocide and Colonization*. San Francisco, CA: City Lights.

Churchill, W. (2003). *Life in Occupied America*. Oakland, CA: AK Press.

——— (2004). *Kill the Indian, Save the Man: The Genocidal Impact of American Indian Residential Schools*. San Francisco, CA: City Lights.

Churchill, W. & Vander Wall, J. (1990). *Agents of Repression: The FBI's Secret Wars Against the Black Panther Party and the American Indian Movement*. Boston, MA: South End Press.

Clegg, L. (1992/2002). The First Americans. In Ivan Van Sertima (Ed.). *African Presence in Early America*. London: Transaction Publishers.

Corcoran C.A. & Davis, A.D. (2005). A study of the effects of readers' theater In second and third grade special education students' fluency growth. *Reading Improvement*, 42(2), 105–111.

Covey, J. (1992/2002). African Sea Kings in America: Evidence from Early Maps. In Ivan Van Sertima (Ed.). *African Presence in Early America*. London: Transaction Publishers.

Crawford, J. (1995). Cheikh Anta Diop, the "Stolen Legacy," and Afrocentrism. In Albert Mosley (Ed.). *African Philosophy: Selected Readings*. Upper Saddle River, NJ: Prentice Hall.

Daily, D. (2004). *Battle for the BIA: G.E.E. Lindquist and the Missionary Crusade against John Collier*. Tuscan: The University of Arizona Press.

Darwin, C. (2007). *The Descent of Man, and Selection in Relation to Sex: The Concise Edition*; selections and commentary by Carl Zimmer. New York: Plume.

Deloria, V. (1997). *Red Earth, White Lies: Native Americans and the Myth of Scientific Fact*. Golden, CO: Fulcrum.

Descartes, R. (1637/1994). *A Discourse on Method: Meditations and Principles*. London: Everyman.

Diop, C.A. (1955/1974). *The African Origin of Civilization: Myth or Reality*. Chicago: Lawrence Hill Books.

Diop, C.A. (1987). *Precolonial Black Africa: A Comparative Study of the Political and Social Systems of Europe and Black Africa, from Antiquity to the Formation of Modern States*. Translated by Harold J. Salemson. Chicago: Lawrence Hill Books.

Drake, S. (1959). *Discoveries and Opinions of Galileo*. New York: Anchor Books.

Durkheim, E. (1893/2000). *The Division of Labor in Society*. In Timmons Robert and Amy Hite (Eds.), *From Modernization to Globalization: Perspectives on Development and Social Change*. New York: Blackwell Publishers.

Dyck, L. (2001). A personal journey into science, feminist science, and aboriginal science. In K. James (Ed.), *Science and Native American communities: Legacies of Pain, Visions of Promise* (pp. 22–28). Lincoln, NE: University of Nebraska Press.

Eastman, P.D. (1992). *The Cat in the Hat Beginner Book Dictionary*. New York: Random House.

Finch, C. (2007). Race and evolution in prehistory. In Ivan Van Sertima (Ed.). *African Presence in Early Europe*. London: Transaction Publishers.

Four Arrows. (2008). Indigenous pedagogy. In Dave Gabbard (Ed.). *Knowledge & Power in the Global Economy: The Effects of School Reform in a Neoliberal/Neoconservative Age: Second Edition*. New York: Lawrence Erlbaum Associates.

Fox, M. (2001). Reading Magic. San Diego, New York, London: Harcourt, Inc.

Freire, P. (1999). *Pedagogy of Hope: Reliving Pedagogy of the Oppressed*. New York: Continuum.

Freire, P. (2005). *Teachers as Cultural Workers: Letters to Those Who Dare Teach*. Boulder, CO: Westview Press.

Freidman, M. (1955). "The Role of Government in Education." [Online] Available at: http://www.schoolchoices.org/roo/fried1.htm.

Freidman, M. (1962/2002). *Capitalism and Freedom*. London: University of Chicago Press.

Fritzer, P. (2002). *Social Studies Content: For Elementary and Middle School Teachers*. New York: Allyn and Bacon.

Galilei, G. (1610/1959). To the Most Serene Cosimo II de' Medici Fourth Grand Duke of Tuscany. In Stillman Drake (Ed.). *Discoveries and Opinions of Galileo*. New York: Anchor Books.

Galilei, G. (1632). *Dialogues on the Great World Systems*, as translated by Thomas Salusbury, 1661.

Gilbert, A. (2009). Utilizing science philosophy statements to facilitate K-3 teacher candidate's development of inquiry-based science practice. *Early Childhood Education Journal*. DOI: 10.1007/s10643-009-0302-7.

Goble, P. (1978). *The Girl Who Loved Wild Horses*. New York: Aladdin Publishers.

Goes in Center, J. (2001). Land, people, and culture: Using Geographic Information Systems to build community capacity. In K. James (Ed.), *Science and Native American Communities: Legacies of Pain, Visions of Promise* (pp. 119–125). Lincoln, NE: University of Nebraska Press.

Good, R. (2005). *Scientific and Religious Habits of Mind: Irreconcilable Tensions in the Curriculum.* New York: Peter Lang.

Gramsci, A. (1971). *Selections from the Prison Notebooks of Antonio Gramsci.* Edited and translated by Quintin Hoare and Geoffrey Nowell Smith. New York: International Publishers.

Grande, S. (2004). *Red Pedagogy: Native American Social and Political Thought.* New York: Roman & Littlefield.

Greider, W. & Baker, D. (2008). Big Banks Go Bust: America's Financial System in Crisis. (September, 16, 2008). http://www.alternet.org/story/98863/

Grinde, D.A. (1992). Iroquois political theory and the roots of American Democracy. In Chief Oren Lyons and John Mohawk (Eds.), *Exiled in the Land of the Free: Democracy, Indian Nations, and the U.S. Constitution.* Santa Fe, NM: Clear Light Publishers.

Guevara, C. (1969). *Guerrilla Warfare.* New York: Vintage.

Gutstein, E. (2006). *Reading and Writing the World with Mathematics: Toward a Pedagogy for Social Justice.* New York: Routledge.

Gutstein, E. & Peterson, B. (2005). *Rethinking Mathematics: Teaching Social Justice By the Numbers.* Milwaukee, WI: Rethinking Schools.

Hammond, L. (2001). Notes from California: An anthropological approach to urban science education for language minority families. *Journal of Research in Science Teaching,* 38, 983–999.

Hankins, T. (1985). *Science and the Enlightenment.* New York: Cambridge University Press.

Harding, S. (1993). Eurocentric scientific illiteracy: A challenge for the world community. In S. Harding (Ed.), *The Racial Economy of Science: Toward a Democratic Future* (pp. 1–29). Bloomington, IN: Indiana University Press.

Harlan, J. & Rivken, M. (2008). *Sciences Experiences for the Early Childhood Years: An Integrated Affective Approach* (9th ed.) Upper Saddle River, NJ: Pearson.

Harris, V. (1992). Multiethnic children literature. In K.D Woods and A. Moss (Eds.), *Exploring Literature in the Classroom: Content and Methods.* Norwood, MA: Christopher-Gordon.

Hedegaard, M. (1990). The zone of proximal development as basis for instruction. In Luis C. Moll (Ed.). *Vygotsky and Education: Instructional Implications and Applications of Sociohistorical Psychology.* New York: Cambridge University Press.

Hersh, S. & Peterson, B. (2005). Poverty and world wealth. In Eric Gutstein and Bob Peterson (Eds.), *Rethinking Mathematics: Teaching Social Justice By the Numbers.* Milwaukee, WI: Rethinking Schools.

Hill, D. & Kumar, R. (2009). Neoliberalism and Its Impacts. In Dave Hill and Ravi Kumar (Eds.), *Global Neoliberalism and Education and Its Consequences.* New York: Routledge.

Holder, W. (2007). *Classroom Calypso: Giving Voice to the Voiceless.* New York: Peter Lang.

Hughes, D. (1983). *American Indian Ecology.* El Paso, TX: Texas Western Press.

Hume, D. (1888/2003). *A Treatise of Human Nature.* New York: Dover.

Hursh, D. (2008). Neoliberalism. In David Gabbard (Ed). *Knowledge & Power in the Global Economy: The Effects of School Reform in a Neoliberal/Neoconservative Age. Second Edition.* New York: Lawrence Erlbaum Associates.

Israel, J. (2002). *Radical Enlightenment: Philosophy and the Making of Modernity 1650-1750.* Oxford: Oxford University Press.

Israel, J. (2006). *Enlightenment Contested: Philosophy, Modernity, and the Emancipation of Man 1650–1752*. Oxford: Oxford University Press.
James, D. (1995). "'The instruction of any' and moral philosophy." In Albert Mosley (Ed.). *African Philosophy: Selected Readings*. Upper Saddle River, NJ: Prentice Hall.
James, G.M. (1954/2005). *Stolen Legacy: Greek Philosophy Is Stolen Egyptian Philosophy*. Deweyville, Virginia: Khalifah's Booksellers & Associates.
James, J. & McVay, M. (2009). Critical literacy for young citizens: First graders investigate the first thanksgiving. *Early Childhood Education Journal*, 36, 347–354.
James, K. (2001a). Fires need fuel: Merging science education with American Indian community needs. In K. James (Ed.), *Science and Native American Communities: Legacies of Pain, Visions of Promise* (pp. 1–8). Lincoln, NE: University of Nebraska Press.
James, K. (2001b). Sons of the sun, daughters of the Earth. In K. James (Ed.), *Science and Native American communities: Legacies of Pain, Visions of Promise* (pp. 107–110). Lincoln, NE: University of Nebraska Press.
Jeffers, S. (1991). *Brother Eagle, Sister Sky*. New York: Dial Books.
Joos, M. (1967). The style of the five clocks. In Abrahams, R.D. & Troike, R.C. (Eds.), *Language and Language Diversity in American Education*. 1972. Englewood Cliffs, NJ: Prentice Hall, Inc.
Jordan, K. (1992/2002). The African Presence in Ancient America: Evidence from Physical Anthropology. In Ivan Van Sertima (Ed.), *African Presence in Early America*. London: Transaction Publishers.
Katz, W.W. (1987). *False Face*. Toronto, Ontario: Groundwood Books.
Keynes, J.M. (1936/1997). *The General Theory of Employment, Interest, and Money*. Amherst, NY: Prometheus.
Kincheloe, J. (2001). *Getting Beyond the Facts: Teaching Social Studies/Social Sciences in the Twenty-first Century: Second Edition*. New York: Peter Lang.
Kincheloe, J. (2004). Why a book on urban education? In Shirley Steinberg and Joe L. Kincheloe (Eds.), *19 Urban Questions: Teaching in the City*. New York: Peter Lang.
Kincheloe, J. (2005). *Critical Constructivism Primer*. New York: Peter Lang.
Kincheloe, J. (2009). Christian Soldier Jesus: The Intolerant Savior and the political Fundamentalist Media Empire. In Shirley R. Steinberg and Joe L. Kincheloe (Eds.), *Christotainment: Selling Jesus through Popular Culture*. Boulder, CO: Westview.
Kincheloe, J. & Steinberg, S. (2004). *The Miseducation of the West: How Schools and the Media Distort Our Understanding of the Islamic World*. London: Praeger.
Kohn, A. (2004). NCLB and the effort to privatize public education. In Deborah Meier and George Wood (Eds.), *Many Children Left Behind: How the No Child Left Behind Act Is Damaging Our Children and Our Schools*. New York: Beacon.
Kuhn, T. (1996). *The Structure of Scientific Revolutions: Third Edition*. London: The University of Chicago Press.
Juhasz, A. (2006). Global water wars. In Jerry Mander and Victoria Tauli-Corpuz (Eds.), *Paradigm Wars: Indigenous Peoples' Resistance to Globalization*. San Francisco, CA: Sierra Club Books.
Lackey, R., Lach, D., & Duncan, S. (2006a). "Introduction: The challenge of restoring wild salmon." In Robert T. Lackey, Denise H. Lach, and Sally L. Duncan (Eds.), *Salmon 2100: The Future of Wild Pacific Salmon*. Bethesda, MD: American Fisheries Society.

Lackey, R., Lach, D., & Duncan, S. (2006b). "Wild salmon in Western North America: The historical and policy context." In Robert T. Lackey, Denise H. Lach, and Sally L. Duncan (Eds.), *Salmon 2100: The Future of Wild Pacific Salmon*. Bethesda, MD: American Fisheries Society.

Leafgren, S. (2008). Reuben's fall: Complicating "goodness" and schoolroom disobedience. *International Journal of Children's Spirituality*, 13, 331–344.

Lefkowitz, M. (1997). *Not Out Of Africa: How "Afrocentrism" Became an Excuse to Teach Myth as History*. New York: Basic Books.

Leap W. (1993). *American Indian English*. Salt Lake City, UT: University of Utah Press.

Lemkin, R. (1944). *Axis Rule in Occupied Europe: Laws of Occupation, Analysis of Government, Proposals for Redress*. Washington, DC: Carnegie Endowment for International Peace.

Lewin, T. (2008). Report urges changes in teaching math. *New York Times*. March, 14.

Lippmann, W. (1920/2008). *Liberty and the News*. Oxford: Princeton University Press.

Lippmann, W. (1922). *Public Opinion*. Boston, MA: Little, Brown and Company.

Lippmann, W. (1927). *The Phantom Public: A Sequel to "Public Opinion."* New York: Macmillan Company.

Lippmann, W. (1937/2005). *The Good Society*. London: Transaction.

Lippmann, W. (1943). *U.S. Foreign Policy: Shield of the Republic*. Boston, MA: Little, Brown and Company.

Llewellyn, D. (2002*)*. *Inquire Within: Implementing Inquiry-Based Science Standards*. Thousand Oaks, CA: Corwin Press.

Loewen, J. (1995). *Lies My Teacher Told Me: Everything Your American History Textbook Got Wrong*. New York: Touchstone.

Longfellow, H.W. (1982). *The Song of Hiawatha*. New York: Bounty Books.

Lumpkin, B. & Zitzler, S. (1992/2008). Cairo: Science Academy of the Middle Ages. In Ivan Van Sertima (Ed.). *Golden Age of the Moor*. London: Transaction Publishers.

Lyons, O. (1992). The American Indian in the past. In Oren Lyons and John Mohawk (Eds.), *Exiled in the Land of the Free: Democracy, Indian Nations, and the U.S. Constitution*. Santa Fe, NM: Clear Light Publishers.

Lyons, O. (2007). Foreword. In Miriam Jorgensen (Ed.). *Rebuilding Native Nations: Strategies for Governance and Development*. Tuscan: The University of Arizona Press.

Lyons, O. & Mohawk, J. (1992). *Exiled in the Land of the Free: Democracy, Indian Nations, and the U.S. Constitution*. Santa Fe, NM: Clear Light Publishers.

Macedo, D., Dendrinos, B. & Gounari, P. (2003). *The Hegemony of English*. Boulder, CO: Paradigm.

Malott, C. (2007). "Cuban education in Neo-Liberal Times: Socialist revolutionaries and state capitalism." *Journal for Critical Education Policy Studies*. 5(1). [Online] Available at: http://www.jceps.com/?pageID=article&articleID=90.

Malott, C. (2008). *A Call to Action: An Introduction to Education, Philosophy, and Native North America*. New York: Peter Lang.

Malott, C. (2009). Education in Cuba: Socialism and the encroachment of capitalism. In Dave Hill and Ravi Kumar (Eds.), *Global Neoliberalism and Education and Its Consequences*. New York: Routledge.

Malott, C. & Pena, M. (2004). *Punk Rockers' Revolution: A Pedagogy of Race, Class, and Gender.* New York: Peter Lang.

Malott, C. & Pruyn, M. (2006). Marxism and Critical Multicultural Social Studies Education. In *The Social Studies Curriculum: Purposes, Problems and Possibilities.* Wayne Ross (Ed.), New York: SUNY Press.

Malott, D.M.C. & Malott, C. (2008). Culture, capitalism and Social Democracy in Jamaica. In Brad Porfilio and Curry Malott (Eds.), *The Destructive Path of Neoliberalism: An International Examination of Education.* Rotterdam, The Netherlands: Sense.

Marshall III, J. (2001). *The Lakota Way: Stories and Lessons for Living.* New York: Penguin Compass.

Martin, R. (1992). *The Rough Face Girl.* New York: G.P. Putnam's Sons.

Martinez, M., Roser, N.L. & Strecker, S. (1999). "I never thought I could be a star": A readers theater ticket to fluency. *The Reading Teacher,* 52(4), 326–334.

Marx, K. (1867/1967). *Capital: Volume 1: A Critical Analysis of Capitalist Production.* New York: New World Paperbacks.

Marx, K. (1894/1991). *Capital: Volume 3: A Critique of Political Economy.* New York: Penguin Classics.

Marx, K. & Engels, F. (1848/1978). *Manifesto of the Communist Party.* In Robert Tucker (Ed.), *The Marx-Engels Reader: Second Edition.* New York: Norton.

Maslow, A. (1968). *Toward a Psychology of Being*: Second Edition. New York: Van Nostrand Reinhold Company.

Mathison, S., Ross, W. & Vinson, K. (2006). Defining the social studies curriculum: Influence of and resistance to curriculum standards and testing in social studies. In Wayne Ross (Ed.), *The Social Studies Curriculum: Purposes, Problems and Possibilities.* New York: SUNY Press.

Matthews, B. (2004). Promoting emotional literacy, equity and interest in science lessons for 11–14 year olds; the 'Improving Science and Emotional Development' project. *International Journal of Science Education,* 26, 281–308.

Matthiessen, P. (1992). Foreword. In Oren R. Lyons and John C. Mohawk (Eds.), *Exiled in the Land of the Free: Democracy, Indian Nations, and the U.S. Constitution.* Santa Fe, NM: Clear Light Publishers.

McIntosh, P. (1988). *White Privilege: Unpacking the Invisible Knapsack.* Wellesley, MA: Wellesley College Center for Research on Women.

McKenna, M.C. & Kear, D. (1990). Measuring attitude toward reading: A new tool for teachers. *The Reading Teacher,* 43(9), 626–638.

McNally, D. (2001). *Bodies of Meaning: Studies on Language, Labor, and Liberation.* New York: SUNY.

McNeil, L. (2003). The educational costs of standardization. In Linda Christiansen and Stan Karp (Eds.), *Rethinking School Reform: Views from the Classroom.* Milwaukee, WI: Rethinking Schools.

Menominee Indian Tribe of Wisconsin (http://www.menominee-nsn.gov/). "Brief History." Accessed 3-15-2009.

Merryfield, M. & Subedi, B. (2006). Decolonizing the mind for world-centered global education. In Wayne Ross (Ed.), *The Social Studies Curriculum: Purposes, Problems and Possibilities.* New York: SUNY Press.

Mohawk, J. (1992). Indians and democracy: No one ever told us. In Chief Oren Lyons and John Mohawk (Eds.), *Exiled in the Land of the Free: Democracy, Indian Nations, and the U.S. Constitution.* Santa Fe, NM: Clear Light.

Mohawk, J. & Lyons, O. (1992). Introduction. In Oren R. Lyons and John C. Mohawk (Eds.), *Exiled in the Land of the Free: Democracy, Indian Nations, and the U.S. Constitution.* Santa Fe, NM: Clear Light Publishers.

Montano-Harmon, M.R. (1991). Discourse features of written Mexican Spanish: Current research in contrastive rhetoric and its implications. *Hispania* 74(2), pp. 417–425.

Moraes, M. (1996). *Bilingual Education: A Dialogue with the Bakhtin Circle.* Albany, NY: SUNY.

Morin, J.A. (2003). *Social Studies Instruction Incorporating the Language Arts.* New York: Allyn and Bacon.

Murphy, C. & Beggs, J. (2003). Children's perceptions of school science. *School Science and Review,* 84, 109–116.

National Council for the Social Studies. (accessed October 24, 2008). Curriculum Standards for Social Studies: I. Introduction. www.socialstudies.org/standards/introduction.

Newton, I. (1952/1987). *Mathematical Principles of Natural Philosophy.* London: William Benton.

Nodelman, P. (1999). The pleasures of children's literature. Pearson, Allyn & Beacon.

Norton, D. (2003). *Through the Eyes of the Child.* (6th edition) Upper Saddle River, NJ: Pearson Prentice Hall.

Obama, B. & Biden, J. (accessed 10-04-08). "Education." http://www.barackobama.com/issues/education.

Ortiz-Franco, L. (2005). Chicanos have math in their blood: Pre-Columbian mathematics. In Eric Gutstein and Bob Peterson (Eds.), *Rethinking Mathematics: Teaching Social Justice By the Numbers.* Milwaukee, WI: Rethinking Schools.

Payne, R. (1998). *A Framework for Understanding Poverty.* Highlands, TX: RFT Publishing Co.

Perlman, F. (1985). *The Continuing Appeal of Nationalism.* Detroit, MI: Black & Red.

Peterson, B. (2005). Teaching math across the curriculum. In Eric Gutstein and Bob Peterson (Eds.), *Rethinking Mathematics: Teaching Social Justice By the Numbers.* Milwaukee, WI: Rethinking Schools.

Pewewardy, C. (1998). A Barbie-Doll Pocahontas. In Bill Bigelow and Bob Peterson (Eds.), *Rethinking Columbus: The Next 500 Years.* Milwaukee, WI: Rethinking Schools. p. 61.

Phillips, S. (1973). Participant structures and communicative competence: Warm Springs children in community and classroom. In A. Duranti (Ed.), *Linguistic Anthropology.* 2001. Malden, MA: Blackwell Publishing.

Pollock, P. (1996). *The Turkey Girl.* Boston, New York, London: Little, Brown and Company.

Popper, K. (1937/2007). *The Logic of Scientific Discovery.* New York: Routledge.

Porfilio, B. & Malott, C. (2008). Introduction: The neoliberal social order. In Bradley Porfilio and Curry Malott (Eds.), *The Destructive Path of Neoliberalism: An International Examination of Urban Education*. Rotterdam, The Netherlands: Sense.

Reese, D. (2007). Proceed with caution: Using Native American folktales in the classroom. *Language Arts*, 84(3), 245–256.

Rinehart, S.D. (1999). "Don't think for a minute that I'm getting up there": Opportunities for readers' theater in tutorial for children with reading problems. *Journal of Reading Psychology*, 20, 71–89.

Robbins, W. (1999), "The World of Columbia River Salmon: Nature, Culture and the Great River of the West." In Joseph Cone and Sandy Ridlington (Eds.), *The Northwest Salmon Crisis: A Documentary History*. Corvallis, OR: Oregon State University Press.

Ross, W. (2000). Diverting democracy: The curriculum standards movement and social studies education. In David W. Hursh and E. Wayne Ross (Eds.), *Democratic Social Education: Social Studies for Social Change*. New York: Falmer.

Roth, W.M. & Barton, A.C. (2004). *Rethinking Scientific Literacy*. New York: Routledge.

Russell, B. (1945/1972). *The History of Western Philosophy*. New York: Simon & Schuster.

Sakaibara, C. (2008). Our home is drowning: Inupiat storytelling and climate change in Point Hope, Alaska. *Geographic Review*, 98(4), 456–475.

Samuels, S.J. (1979, 1997). The method of repeated readings. *The Reading Teacher*, 50(5), 376–381.

Sarton, G. (1952). *Ancient Science through the Golden Age of Greece*. New York: Dover Publications.

Sarton, G. (1959). *Hellenistic Science and Culture in the Last Three Centuries B.C.* New York: Dover Publications.

Savage, J. (2000). *For the Love of Literature*. New York: McGraw Hill.

Saxe, D. (1991). *Social Studies in Schools: A History of the Early Years*. Albany, NY: SUNY.

Scobie, E. (1985/2007). The Black in Western Europe. In Ivan Van Sertima (Ed.), *African Presence in Early Europe*. London: Transaction Publishers.

Seale, D. & Slapin, B. (1998). *Through Indian Eyes: The Native Experience in Books for Children* (4th edition). New York: University of California.

Sendak, M. (1962). *Alligators All Around*. New York: Harper Trophy.

Sendak, M.(1988). *Where the Wild Things Are*. New York: HarperCollins.

Seurujarvi-Kari, I. (1994). Irja Seurujarvi-Kari: Nordic Saami Council (Northern Europe). In Alexander Ewen (Ed.), *Voice of Indigenous Peoples: A Plea to the World*. Santa Fe, NM: Clear Light Publishers.

Slapin, B. & Seale, D. (1998). *Through Indian Eyes*. Berkeley, CA: McNaughton & Gunn, Inc.

Smith, A. (2005). *Conquest: Sexual Violence and American Indian Genocide*. Cambridge, MA: South End Press.

Smith, M. (1996/2003). *The Aztecs* (2nd edition). Oxford: Blackwell Publishing.

Smith, P. (1984). *The Rise of Industrial America: A People's History of the Post-Reconstruction Era: Volume 6*. New York: Penguin Books.

Spector, B., Burkett, R., & Leard, C. (2007). Mitigating resistance to teaching science through Inquiry: Studying self. *Journal of Science Teacher Education*, 18, 185–208.

Spindler, G. & Spindler, L. (1971). *Dreamers Without Power: The Menomini*. Prospect Heights, IL: Waveland Press.

Spindler, G. & Spindler, L. (1984). *Dreamers With Power: The Menominee*. Prospect Heights, IL: Waveland Press.

Steel, R. (2008). Foreword. In Walter Lippmann. *Liberty and the News*. Oxford: Princeton University Press.

Stewart, M.P. (2002). Judging authors by the color of their skin? Quality Native American children's literature. *Melus*, 27(2), 179–196.

Stott, J. (1995). *Native Americans in Children's Literature*. Phoenix, AZ: Oryx Press.

Taylor, R.H. (2000). Indian in the cupboard: A case study in perspective. *Qualitative Studies in Education*, 13(4), 371–384.

Teller, L. (1985). The elements of metaphor in Menominee oral tradition: Myth, legend, and naming practices. Unpublished manuscript.

Thornton, R. (1987). *American Indian Holocaust and Survival: A Population History Since 1492*. London: University of Oklahoma Press.

Thornton, S. (2005). *Teaching Social Studies that Matters: Curriculum for Active Learning*. New York: Teachers College.

Trelease, J. (1995). The Read Aloud Handbook. New York: Penguin Books.

Tyler, B. & Chard, D. (2000). Using readers' theater to foster fluency in struggling readers: A twist on repeated readings strategy. *Reading and Writing Quarterly: Overcoming Learning Difficulties*, 16(2), 163–168.

Van Sertima, I. (1976/2003). *They Came Before Columbus: The African Presence in Ancient America*. New York: Random House.

Van Sertima, I. (1992/2008). The Moor in Africa and Europe. In Ivan Van Sertima (Ed.). *Golden Age of the Moor*. London: Transaction Publishers.

von Wuthenau, A. (1992/2002). Unexpected African faces in pre-Columbian America. In Ivan Van Sertima (Ed.). *African Presence in Early America*. London: Transaction Publishers.

Vygotsky, L. (1962). *Thought and Language*. London: The MIT Press.

Vygotsky, L. (1978). *Mind in Society: The Development of Higher Psychological Processes*. London: Harvard University press.

Watters, J. & Diezmann, C. (2007). Multimedia resources to bridge the praxis gap: Modeling practice in elementary science education. *Journal of Science Teacher Education*, 18, 349–376.

Wee, B., Shepardson, D., Fast, J. & Harbor, J. (2007). Teaching and learning about inquiry: Insights and challenges in professional development. *Journal of Science Teacher Education*, 18, 63–90.

Wilentz, S. (2008). General editor's introduction. In Walter Lippmann. *Liberty and the News* (1920/2008). Oxford: Princeton University Press.

WisKids Count. (2000). Wisconsin Council on Children and Families, Inc.

Worthy, J. & Broaddus, K. (2002). Fluency beyond the primary grades: From group performance to silent, independent reading. *The Reading Teacher*, 55(4), 334–343.

Worthy, J. & Prater, K. (2002). "I thought about it all night": Readers theater for reading fluency and motivation. *The Reading Teacher*, 56(3), 294–297.

Young, T.A. & Vardell, S. (1993). Weaving reader's theater and nonfiction into the curriculum. *The Reading Teacher*, 46, 396–406.

Zimmer, C. (2007). Selections and commentary. In Charles Darwin. *The Descent of Man, and Selection in Relation to Sex: The Concise Edition*. New York: Plume.

Zinn, H. (1995). *A People's History of the United States: 1492—Present*. New York: Perennial.

Zinn, H. (1997). *The Zinn Reader: Writings on Disobedience and Democracy*. New York: Seven Stories.

Studies in the Postmodern Theory of Education

General Editors
Joe L. Kincheloe & Shirley R. Steinberg

Counterpoints publishes the most compelling and imaginative books being written in education today. Grounded on the theoretical advances in criticalism, feminism, and postmodernism in the last two decades of the twentieth century, Counterpoints engages the meaning of these innovations in various forms of educational expression. Committed to the proposition that theoretical literature should be accessible to a variety of audiences, the series insists that its authors avoid esoteric and jargonistic languages that transform educational scholarship into an elite discourse for the initiated. Scholarly work matters only to the degree it affects consciousness and practice at multiple sites. Counterpoints' editorial policy is based on these principles and the ability of scholars to break new ground, to open new conversations, to go where educators have never gone before.

For additional information about this series or for the submission of manuscripts, please contact:

> Joe L. Kincheloe & Shirley R. Steinberg
> c/o Peter Lang Publishing, Inc.
> 29 Broadway, 18th floor
> New York, New York 10006

To order other books in this series, please contact our Customer Service Department:

> (800) 770-LANG (within the U.S.)
> (212) 647-7706 (outside the U.S.)
> (212) 647-7707 FAX

Or browse online by series:
> www.peterlang.com